Honor and Political Imagination

Honor and Political Imagination

SMITA A. RAHMAN

OXFORD
UNIVERSITY PRESS

Oxford University Press is a department of the University of Oxford.
It furthers the University's objective of excellence in research, scholarship,
and education by publishing worldwide. Oxford is a registered trade mark of
Oxford University Press in the UK and certain other countries.

Published in the United States of America by Oxford University Press
198 Madison Avenue, New York, NY 10016, United States of America.

© Oxford University Press 2024

All rights reserved. No part of this publication may be reproduced, stored in a retrieval system, transmitted, used for text and data mining, or used for training artificial intelligence, in any form or by any means, without the prior permission in writing of Oxford University Press, or as expressly permitted by law, by license or under terms agreed with the appropriate reprographics rights organization. Inquiries concerning reproduction outside the scope of the above should be sent to the Rights Department, Oxford University Press, at the address above.

You must not circulate this work in any other form
and you must impose this same condition on any acquirer

Library of Congress Cataloging-in-Publication Data
Names: Rahman, Smita A., author.
Title: Honor and political imagination / Smita A. Rahman.
Description: New York, NY : Oxford University Press, [2024] | Includes index.
Identifiers: LCCN 2024032935 (print) | LCCN 2024032936 (ebook) |
ISBN 9780197642115 (hardback) | ISBN 9780197642139 (epub)
Subjects: LCSH: Political culture—United States. | Honor—Political aspects—United States. | Collective memory—Political aspects—United States. | Political science—United States—Philosophy.
Classification: LCC JA75.7 .R34 2024 (print) | LCC JA75.7 (ebook) |
DDC 306.20973—dc23/eng/20240820
LC record available at https://lccn.loc.gov/2024032935
LC ebook record available at https://lccn.loc.gov/2024032936

DOI: 10.1093/oso/9780197642115.001.0001

Printed by Marquis Book Printing, Canada

For Baba

Contents

Preface	ix
Introduction: The Enduring Appeal of Honor	1
1. "You Win or You Die": Honor, Recognition, and Subjectivity in *Game of Thrones*	25
2. Honor among Spies: The Cold War Mom, Family, and Identity in *The Americans*	51
3. The Ornamental Politics of Honor: *Wolf Hall*, Machiavelli, and the Art of Power	67
4. Honor, Heroism, and Tragedy in *The Iliad*	94
5. Honor, Nostalgia, and Democratic Anxiety in the Marvel Cinematic Universe's *Captain America*	125
Conclusion: The Agonism of Honor	156
Notes	159
Bibliography	171
Index	177

Preface

Consider three differing invocations of honor by recent U.S. presidents: President Trump once joked that he wanted to give himself the Medal of Honor; President Obama honored his own vice president with the Presidential Medal of Freedom; and former presidents Clinton, George W. Bush, and Obama came together to encourage support for building a national museum to recognize Medal of Honor recipients (slated to open in Arlington, Texas, in 2024). It is telling that as a moment of levity or as a gesture of recognition for public service or as a repository of collective memory, honor persists in varied forms in political life to this day. It pops up in political speeches to venerate character or to bemoan its lack, often accompanied by a hefty dose of nostalgia. It is threaded into discussions of nationalism and patriotism, it is an essential component of military training, and it is often invoked in the celebration of heroic acts. Honor clearly endures in these familiar forms, but a more complex and layered version of it emerges in the political imagination in creative renderings in popular culture, in the form of television, film, and fiction, allowing one to grasp its various sensory and aesthetic dimensions, consider its myth-making potential and its tragic consequences, and explore its ability to both inspire heroic action and evoke destructive rage.

Honor is a complicated and multivalent concept to write about, not least because it means so many different things to different people. Honor can be external, as a code of honor that is rooted in tradition and cultural norms, or it can be deeply internal and woven into one's very sense of oneself as a subject, or it can be ornamental and take the form of medals, badges, and titles that are bestowed on one by others and therefore always vulnerable to recognition. It is difficult to think of honor without considering its temporality, which takes the form of pastness. Honor is more often than not considered to be obsolete, musty, and tethered to a distant past of jousting knights and profound inequality. And yet it endures in the present, and it is its very conceptual slipperiness that allows it to inspire political action, even as it binds and blinds one to the consequences of a rigid attachment to it. Honor persists in the political imagination and generates mythic sources of meaning for those who draw inspiration from it for heroic (and often reckless) acts.

In our contemporary world, it is often thought of as respect or dignity and closely connected to duty (particularly patriotic duty to the nation). In ancient epic and in the Homeric world, honor meant something more. It inspired heroes, it ennobled the contest, and it was inescapably tragic. This tragic aspect of honor, where it leads to suffering, grief, and rage, is often smoothed out of contemporary accounts of honor in political theory that seeks to recover a more anodyne version of it for liberal and democratic politics. This book resists that impulse and argues that the concept of honor that endures in the political imagination is much more layered. It explores the craggy contours of honor through the analysis of several different visual and literary texts in popular culture—from HBO's smash hit *Game of Thrones* to FX's thrilling espionage drama *The Americans*, Hilary Mantel's award-winning and remarkably modern *Wolf Hall* trilogy of historical novels, Homer's epic *Iliad*, and finally the Marvel Cinematic Universe's depiction of *Captain America*. These texts are put into conversation with a wide range of sources in classical, modern, and contemporary political theory on honor, ranging from Aristotle, Machiavelli, and Nietzsche, to Kwame Anthony Appiah, Sharon Krause, and more.

This book seeks to underline various aspects of honor's multivalence to account for its enduring appeal by exploring the links between honor, subjectivity, and recognition; the intersection of honor, motherhood, and family; the aesthetics of ornamental honor and the political life of sensation; the constitutive role that honor plays in the trauma and tragedy of war; and the interplay between honor, democratic anxiety, and nostalgia. It argues that there is a push and pull in honor, where it can inspire one to act with courage and moral conviction and generate a mythic grandeur that remains part of the aesthetics of political life, but at the same time it can be profoundly destructive and anesthetize one to the terrible consequences of its pursuit. There may be a place for honor in the political imagination, but this book attempts to show that it remains a contested and complicated one.

This book began, as so many do, with a series of conversations. In my case, these took place over many decades with my father, Ishfaqur Rahman, who sadly passed away before the book's completion. Growing up in Bangladesh, in a family accidentally mired in politics, we had many occasions to reflect together on the tragic consequences of honor. My debt to him is profound, and my love for him, his wisdom, his deep generosity, and his fundamental kindness is immeasurable. Simply put, he shaped and continues to shape my thinking and my love of ideas.

I am indebted to many for their support throughout the years it took me to write this book. My thanks to my editor, Angela Chnapko, at Oxford University Press, for her steady encouragement throughout the process. I also want to thank the two anonymous reviewers who provided feedback that helped me clarify and develop some of the core ideas in this book, and to the many commenters at various conferences over the years who pushed me to sharpen my insights. My thanks to William Connolly, Matthew Scherer, Elisabeth Anker, James Martel, Shirin Deylami, and Katherine Gordy for their consistent support, the inspiring conversations, and their friendship.

I am fortunate to work at DePauw University, where the commitment to teaching in the liberal arts is matched by strong institutional support for scholarship. This book would not have been completed without the generous award of the three-year Larz A. Whitcomb Faculty Fellowship that allowed me to develop the project in its early stages, and a Fisher Fellowship that gave me much needed time off from teaching at the end of the process to complete the manuscript. My thanks to Dean of Faculty Bridget Gourley, for her dedicated support of my research, and to my colleague in classical studies Michael Seaman, for his inspired suggestion to read about *The Iliad* in the context of Vietnam. Many of us hope to find moments of synergy between our scholarship and our teaching, and I have been fortunate to find it time and again at DePauw. I taught a seminar on the politics of honor twice as I was researching and writing this book, and my students helped me sharpen my ideas and rethink many of my assumptions. I am grateful to them all, and, in particular, I want to thank Marko Mavrovic, Megha (Summer) Pappachen, and Rowan Adams for their insights. I also want to thank my colleagues in the Political Science Department for all their support over the years, and especially Deepa Prakash, Salil Benegal, and Sunil Sahu.

These past few years of pandemic life and loss were lightened and made easier thanks to the friendship of Kim Hartley and Mike Barbee. I am also thankful to Jimmy R. Watkins for his steady encouragement. I remain profoundly grateful for my mother, Yasmin Rahman, who is a model of perseverance and dignified grace. My continued thanks to my partner in life and ideas, Rob Watkins, for his endless patience and support. This book would never have been completed without him. Finally, my deep gratitude and thanks to Kai Rahman-Watkins, who did the design editing for the book cover, and who inspires me every single day with his creativity, humor, and kindness.

Introduction

The Enduring Appeal of Honor

In an unusual appearance in the press room in Fall 2017 the White House chief of staff General John Kelly made an interesting set of observations that compared our political present to a more traditional and seemingly upright past. "You know when I was a kid growing up, a lot of things were sacred in our country. Women were sacred, looked upon with great honor. That's obviously not the case anymore, as we've seen from recent cases. Life—the dignity of life—is sacred. That's gone. Religion, that seems to be gone as well," he said.[1] In his comments Kelly seemed to be lamenting the loss of a chivalric past (which, to be clear, lounged grandly on a system of violent exclusion and deep prejudice) that is no longer available to us. In particular, he linked the idea of the sacred with the concept of honor, which in turn was linked to its close cousin, dignity. In Kelly's language, our present political moment was cast as profane and corrupt, unmoored from religion and tradition and cloaked in the shadows of moral bankruptcy. It was characterized as an age without honor and therefore without the guardrails of decency to govern behavior. It is not surprising to see the concept of honor invoked in this context in our contemporary political discourse, doused heavily in the language of remembrance of things past and often with a hypermasculine tint. (Look no further than Jordan Peterson and his acolytes for the most reductive examples of such thinking or, much more profoundly, to Harvey Mansfield's work on masculinity.) Invoking honor in this manner seeks to restore balance and constancy to a chaotic present that in these renderings has been unmoored by radical feminists, populist movements for racial equality, and advocates of gay and trans rights.

Of course, such a contrast ignores the myriad factors that have given rise to political polarization (and is not particularly compelling on its own as a point of political analysis), but in its invocation of honor as central to our political present it does highlight an interesting conundrum that is worth thinking about. What accounts for the enduring appeal of honor in the political imagination today? Is honor simply a relic of the chivalric past to be cast aside with the rusty suits of armor and restrictive corsets of its era, as emblematic of a time that was marked by radical inequality and oppression and therefore to be happily consigned to the dustbin of history? Or does a fugitive fragment of the concept of honor persist in our present and have something productive to offer it? If we take the possibility of the latter seriously, how can we best come to grips with its enduring appeal? In other words, is honor an anesthetic, a dangerous sedative that dulls the senses and blinds us to the risks and consequences of the heroic quest for glory? Is it a constraining virtue that stubbornly binds us to a foolhardy course of action? Is honor simply and bluntly masculine, or does it remain so by default, as a consequence of not thinking through its appeal as a source of agency in contemporary politics? Is there a tragic version of honor that can be excavated from myths and epics (and novels and television shows and films) and that takes seriously the heroic (and superheroic) desire to affirm and celebrate life, but which still remains acutely aware of the ties that bind us all as subjects formed by power?

This book is an attempt to puzzle through many of these questions through close readings of the enduring appeal of honor in the political imagination by exploring its rendering in contemporary visual and literary culture. Invocations of honor are infrequent in political discourse, but the concept itself remains firmly rooted in popular culture in television shows, novels, and films, all of which characterize honor in various ways. Honor in such depictions is both internal, where it is seen as an individual virtue akin to dignity or respect and often conflated with its close cousin duty, and external, where it takes the form of titles, medals, and other ornaments that are bestowed by others. Regardless of the form it takes, what is intriguing about these contemporary renderings of honor is how deeply tragic they are in their repeated emphases on the costs of following a traditional code. More often than not in these retellings the emphasis is placed on the blinding and binding consequences of a strict adherence to honor. In the political imagination, honor is seen as taking a toll on the family and leading to rash political decision-making and heroic actions by the honorable subject, who too often ignores how deeply their subjectivity is bound up in their relations with others and the regimes of power they are embedded in. Despite these costs and the often reckless actions it inspires, honor endures in the political imagination, in part because of its mythic appeal and its capacity to imagine, to inspire, and to enchant. However, even the most enduring of myths and legends are deeply tragic at their core: Pandora opening the box that unleashes disease and sadness and death upon the world, Narcissus tumbling to a watery death in his own reflection, and always, always Achilles, the paradigmatic figure of wounded honor who almost cost the Greeks a war in his unrelenting obsession with his honor and who returned to the battlefield only after the tragic loss of his beloved Patroclus, his epic glory streaked through with unbearable grief and blinding rage. Such is the case for honor, which inspires heroic action, with tragic consequences.

This book attempts to restore or, perhaps more appropriately, rewind the tragic thread to the concept of honor in the political, to imbue it with the recognition of power and the complexity of intersubjective relations. It therefore departs from the directions laid out by two of the most compelling recent works on honor in contemporary political theory, one of which boosts it to the forefront as a source of moral revolution (Anthony Appiah's work) and the other of which softens it into a virtue that can revitalize liberalism and democratic agency (in Sharon Krause's version). This book is precisely not an attempt to articulate the contours of the concept of honor itself in philosophical terms as others have already done with great diligence and specificity.[2] The theoretical approach to the concept of honor put forward in this book is therefore not to try to pin it down with definitional clarity, but rather to show how the very conceptual slipperiness of honor and its multivalence and conflation with related concepts of duty, patriotism, and heroism account for its enduring appeal. Here, the words of Wendy Brown are instructive, who when describing the concept of democracy in her fantastic book *Undoing the Demos* describes it as concept that is both "contested and promiscuous."[3] Rather than try to make a case for the significance of internal honor (as a virtue, a code, or a source of agency) or external honor (as titles or ornaments bestowed by others), this book explores the depths and furrows of honor in the political imagination in order to, first, develop a critique of honor and, second, explore its connections to heroic agency, myth, and tragedy to account for its affirmative and enduring appeal.

The critique of honor is developed in the first part of the book by exploring how it is both binding and blinding in its attachment to tradition and duty, which acts as a kind of sedative that allows the honorable subject to elide power relations and the complexities of intersubjective formations. The second half of the book extends the critique of honor in the first half, to develop an account of honor that is at once affirmative and tragic, exploring honor's capacity for art and artifice, the often tragic consequences of heroic agency, and its relationship to nostalgia and democracy. The book proceeds through an examination of the concept of honor in the political imagination through a close reading of a series of eclectic sources in contemporary popular culture. The first half of the book explores the binding and blinding aspects of honor by analyzing the arc of the honorable Ned Stark in *Game of Thrones* and the vexed inheritance he leaves behind for his family, and then by exploring the figure of Elizabeth Jennings in the Cold War espionage drama *The Americans*, who complicates the masculine narrative of the concept of honor with her nuanced depiction of honor, duty, and motherhood. The second half of the book examines both the aesthetic and tragic aspects of honor, first by exploring Hilary Mantel's award-winning novel *Wolf Hall* and its transformative rendering of its protagonist, Thomas Cromwell, as a Machiavellian figure of intrigue who uses ornamental honor skillfully to achieve great political success, and through Achilles in *The Iliad*, the tragic hero par excellence of the Greeks, the tornado of wounded honor and carnage who continues to shape so much of how we view honor today, even as elements of his story remain hidden from view. The book concludes with an analysis of the myth-making, militarism, and nostalgia that is on display in the Marvel Cinematic Universe's version of *Captain America* in order to examine the relationship between honor and democratic anxiety in political imagination.

Honor, Obsolescence, and Pastness

Every recent treatment of the concept of honor starts with the same caveat: that such a concept might be outmoded, antiquated, or, in Peter Berger's formulation, even obsolescent.[4] There is a curious temporality to the notion of honor through which it appears to be deeply embedded in a chivalric past of knights and jousts, cigar-smoking gentlemen and dueling pistols, and from which it resists any attempt to tug it free into the present. But the appeal of honor, at least for a certain traditionalist and conservative politics, lies precisely in this pastness. Honor seems to hark back to a more orderly time, when moral codes and norms of behavior demarcated social interactions clearly for many, and when, as John Stuart Mill famously described it, the "despotism of custom" held sway.[5] The distinct odor of mothballs and cedar chests clings to the idea of honor, as a relic of the distant past with very little to offer us today. In Berger's formulation, "Honor occupies about the same place in contemporary usage as chastity. An individual asserting it hardly invites admiration and one who claims to have lost it is an object of amusement rather than sympathy."[6] Berger notes that much of this characterization of quaintness has to do with the association honor has with aristocracy and hierarchy and that it "is certainly true that western notions of honor have been strongly influenced by the modern codes of chivalry and that these were rooted in the social structures of feudalism."[7]

This conservative and traditionalist pull of honor is apparent in the appeal to pastness that permeates much of James Bowman's recent work, *Honor: A History*. In this text, Bowman attempts to define two kinds of honor—first, a reflexive honor (which is described quite problematically in the book as the "the honor of the savage" but which one might more productively describe as a visceral urge to defend one's honor) and, second, a concept of cultural honor (which describes stories, traditions, and norms of particular societies).[8] Much of Bowman's book is focused on lamenting the erosion of cultural honor in the West, with various forces held responsible for its decline and fragmentation—modern feminism, a therapeutic culture, the renewed emphasis on the trauma of war after Vietnam, the rise of celebrity culture—all of which combine to sever honor from the bankrupt present. He writes, "[A]ny coherent idea of honor was amputated from Western culture three-quarters of a century or so ago, leaving nothing behind but a few sensitive moral nerve endings that make themselves felt every now and then when our residual sense of propriety and public virtue is outraged and we don't quite know why."[9] Still, even for Bowman, who laments the erosion of the cultural honor of the past, there remains an understanding that it is necessary in the present (though for him it has to be revived in order to deal with "honor-crazed Muslim fanatics who are blowing up women and children" and who must be opposed by a "hard residuum of masculine honor of our own").[10] In this account, honor is regarded as incompatible with democratic, liberal, and progressive politics and needs to draw on a renewed chivalry in order to survive in the present.

Another contemporary work on honor, by Robert Oprisko, has examined its philosophical dimensions in a rigorous exploration of its phenomenology. Oprisko makes a valiant effort to pin down and define the various aspects and models of this notoriously slippery concept, though he too acknowledges that it is "a multiphenomenal category of concepts," which when "elevated to a wholly inclusive level of abstraction, binds individuals together and forms society, but it also tears them apart."[11] Oprisko's book comprehensively details the existing literature on honor and establishes both a typology and a phenomenology of honor by accounting for its various dimensions, with chapters that focus on external honor, horizontal honor, esteem, affiliated honor, glory, and dignity, among others. Even the list of terms carefully mapped out by Oprisko in this exhaustive study underlines the multivalence and conceptual slipperiness of the concept itself. Honor, it appears, contains multitudes.

More recent work, notably a fascinating article by Haig Patapan, has underlined that there are contradictory impulses in the discussions of the politics of modern honor—at once a neglect or disdain of honor as quaint and, simultaneously, an attempt to elevate it in political theory and promote its analysis in slightly different form, as dignity, self-esteem, and recognition.[12] There is some suggestion that we have freed ourselves from the mystifications of honor when we focus on its cousins, but it might actually be that this transfiguration of honor into dignity and respect retains some of the agentic force of honor in more pliable and faintly moral form but has the consequence of stripping from it its mythic force. This brief exploration of some of the contemporary literature on honor therefore makes clear that as rooted as it is in its pastness, honor remains present and enduring in fragmented and reformulated ways.

One of the sadder consequences of liberalism's insistence on the thinness of rationalism for its many solutions is the stripping away of myth and heroic agency and along with it the tragic orientation that such ideas bring to political analysis. This book proceeds in a different direction, veering away from the austere confines of the logic of liberalism and turning instead to the tragic for its orientation. Decades of rationalism and individualism have done little to erode our desire for heroes (or superheroes, if we allow the Marvel Cinematic Universe to take its place alongside Homer), for the tragic fall and the redemptive arc, for stories that set passions aflame and make us weep for the beauty of a broken world. We are never outside of myth, and we are never divorced from narratives that help us imagine, even if all they conjure up are the heroes who die in the reckless pursuit of glory.

This book is not a call for the return of vainglory, indeed far from it, but instead an attempt to reckon with the enduring power of honor in contemporary political culture and the myth-making desire for heroism that accompanies it, even as we attend to the tragic nature of such heroic agency. Wendy Brown posed a provocative question several years ago when she asked, "What, other than anarchy or free fall, is harbored by the destabilization of constitutive cultural or political narratives?"[13] She asked how we might navigate these "tattered narratives of modernity" which are "troubled yet persistent" in politics.[14] Honor is an interesting concept to explore through Brown's diagnosis of politics out of history because it is an eroding and frayed cultural and political narrative, but it is also posed by many as the salve to the crisis of its own disintegration. The longing for the kind of pastness that a call to honor brings today (as it did for John Kelly) is redolent with nostalgia and the desire for fixity that can soothe "a world that is contingent, unpredictable, not fully knowable, and directed neither by external forces, nor by internal logics."[15] Brown's analysis of Derrida's "hauntology" is useful here in grappling with politics out of history in our late modern era. If the past is not truly past, as Faulkner memorably noted, but remains present in fugitive traces, how do such hauntings help shape the future? Brown perceptively notes that "we inherit not 'what really happened' to the dead but what lives on from that happening, what is conjured from it, how past generations and events occupy the forcefields of the present, how they claim us, and how they haunt, plague, and inspire our imaginations for the future."[16] Brown's framing here is a much more productive way to think honor that allows us to get out of the bind that contemporary political theory places it in, to think of it as something other than a dusty relic of the past or a reformulated and less thorny political virtue for the present. Brown's language offers another path, to recast the disruptive and multivalent concept of honor in complex temporal terms—as an inherited ghost from a chivalric era that haunts and plagues the present but which may still retain the capacity to inspirit our imagination for the future if we attend to its mythic and tragic potential.

Codes of Honor, Tradition, and Power

In recent years, Kwame Anthony Appiah has made an attempt to think deeply about honor and the role it might continue to play in the present. His book *The Honor Code* is a fascinating and illuminating work on the various moral and political dimensions of honor, eloquently written for a wider audience. Appiah's careful analysis of several case studies, ranging from the end of the duel to the disappearance of Chinese foot-binding, the abolition of slavery, and honor killing in tribal areas of Pakistan, are useful for highlighting the role that codes of honor play in what he terms "moral revolutions." Appiah wants to reclaim a role for honor in contemporary politics but is not entirely convincing in his argument that honor plays a crucial role in moral change. Appiah's wide-ranging popular study of honor is persuasive in the linkage it creates between honor and social identity but is undermined by the way he connects honor far too closely with the liberal assumption of progress that always promises a better future. However, what is compelling about his work is how he locates the moments during which the codes of honor become obsolete or stop functioning or change form, which contains important insights for how honor is connected to and contingent on power relations. In the various cases he explores (two of which are highlighted in this introduction: the collapse of the duel and the disappearance of foot-binding), there are moments when honor becomes disconnected from tradition and the elite sources from which it draws its power and sustenance. When honor is untethered from power, and hence from legitimation, it loses its broad moral appeal to people. When it becomes unshackled from the hooks of tradition, the honor code collapses and the accompanying cultural and political change is swift. Tracing this dynamic through Appiah's work and reading it against the liberal and moral exhortations of his writing reveals something much more interesting: the degree to which codes of honor are tethered to regimes of power that sustain it and how the constraints of tradition produce docile subjects that remain submissive in their desire for status and recognition. Examining the role that power plays in the construction of these "honor worlds," as Appiah terms them, allows for a closer exploration of honor and subjectivity, a set of connections that are explored in further depth and detail in chapter 1 of this book.

Appiah introduces his book as an analysis of crucial moments when moral revolutions happen. He writes that he was surprised that when moral change happened it was not because people were convinced by new and better arguments, but rather that "in each of these transitions, something that was naturally called 'honor' played a central role."[17] He links honor from the outset with identity formation and more explicitly with Hegelian recognition, noting the connection between identity and "our deep and persistent concern with status and respect" and that we as human beings "need others to recognize us as conscious beings and to acknowledge that we recognize them."[18] This connection between Hegelian recognition, subjectivity, and the particular vulnerability of honor is explored in depth in chapter 1, but for now it suffices to note how closely this popular invocation of honor is tied to status and respect as a form of legitimation. Appiah further seeks to "claim a crucial place for honor in our thinking about what it is to live a successful human life" by linking it to the Aristotelian concept of *eudaimonia* by focusing on how honor serves as a connective tissue for social life.[19] This leads him to his clearly stated purpose, that "it is perhaps not too much to hope that if we can find the proper place for honor now, we can make the work better."[20] While admirable, this is entirely too optimistic because, as the rest of the book makes clear, honor does not appear in isolation, freed from its embeddedness in cultural norms and traditions, but, more often than not, remains the privilege of a select few, whether it is the British aristocrats who give up on dueling only when the grubby masses begin to adopt it or the Chinese nobility who quickly give up the painful practice of foot-binding when it clearly becomes a hindrance to their status on the global stage.

Appiah begins his analysis with an exploration of the death of the duel in Britain, a practice that was in place for centuries before its sudden demise. Despite the many objections raised by the church and the law (it was already an illegal activity in Britain during the time of the duel discussed in the case), the practice persisted in the ranks of the nobility. Several Enlightenment philosophers, most famously Hume, Bacon, and Smith, raised objections to it as a mechanism for avenging assaults on one's honor. Despite the ambivalence toward the practice, the duel continued in elite circles, in part because of tradition, in part because of a persistent code of honor that "required that, once an allegation . . . had been made, you had to clear your name: you had to establish that it wasn't true. And the first way to do this was to ask for and receive a public apology. If the apology was denied, the same code required you to challenge your accuser to a duel; and that would show, among other things, that you were willing to risk your life rather than be thought to be guilty of something dishonorable."[21] The duel was a central part of the chivalric two-step of the code of honor that bound European nobility, buttressed by the weight of inheritance and propped up by the power custom. As Appiah notes, even though dueling was illegal in Britain at the time, "the reason duelists were not condemned was that the official legal norm conflicted with the social consensus among the British elite."[22]

The practice of dueling persisted among the British nobility for these reasons of social identity and conformity, but the logic of honor that undergirded it is worth exploring in a bit more detail as it reveals the crucial role that power played in its enduring appeal. Appiah writes that "at the heart of honor, then, is this simple idea: Having honor means being entitled to respect."[23] However, this construction begs the question: Is this linkage between honor and respect available only for a few? Certainly, the desire for recognition by others is crucial to the concept of honor, but at least in the chivalrous arena of dueling what also emerges as critical is its sense of entitlement. Honor, or the claim to respect that accompanies it, and the insults that can so easily slight it, asserts a kind of privileged power that demands submission and recompense. If one craves respect or recognition, is one also entitled to it? If so, the conflation between honor and respect that undergirds the practice of dueling seems to operate in the purview of an elite few.

It is also worth noting how such a pursuit of the entitlement of honor moves it away from its tragic potential. In Nietzsche's terms, the practice of dueling as a form of recompense for the assault on one's honor can be read in terms of the ascetic morality of the small man who wallows in the resentment engendered by not receiving his just dues rather than the overman who affirms his strength and glories in it amid the suffering of life. This separation from the tragic is clear in the one reference Appiah makes to Achilles's boasting of his own strength and power in *The Iliad*, which he contrasts with the British code of honor around dueling which sees such self-promotion as ungentlemanly. Honor, in the practice of dueling, has already been drained of its tragic underpinnings, as is evident in Appiah's dismissal that "you showed your worth in action, not by singing your own praises."[24] Instead of the tragic, the death of the duel veers toward the comic and makes clear how the binding power of tradition requires of its subjects that they "conform to the standard for its own sake."[25]

Appiah tells the story of the duel between the Duke of Wellington and the Earl of Winchilsea, one of the last duels among the British nobility, in which both men participated reluctantly. The Duke of Wellington was, of course, one of the most famous men in the country, the prime minister of England, and the commander of British forces at the Battle of Waterloo. The Earl of Winchilsea was a vigorous advocate for the Protestant Church who opposed Wellington's efforts to increase Catholic representation in Parliament. He accused the Duke of infringing on liberties and introducing "Popery into every department of the state."[26] The Duke asked for an apology, the Earl declined, and the Duke felt compelled to ask for a duel to pay for the assault on his honor. In his text, Appiah walks through the drama of the duel itself in great detail, but for the purposes of this book it is worth noting simply that by this era the practice of the duel had been reduced to an empty performative gesture. During the duel, the Duke missed his target and the Earl intentionally discharged his weapon into the air, but both felt compelled by their code of honor to go through with it. The widespread mockery that greeted the news of this farcical duel laid bare the dependence of honor on the recognition of others and its vulnerability to the shifting of cultural norms. In Appiah's words, Wellington's encounter was judged as "juvenile by a standard other than the gentlemanly honor that had long sustained the practice."[27] It was recognized by the public for the empty performance that it was, and questions were raised about the Duke's temperament for exposing himself to such a dangerous means of restitution. But why exactly was a duel among the nobility greeted with such scorn? The answer lies in the erosion of the power of legitimation around the practice and the code of honor that sustained it for centuries. Appiah quotes V. G. Kiernan, the noted historian of the European duel, who wrote that "the class whose norm it was gradually lost its central place in British public life. The ruling aristocracy was being superseded in the early nineteenth century, as Marx famously argued, by a new class."[28] The practice of dueling was linked closely to the power of the aristocracy in British society and the traditions that undergirded it and the subjects it produced. Clearly the code of honor that led to the entitlement and requirement of dueling was sustained by a regime of power that gave it legitimation, the erosion of which pulled at the thread of the entire tapestry of that "honor world." The code of honor that sustained the practice of dueling among the British nobility lost its discursive power and became the subject of mockery only when the practice was adopted by broader and less elite audiences for whom it was not originally intended.

Similarly, the Chinese practice of foot-binding girls and women continued despite the efforts of many to eliminate it, until it was connected to a concern for national honor that was "shared by many in the educated classes who shaped China's transformation from an empire into a modern state."[29] A generation of elites who became increasingly aware of the need to open up to the outside world economically and culturally came to see that such a practice viewed from a foreign perspective might just as easily be seen as a source of collective shame. An honorable practice of femininity and beauty that held fast for generations could no longer survive once it became untethered from elite influence and lost its hold on power. It disappeared almost overnight. As Appiah notes, "Simply put, since footbinding is embedded in a system of status, its abandonment by the elite deprives it of its appeal; a mechanism that echoes in reverse the case of the duel in England, where it was its uptake by people who were not gentlemen that reduced its ability to secure gentlemanly honor."[30] The mechanisms that caused a traditional honorable practice to disappear differed in the two cases, but in both instances the loss of elite status and power led to the erosion of the norm. Appiah's analysis of these cases therefore provides compelling evidence of how clearly traditional codes of honor are connected to structures of power. That might not be the intent of Appiah's work, which is focused on the role honor plays in his somewhat teleological view of moral progress, but his analysis lays bare how clearly codes of honor are tied to power and authority and how the creation and cultivation of honor is always vulnerable to and contingent on the recognition of others.

The concept of group identity, or what the great 14th-century Islamic philosopher Ibn Khaldun termed *asabiyah*, or group-feeling, seems to be active in both these discussions of honor codes. One's membership in a community inspires both connection and power, and looking at political identity from the perspective of belonging to a group can sometimes provide greater insight than consistently viewing it from the traditionally individualistic perspective of Western liberal thought. A significant problem with the latter perspective is that it strains to explain the complexity of intersubjective relations with the thin framework of rationalism, which reduces most of political agency to the rational decision-making of the individual actor, whereas attending to group feeling from the outset, even in this most schematic manner, allows for the emphasis to be placed on dependence on, vulnerability to, and recognition from others in the analysis of political identity. In the *Muqaddimah*, Ibn Khaldun identified *asabiyah* as the key factor in determining the success or the erosion of a political regime, noting that "this is because group feeling gives protection and makes possible mutual defence, the pressing of claims, and every other kind of social activity ... [because] familiar customs determine human nature and character."[31] While we might reject the determinism of his formulation, Ibn Khaldun's analysis of group feeling is nevertheless instructive in exploring the "honor worlds" that Appiah delineates. In each of these cases the group feeling constructs a traditional code of honor and is simultaneously strengthened by it. When the group feeling erodes, because of diminished political and economic power as with the aristocracy in Britain or a changing perception among the educated elite in China, the code of honor that feeds into it is similarly diminished. In both these examples one's status and recognition within the group is fundamental to the construction of oneself as a political subject. As these discursive forms of power erode, so does the sense of the subject as an honorable source of change diminish.

Honor, Liberalism, and Agency

If an analysis of traditional codes of honor reveals a deep embedding in power relations at their core, how is it possible for honor to function as a liberal virtue today, given liberalism's foundational commitment to individualism and rationalism? Perhaps, like Bowman, the very premise can be dismissed as fundamentally incompatible. However, in *Liberalism with Honor*, Sharon Krause makes a valiant attempt to recover honor as a source of liberal agency. In her rendering honor is viewed in multiple ways: as high and principled ambition, as a quality of character, as public recognition, and in its connection to self-respect and human dignity. Most interesting of all is her initial framing of the value of honor in contemporary politics, which gestures at the necessity of a kind of heroic agency without going quite that far. In her account, honor becomes a bulwark against the erosion of liberty— a kind of superpower that allows men and women to risk their lives to defend their liberty.[32] She writes at the very beginning that the book is animated by a "fear of majority tyranny," which makes her interested in "political agency, because it is agency that generates the possibility of resistance to majorities that go bad."[33] From the outset, then, Krause conceives of honor as a safeguard, a guardrail on the rocky cliffs of democracy, something to imbue the individual with a proper sense of civic virtue and embolden them to use their agency for the larger good.

Honor is conceived in a form that ties it to agency directly, but also to a thin formulation of agency that eschews an analysis of power and the complexity of intersubjective relations. Krause's definition of agency is therefore worth attending to as it is quite disconnected from power relations and is clearly classically liberal in its formulation. She writes that "agency implies an awareness of oneself *as* agent, a confidence in one's ability to act, rather than simply react, and to shape, not merely endure, events and circumstances of one's life. The theme of agency has been relatively unexplored by political theorists in recent years, particularly the sources of agency, or the forms of motivation that support it. Honor is one such source" (emphasis in original).[34] Such an account seems to be that of an "unchastened agency," one that emerges from internal self-awareness and confidence in one's ability to act with scant awareness of how we as subjects are always constructed by and through power relations, through the norms that shape and produce us, to the *asabiyahs* that bind and perhaps even empower us. Indeed, for Krause, the chastening of power and subjectivity is precisely what has led to the diminishing of the importance of agency in contemporary political theory. She writes that we have been "educated by a generation of theorists about the power of our circumstances to construct our identities and determine our actions. Race, class, and gender are sometimes given all the credit for what we do or fail to do."[35] In her analysis, all of this talk of power and difference has rubbed away at the possibility of political agency altogether, reducing us to paralysis by unlimited choices or inexorable power. In its place she seeks to retrieve and rework honor as a liberal virtue that can "invigorate the civic sources of liberal democracy" and bring "a new purpose and new resources to this effort."[36]

While the notion that attention to power relations and the complexity of subjectivity makes action impossible is difficult to take at face value, given the wide range of racial, postcolonial, feminist, and queer activism it has produced over several decades, not to mention several centuries of classical literature that managed to cultivate an idea of heroism despite its tragic recognition of life, it is still worth attending to the grounds on which Krause seeks to recover honor for contemporary liberalism. This is where an interesting thread begins to emerge in her writing that gestures briefly at the usefulness of tragic heroism while eschewing that language almost completely as she writes that "honor rises above the natural limits on human action imposed by the motive of egoistic interest. As a result, it can animate riskier and more difficult actions, even actions that involve the risk of life."[37] For Krause the appeal of honor lies in the middle ground it carves out between altruism and self-interest and "makes honor a powerful source of individual agency especially in cases where the risks of action are high and its benefits uncertain, as when one rises to defend individual liberties against encroaching political power or the threat of majority tyranny."[38] She argues that in order to be better citizens, and occasionally great ones, we still need to make a place for honor at liberalism's table, for "the heroic qualities at the heart of honor answer to this need: high and principled ambition, courage, pride, and the powerful desires for self-respect and public distinction."[39]

Krause is not wrong in noting the agentic power of honor, but bypassing its connection to tradition and power also allows her to downplay its foolhardiness and the myopia it can engender in its rigid insistence on following its internal code. If the project of civic renewal and saving liberalism is not a sufficient exhortation, then such an unchastened account of agency is worth exploring in greater depth. Even at the core of liberalism lies Hobbes's influential and blistering denunciation of honor and the destructive pursuit of glory (what Haig Patapan has recently termed "Hobbes' ruthless debunking of honor").[40] Krause notes this familiar critique, writing that "even liberals (and quasi liberals) such as Hobbes and Locke saw the love of honor as a contributor to the ills of humanity's natural condition, on the grounds that it may make persons quixotically idealistic and even warlike, the desire to be a hero may turn into the desire to slay dragons or search perpetually for (and even invent) opportunities for heroism."[41] Such a danger has always been part and parcel of the tragic appeal of honor, but Krause sidesteps this critique by arguing that more moderate forms of honor guided by liberal codes are both compatible and desirable today. Her pivot here rests on a fundamental distinction she draws between the past and the present, a line of demarcation that is difficult to sustain in political life.[42] She argues that the Hobbesian critique of honor relied on the "fixed hierarchy of traditional society" and that one's sense of honor was tied to the inheritance of that social role.[43] By contrast, she argues that "individuals in the modern world are not identified with any social roles in particular, especially not hereditary roles.... [S]ocial roles and the expectations that go with them continue to exert a powerful influence on individuals today. But most of our roles are chosen rather than inherited."[44] The latter formulation is captive to liberalism's insistence on choice and the atomistic freedom of its subjects. To return for a moment to Brown, it is precisely the inheritance of these tattered narratives from the past that continue to haunt and inspire us today. Krause is at once too willing to pull out of honor its redemptive power of agency and too quick to strip away its attachment to tradition and the blindness of its pursuit of glory. She wants all of the revitalizing agency that honor proffers but wants it unchastened, or at least stripped from its dependence on power relations.

The atomistic individual who has such an unchastened capacity for political agency is at the heart of liberalism, and Krause makes no attempts to separate herself from that project. Instead her book is an effort to revitalize liberalism for our time. In doing so, she further compounds and re-entrenches this thin notion of individualism and ties it to the concept of honor more tightly. She reduces the latent and mythic capacity of honor to inspire to just another form of choice. In his layered and perceptive book on freedom and vengeance in film, Robert Watkins offers a convincing critique of such an account of the liberal subject. He writes that "the familiar but fantastic construction of the sovereign individual has the effect of abstracting from the troubling realities of unchosen powers, relations, and determinations that not only restrict but enable our lives."[45] This is precisely what Krause manages to accomplish as she abstracts the concept of honor from tradition, myth, and the vulnerability of recognition by others and reduces it to yet another liberal virtue. Not only does this lead to a "fantastic" account of the individual, as Watkins proclaims; it also erases from the concept its tragic potential. Subjectivity, which highlights the formation of the subject by and its dependence on power relations, gets a lot closer to the complexity of the concept of honor, which is at once beholden by tradition and hopeful of ushering in a utopian future, at once full of heroic verve, and at once dependent, precariously so, on others for its status. Watkins writes, "[I]n other words, whereas individualism connotes choice, subjectivity suggests an accounting for the unchosen—those influences that despite being not chosen, are still active and influential."[46] Watkins's emphasis on subjectivity therefore stands in direct contrast to Krause's insistence on choice over inheritance. In his attention to the myriad ways in which the unchosen continues to shape and influence agency he brings to the forefront the complex subjectivity that I argue operates at the heart of the idea of honor. Further, it allows for a more multifaceted approach to agency itself that goes well beyond the limits of liberalism, arguing that "a critical analysis of individualism and the associated sovereignty of choice intimates the need to not merely better appreciate the unchosen, structural context in which agency takes place, but also to rethink agency itself as less free, more negotiated and subject to some external determination."[47]

Honor, Glory, and Inheritance

The attempt to restore honor as a liberal virtue to revitalize political agency seems even more problematic if one returns to the canonical sources of modern political thought to examine the treatment of honor more closely. Several writers in the modern era engage with the concept of honor: Machiavelli in his discussion of republicanism in the *Discourses* but even more interestingly in aesthetic form in the *Prince* (which is explored in a subsequent chapter in more detail), Hobbes's critique of the dangerous pursuit of glory that accompanies honor, and Montesquieu's analysis of honor as both a form of protection and an inheritance. In doing so, they emphasize that honor contains within itself elements of both the chosen and the unchosen. As Patapan argues in his recent article, "modernity inaugurates a decisive break from classical and pious conceptions of honor, an innovative perspective that continues to shape our contemporary conceptions of honor, and the political institutions that emerge from them."[48] Returning to Hobbes and Montesquieu briefly reveals a much thornier and more problematic concept of honor that is difficult to separate quite so cleanly from its reckless ambition and essential myopia regarding its impact on others. Honor, and the pursuit of it, can be a dangerous sedative to introduce into political thinking as it dulls the senses from the essential recognition of one's dependence on others.

Honor emerges as a much more complex and difficult concept in this literature than in Krause's moderated liberal version, which restores it in a more pliable form as self-respect and the desire for individual self-mastery: "[I]nsofar as honor supports individual agency without promising or requiring the perfection of the soul, it is compatible with liberal forms, purposes and character."[49] But it is less than clear that the concept of honor can be shorn so cleanly from its inheritance, from the unchosen and structural context in which it operates, to borrow again from Watkins's language. The kind of agency it engenders results more often than not in the blinding pursuit of glory, and Krause has greater faith in the bulwarks of democratic society to restrain its reckless pursuit than it perhaps deserves. In her portrayal, the liberal subject who can revitalize civil society is "the honorable person [who] wants to be the kind of person who lives up to her code, but her concern with appearances does not diminish her allegiance to a set of independent principles and the inner desire for self-respect."[50] In Krause's rendering the allegiance to a code of honor is strong enough to endure, even when the social consequences for doing so shift. This stands in contrast to Appiah's account of the widespread comic dismissal Wellington faced after his empty duel, where he adhered to a traditional code that demanded a particular performance, only to be mocked by the public since the power of the practice had rapidly diminished and its social capital had eroded. In the instances Appiah describes, shifts in traditional codes of honor can and do occur, and indeed are most likely to take place when they become untethered from the regimes of power that sustain them.

To unpack this further, the lasting allegiance to an independent set of principles that Krause admires as central to the concept of honor is precisely the aspect of honor that Hobbes decries in *Leviathan*. Throughout chapter 10, Hobbes clearly links honor to power and to the recognition and validation of others and does so much more explicitly than either Krause or Appiah. He begins with the fundamental and inescapable link between reputation and power, writing that "reputation of power, is Power ... because it draweth with it the adherence of those who need protection," and further, that "what quality soever maketh a man beloved, or feareth of many; or the reputation of such quality is Power."[51] For Hobbes it is precisely the power exerted by reputation and "the manifestation of the Value we set on one another ... that ... is commonly called Honoring or Dishonoring."[52] He only then connects the public worth of a man to dignity, which is interesting since so much of the discourse of honor in recent research ties it instinctively to respect and dignity but seems to fundamentally miss how shot through this virtue is with power. He notes that there is always an element of the recognition of power in honor and ties it clearly to custom: to ask one for aid is "a sign we have an opinion he has the power to help," "to obey," and "to do those things to another, which he takes for signes of Honour, or which the Law or Custome makes so, is to Honour; because in approving the Honour done by others, he acknowledgeth the power which others acknowledge."[53] As if the ties between honor, custom, and the acknowledgment or recognition of others could not be clearer, Hobbes goes even further, making the link between honor and power explicit: "Honour consisteth onely in the opinion of Power."[54]

The joy that one feels about one's own power when grounded in one's own experiences Hobbes characterizes as glorying that can be understood to be confidence, but there is a more toxic and dangerous form that can rise from the pursuit of honor. Hobbes writes of honor that "if grounded on the flattery of others, or onely supposed by himself, for delight in the consequences of it is called VAINE-GLORY."[55] For Hobbes, the reckless pursuit of honor leads to vainglory, and this is precisely why he considers it to be a dangerous form of agency for politics. Hobbes's analysis serves as an important correction to Krause's idea that honor can be moderated and sanded down by the institutions of liberalism. The agentic power of honor is very real, but it is difficult to harness and not so easily moderated by prudence and self-awareness. Indeed, it leads to a kind of myopia about the consequences of one's actions, perhaps even a tragic blindness. Hobbes makes this abundantly clear when he writes, "Vain-glorious men, such as estimate their sufficiency by the flatter of other men, or the fortune of some precedent action, without assured ground of hope from the true knowledge of themselves, are inclined to rash engaging; and in the approach of danger, or difficulty, to retire if they can: because not seeing the way of safety, they will rather hazard their honour, which may be salved with an excuse; than their lives, for which no salve is sufficient."[56] Even so, Hobbes's dismissal of honor as leading to the destructiveness of vainglory remains entirely too rationalist. This is Hobbes, after all, who believes fundamentally in a clarifying and enlightening power of reason and who roots his entire political project in the capacity to "read thyself," suggesting that through the meticulous observation of one's own nature, one can come to understand the nature of all mankind, as long as one proceeds in a rational and orderly manner and with clear and perspicuous language. As such, Hobbes's critique of honor doesn't quite get to the core of its tragic agency, but it does highlight the dangerous myopia that a blind pursuit of honor can bring.

Unlike Hobbes, Montesquieu is far more positive about the role that honor plays in contemporary politics, but his account too contains an inescapable note of the tragic, if not much of a melody. For him, as for Krause, who draws heavily on his construction of honor for her rewriting of its agentic power, honor functions as a kind of political virtue, as a defense against tyranny, and is therefore necessary for republican and constitutional government. For him, it seems to serve in opposition to despotic government, which rules by fear. Thus, while honor seems to be the essence of good government for Montesquieu he curiously nods at its myth-making potential when he notes the value of something he calls "false honor." In *The Spirit of the Laws*, Montesquieu writes that honor is "the prejudice of each person and each condition, takes the place of the political virtue of which I have spoken and represents it everywhere. It can inspire the finest actions; joined with the force of the laws, it can lead to the goal of government as does virtue itself."[57] Honor is therefore a form of political virtue that can inspire agency. Unlike Hobbes, Montesquieu, while similarly noting the destructiveness of the pursuit of glory (he writes that "ambition is pernicious in a republic"), does not conflate such a pursuit with honor.[58] Honor has an almost gravitational pull for him; it is at the center of the entire enterprise, giving cohesion and life force to the body politic. He writes that "honor makes all the parts of the body politic move; its very action binds them, and each person works for the common good, believing he works for his individual interests."[59]

As he goes further into his analysis of honor, though, a more fugitive and tragic strain becomes visible. He asserts that the "honor that guides all the parts of the state is a false honor, but this false honor is as useful to the public as the true one would be to the individuals who could have it."[60] There is a whiff of fantasy here, maybe a noble lie, or perhaps more accurately a nod at the myth-making potential of honor (and its twin, patriotism) and how it can help create a common narrative framework to tie people together in a republic. He even notes the inflexible nature of honor, writing that it "has its laws and rules and is incapable of yielding, as it depends on its own caprice and not on that of another."[61] Thus, even as he notes its value for cementing the *asabiyah* of a republic and its myth-making potential in the narrative glue it provides for a nation, Montesquieu cannot escape the performative bonds that accompany honor and often make it bitter and unyielding in its adherence to its traditional code or its myopic pursuit of glory. The final tragic note that Montesquieu sounds is when he writes that honor "glories in scorning life" and that this is precisely its source of resistance to despotism as it "has consistent rules and sustains its caprices" and can therefore not be ruled by the tyranny of fear.[62] It is this scorn for life that gives honor its heroic agency but is also the source of its tragic downfall as it blinds those who pursue it at all costs to the regimes of power and the bonds of tradition that undergird it.

Toward a Tragic Theory of Honor

This exploration of the politics of honor in modern and contemporary thought has brought to the forefront the fragmenting and multiplicity of its persistence in political life. Honor remains present in many forms, some of which are closely related to each other. This book theorizes the concept of honor as it emerges in the political imagination through an analysis of several different popular texts of literary and visual culture. The aim here is not to pin down the concept of honor with definitional clarity but rather to show how the very conceptual slipperiness and multivalence of honor and its conflation with related concepts of duty, patriotism, and heroism account for its enduring appeal. Honor, and the pursuit of glory, retain their hold on the popular imaginary with their traces of mythic heroism, but they also remain inescapably tragic, even in the most optimistic and pliable accounts. The concept of honor contains within it an interesting temporal dimension: it remains tethered to the past even as it haunts and perhaps also inspires the present as it reaches toward the future. It is one of those undergirding narratives of the political that is tattered but enduring in our fragmented and globalized world of difference precisely because of its power to inspire heroic agency, even as it falters in tragic ways. It is a complex idea that cannot be separated from its embeddedness in power, its inherent vulnerability to public recognition, the pressing force of tradition, the demands of patriotic duty, and the kinds of subjectivities it constructs. Honor is too appealing and seductive an idea to simply be left to dry on the branches of traditionalism to harden into a brittle reactionary politics. A concept of honor, while often leading to myopia and the reckless pursuit of vainglory, still has the capacity to infuse our politics with mythic appeal—to give to it the affirmative power of heroic action that embraces life and seeks to overcome resentment and wallowing in a past that it cannot will away. Rather than rehabilitate honor and recover an anodyne version of it for liberalism, as Krause does, or as the key to moral revolution, as Appiah does, this book attempts to underline the affirmative and tragic notes of honor at the same time as it exposes its blinding and binding qualities.

The ensuing chapters of book examine the enduring concept of honor and the continued presence of the past by analyzing an eclectic selection of texts from contemporary visual and literary culture. The first two chapters develop a critique of honor and explore how it both binds and blinds political subjects. Chapter 1 is centered on a close reading of the popular HBO television show *Game of Thrones*, a fantasy series that is surprisingly grounded in gritty realism. The show continually plays against the narrative tropes of the fantasy genre by consistently undermining the traditional heroic narrative and the audience's expectations of revenge and justice. This chapter closely analyzes the character arc of the protagonist of the first season, Lord Eddard Stark, known as Ned, who embodies the traditional narrative tropes of honor and heroism on the show and is an incongruous fit for the political intrigues and scheming of Westeros. The chapter explores Ned Stark's narrative arc to sketch out a more complex understanding of the politics of honor that is grounded in the conceptual framework of subjectivity and the politics of recognition. It begins by examining the tight nexus between tradition and honor that is viscerally woven through the identity of the Starks and underlines this connection through a close reading of Aristotle's writing on honor and family in the *Nichomachean Ethics*. For Ned Stark, the weight of past tradition continually exerts a role in the present. The burden of the inherited and unchosen past makes his code of honor that much more rigid, a garment that binds and constrains his every move and at times leads him into what Aristotle calls *hamartia*, or the tragic form of error. The chapter then introduces Hegel's account of chivalric honor to deepen the analysis, arguing that at the very heart of the politics of honor lies the concept of recognition. In the absence of recognition, or when recognition is muted or complicated, honor appears to be something much less determinate and fixed, emerging instead as a concept of particular vulnerability and contestability. This argument is developed further through an engagement with Patchen Markell's work on the limits of recognition and Judith Butler's work on power and subjectivity.

Chapter 2, the second of the two chapters that develop a critique of honor, opens with an analysis of President Trump's speech in front of the CIA's Wall of Honor in the initial days of his presidency and the backlash that followed. This framing allows the chapter to highlight the tight linkage between espionage and honor in political discourse and to show how simplified this narrative is in contemporary political culture (easily shrouded as it is in the language of duty, sacrifice, and patriotism). A much more complex account of the relationship between honor and espionage emerges when its depiction in contemporary popular culture is explored, where the pursuit of honor serves less as a guiding principle for the intrepid spies and more as a kind of anesthetic that dulls their contemplation of the consequences of violence in "the line of duty." The chapter examines this conceptual nexus between honor, espionage, and the formation of identity through a close narrative reading of the FX drama *The Americans*, a drama set in the early 1980s during the Cold War. In particular, it highlights the show's portrayal of motherhood and how it operates within and against the context of Cold War discourse of mothers as a source of corruption. Honor, in much of literature, and certainly in the context of espionage, is often seen as a heroic, masculine, and gendered characteristic. *The Americans*, however, subverts this narrative radically by casting Elizabeth Jennings as the seemingly unquestioning embodiment of this trope, who blends the roles of mother and recruiter in her relationship with her daughter, Paige, and in doing so works to both confirm and subvert traditional Cold War narratives of the mother as a source of contamination, a trope that Michael Rogin referred to as "Cold War Moms." Such a reading of the complex issues of motherhood, identity, and the challenges of family in *The Americans* disrupts the notion of an easy link between honor and espionage in political discourse and, in doing so, suggests that the outcry about the debasement of the Wall of Honor is reflective of a larger anxiety about facing a political present without the comforting sedation of norms of honor and patriotism.

Chapter 3 is the first of two chapters that come together to explore the links between honor and agency by emphasizing its aesthetic, affirmative, and tragic aspects in order to account for its enduring appeal. This chapter examines Hilary Mantel's Booker Prize–winning novel *Wolf Hall*, a masterful work of historical fiction, which eschews the soapy narrative tropes of that genre and instead delivers a deeply researched but creatively rewritten account of Henry VIII's most efficient and ruthless counselor, Thomas Cromwell. For Mantel's Cromwell, honor is essentially fungible—it is a currency to be exchanged and traded, a means to an end in the practice of the art of power. Mantel's revisionist portrayal of Cromwell stands in sharp contrast to the chivalric account of honor embodied by Ned Stark of *Game of Thrones*, which was deeply rooted in and constrained by ancestral tradition and which marked a failure to attend to honor's dependence on the recognition of others. By contrast, Mantel's Cromwell is the master of a tactile political economy; he is a skilled cook, a deft surveyor of kitchen pantries, a sharp appraiser of jewelry and fine tapestries, well versed in the flows of emerging financial markets, and a brutally precise architect of law—a man particularly well suited to "multiplying" the arts of governance and radically expanding his terrain of power. This chapter performs a close reading of *Wolf Hall*'s portrayal of Cromwell alongside Niccolò Machiavelli's *The Prince* to uncover a concept of honor that is at once instrumental to the art of power and an ornamental representation of its deeply aesthetic nature.

Chapter 4 is a detailed examination of honor, heroism and tragedy. It takes the concept of the heroic seriously, with all of its complexities, to move beyond a simple savior narrative to something more complex, unsettling, destabilizing, and possibly affirmative. The epic heroes that are discussed in this chapter have a fundamental grasp of the tragic core within the concept of honor. They consistently affirm the importance of honor and the shared meaning it provides, but they also underline its association with rage, grief, and death. At the heart of this chapter is a close reading of *The Iliad*, a deeply tragic epic poem whose central dramatic focus is the question of honor and the price that honor exacts. The Greek hero, of whom Achilles is paradigmatic, is more complex than the heroes we seem to yearn for today. He is violent, reckless, and dangerous, subject to forces he cannot control, formed by divine power, bound by fate, yet full of human desire. He lives according to a code of honor that is vulnerable to and constructed by power, power that rests on the recognition of others. He is not the atomistic individual at the heart of liberalism. This chapter constructs a critique of the honorable liberal hero through an exploration of the disruptive and contingent links between honor and tragedy in *The Iliad* by drawing on Nietzsche's work on tragedy and the work of classical scholars of heroism, highlighting in particular the links between honor, anger, and grief. It also briefly engages with the fascinating therapeutic work done by Jonathan Shay, who found remarkable parallels between the plot of *The Iliad* and his treatment of posttraumatic stress disorder in his Vietnam War veteran patients. There is something persistently affirmative about the politics of honor in its mythic capacity to impart meaning, but it cannot be unthinkingly imported into contemporary politics without attending to its tragic core.

Chapter 5, the final and concluding chapter of the book, moves from the epic hero to the modern superhero, closely examining the blockbuster and modern mythic appeal of the Marvel Cinematic Universe by analyzing its version of the star-spangled superhero, Captain America. From his origin story as Steve Rogers in the Second World War in the MCU until the torch is passed to the Falcon, who becomes the first Black Captain America, he operates consistently at the intersection of militarism, myth-making, and honor through the various twists and turns his character takes. Captain America consistently weaves multiple pasts into a complex and fragmented present, responding to and calibrating his code of honor to adjust to modern audiences. The character is steeped in nostalgia for a more orderly past, which reveals a deep sense of anxiety about the present. In this moment of democratic erosion across the globe, a superhero cloaked in red, white, and blue might seem to be an incongruous and anachronistic figure to explore, but in the MCU's rendering he begins to incorporate the tragic dimension of honor into a messier version of the American myth that seems startlingly present, with its focus on race and recognition of the failures of American political institutions. As such, the figure of Captain America becomes a useful lens through which to examine the relationship between honor and democratic erosion by providing one more layer of analysis to underline the enduring appeal of honor in the political imagination today.

1

"You Win or You Die"

Honor, Recognition, and Subjectivity in *Game of Thrones*

The fantasy television drama *Game of Thrones* became a cultural phenomenon during its eight-season run, inspiring countless internet memes and gifs and turning into HBO's biggest hit ever in terms of audience numbers and appeal. It was one of the most talked about shows in recent memory, known for its spectacular battles, shocking murders, and graphic sex scenes (and an all too dismissive approach to sexual violence). It became firmly lodged in the popular discourse and remains so today, as evidenced by the smashing success of the recently launched prequel to the original series, *House of the Dragon*, which has captured millions of viewers, many of whom had professed never to return to the fictional world of Westeros after what they deemed to be a disappointing and rushed final season that left many fan favorites in surprising positions. *Game of Thrones* became an entrenched part of the political imagination during its eight seasons. Not only were there countless think-pieces published during and after its airing in various newspapers, magazines, and journals, but it took over Twitter, Reddit, and Facebook, inspired a million memes, and even had its own fan convention (Con of Thrones). It became part of the cultural lexicon, with terms like "the Red Wedding" and "Winter is coming" now familiar to those who have never watched a minute of the show but who can easily grasp the reference. No less a figure than former president Obama asked one of its directors the fate of a character after a particularly shocking twist and confessed himself a fan of the show.[1] *Game of Thrones*, which is adapted from and inspired by the fantasy novel series *A Song of Ice and Fire* by George R. R. Martin (though the fictional series is as yet unfinished and the show outpaced the books after its fifth season), is a sprawling and textured show, with multiple dense and interwoven threads and an enormous and expanding cast of characters. Set in the fantasy lands of Westeros and Essos and loosely inspired by the English War of the Roses and various mythic traditions, it is a darkly tragic and multilayered show about the complexity and essential contingency of politics. In this realm, not only are multiple games of strategy and power politics being played simultaneously to secure the Iron Throne of Westeros, but the entire political tableau is contingent on keeping at bay the larger threat of the otherworldly White Walkers and their Army of the Dead (terrifying zombie-like characters loosely seen as metaphors for climate change), who threaten to overrun all seven kingdoms if the already fraying border in the North of the country fails to hold. In a sense, the largest game being played in the show is how little the endless scheming and power politics in Westeros matter as the entire edifice rests on immense, and perhaps climatic, forces that seem almost impossible to defeat unless the game can be put aside to focus on the existential threat.

While *Game of Thrones* is certainly a fantasy series (there are dragons aplenty and magic is woven throughout its many plots), its fantasy is of a darker and more tragic kind than most. (Indeed, Martin has explicitly called the series a rebuttal to the "Disneyland Middle Ages" trope of fantasy writing.)[2] It is resolutely and somewhat paradoxically grounded in a gritty realism, continually playing against the narrative tropes of the genre by consistently undermining traditional hero and heroine narratives and with them the audience's expectations of revenge and justice. This reworking of the fantasy genre is clearly seen in the very first season of the show, which at first seems to introduce a typical father as hero and protector of the family narrative, only to sharply and tragically undermine this arc. The protagonist of the first season is Lord Eddard Stark, known as Ned, the lord of Winterfell and the warden of the North, who embodies the traditional narrative tropes of honor and heroism on the show and is consequently a less than ideal fit for the political intrigues and scheming of Westeros, which are rarely tethered by considerations of morality and justice. In the complex world of *Game of Thrones*, Ned Stark articulates a rather uncomplicated view of individual political agency, which suffers greatly from his inability to recognize the power relations that are constantly at play. Instead, he holds on tightly to his code of honor, which is rooted in his ancestral traditions and in his firmly held belief that the inherent nobility of his honor will be recognized and respected by all and will prevail above all other considerations at the end of the day. His unyielding attachment to his honor puts him at a serious disadvantage as he stumbles through the many intrigues of the capital of King's Landing, and his inability to win at the game of thrones becomes one of the core themes of the show. As such, the first season sets the tone for the political imaginary of the show's eight-season run, as his tragic failure haunts and shapes his family for seasons to come and remains a throughline in the show's plot as a cautionary tale for many of its characters of the pitfalls of honor in a world of political intrigue.

In this first season, Ned Stark stands in sharp contrast to the others we meet shortly thereafter. Given the subversive aims of *Game of Thrones*, his resolute faith in his code of honor is crushed by the intrigues of a scheming court that is all too familiar with how to play the game of power politics. As the queen of Westeros, Cersei Lannister famously says, "When you play the game of thrones, you win or you die. There is no middle ground."[3] Perhaps the choice is not quite as binary as she suggests, and perhaps honor is more than just a fool's noble error, but the show repeatedly warns us of the questionable assumptions that underline a politics based on a rigid code of honor and the failures they engender, such as its inability to come to terms with the complexity of subjectivity and power, its reliance on recognition by others, and its stubborn belief in the universality of its claims. Ned Stark's sense of honor and duty conflict sharply with the role he is interpellated in as a key figure in the political game of thrones that plays out in King's Landing and ripples through the rest of Westeros. He is impeded by his inability to realize the ways in which his code of honor conditions his very subjectivity and consequently his own psychic recoil from it. Related to this is his misguided belief in the potency of his own political agency, a notion that is divorced from an understanding of the complex relations between subjectivity, recognition, and power.

This chapter explores Ned Stark's narrative arc by focusing primarily on the first season of *Game of Thrones*, where his story begins and ends (though his legacy and impact persist throughout the entire arc of the show and shape the motivations of some if its central characters, who define themselves both through and against him). It offers a critique of honor as both binding and blinding and develops a more complex conception of honor that is grounded in the framework of subjectivity and the politics of recognition. It first analyzes the tight linkage between tradition and honor that is integral to Ned Stark's identity and reads it alongside Aristotle's writing on honor and family in the *Nichomachean Ethics*. For Ned Stark, the weight of his inherited ancestral past continues to exert a role in the present and shapes the obligations he strains to meet. The burden of the past makes his code of honor that much more rigid, a garment that binds and constrains his every move and at times leads him into what Aristotle calls *hamartia*, or the tragic form of error.

It then examines his key political role as the best friend of the king of Westeros, Robert Baratheon, who in the opening episode of the series invites him to be the hand of the king and the second in command of Westeros, therefore ushering him on to center stage in the power games of the capital. This move from the North to the South displaces and destabilizes him in multiple ways. The very fact of his departure leads to deep conflict with his wife Catelyn, who suggests that he is merely using honor as an excuse to justify his choice to leave much of his family behind. The journey from his ancestral lands to the capital is therefore much more than a spatial move; it also places Ned Stark in a very different political context as he leaves behind the predictable and ordered space of family and tradition for the power politics of the capital. The move forces him to trace the limits of his faith in his own code of honor as it increasingly becomes clear that his strict adherence to honor and tradition is incommensurable with the political context of King's Landing, where it simply does not translate into the language games of realpolitik that everyone else is playing. By reading this set of events alongside Hegel's account of chivalric honor, this chapter argues that at the very heart of the politics of honor lies the concept of recognition—honor demands to be recognized by others, and its value (or its "shine") is diminished when that recognition is denied. These arguments are further developed in combination with Patchen Markell's work on the limits of recognition and Judith Butler's work on power and subjectivity. In the absence of recognition, or when recognition is muted or complicated, honor appears to be something much less determinate and fixed, emerging instead as a concept of particular vulnerability and contestability. Finally, the chapter analyzes the legacy of honor that Ned Stark bequeaths to the political imaginary of *Games of Thrones* and how it shapes the motivations of some of its central characters.

"Winter Is Coming": Honor, Tradition, and Family

In his *Politics,* Aristotle famously argues that man is "by nature a political animal."[4] In the Aristotelian schema, the ability to achieve self-sufficiency can occur only within the context of a community. Membership in the community as an active part of the whole is the only way to achieve true happiness. For Aristotle, the polis comes to be "for the sake of living, but it remains in existence for the sake of living well." Man, his household or family (*oikos*), and the larger political community of which it is a part (polis), are therefore linked closely together in degrees of self-sufficiency. Happiness is linked clearly to the survival and thriving of the entire community, and the family unit forms an essential part of that whole. The centrality of family to happiness as an active form of thriving is similarly seen in the account Ned Stark gives of himself. The traditions of the Starks act as a regulative set of principles for him as he governs his lands as the warden of the North. The wisdom handed down through generations of the family, tested by battle and conflict and centuries of coping with forbidding winters, is seen as a core component of both happiness and self-sufficiency. For Ned Stark, however, the attachment to these traditions of House Stark go beyond the notion of happiness and self-sufficiency and ossify into a rigid code of honor. This inherited code is an omnipresent force in Ned Stark's life, one that both constrains and defines him with its assumed and unquestioned power.

In the world of *Game of Thrones*, of all the major houses in the land, House Stark is the one that is most closely associated with the past, which is particularly important given the opening scenes of the series, which show that the forgotten secrets of seemingly eternal winters and the fantastical figures that threatened Westeros in the ancient past are beginning to reemerge in the present. The Starks seem to have access to ancient wisdom and centuries of tradition, and they keep to the Old Gods, which are represented by the haunting weirwood trees, in contrast to the seven gods that are worshiped in most of Westeros in more familiar temples or septs. Throughout the show there are various hints of the lingering mystical powers that the Starks possess that suggest a deep connection between the family and a buried magical past that remains present in faint whispers. Along with that uncanny mystical connection, the Starks also lay claim to some of the earliest models of political governance in Westeros. Ned Stark often reminds us that theirs is the blood of the First Men, the first humans to arrive in Westeros and establish some form of order and rule of law.

The close connection to tradition is repeatedly invoked in the grim and foreboding words of the motto of House Stark: "Winter is coming." The words serve at once as a warning and a link to the past, but they also underline the necessity of preparing for brutal conditions that are completely unpredictable. They are a portent to prepare for the onslaught of forces beyond one's control, to prepare for suffering during a winter that may last for many years, and the words themselves are permeated with a tragic recognition of the impending future. In the icy and bleak North, a region characterized by hardship and a sense of living on the very edge of Westerosi civilization, tradition is the key to survival, and the "old ways" provide a rope to hold on to when the winds start to howl and the snow blankets the earth. But tradition is more than just a code of survival for Ned Stark; it is a source of identity, meaning, happiness, and fulfillment.

Interestingly, in the *Ethics*, Aristotle notes that the idea of happiness, which is grounded in self-sufficiency and active thriving within the community, is often linked to the concept of honor, and sometimes mistakenly so. He writes that political science aims at "happiness, and identif[ies] living well and faring well with being happy, but with regard to what is happiness they differ, and the many do not give the same account as the wise. For the former think it is some plain and obvious thing, like pleasure, wealth, or honor."[5] Honor is therefore linked clearly to happiness, not necessarily as the most effective explanation but only the most obvious one. Aristotle writes, "Happiness, then, is something final and self-sufficient, and is the end of action"[6] and "a virtuous activity of soul, of a certain kind."[7] In order to be happy, one needs the self-sufficiency of family and community, but honor often becomes something that is overlaid on top of this nexus of forces.

In Aristotle's discussion of honor, it becomes clear that while it serves as one of the many constitutive forces that link the individual to their family and the larger community, it can sometimes be problematic. Thus, while honor can lead to happiness, it can also become a tie that binds, leading people into pride and failure. Aristotle complicates the concept of honor by suggesting that "of honor, wisdom, and pleasure, just in respect of their goodness, the accounts are distinct, and diverse. The good, therefore, is not something common answering to an Idea."[8] Multiple formulations of honor are therefore possible, perhaps adapting to different contexts and communities, and too rigid an attachment to a traditional code of honor might not always be the best path to tread. But the links between nobility and honor are often difficult to loosen as they are more likely to closely connect their traditional codes of honor to happiness. Aristotle writes, "A consideration of the prominent types of life shows that people of superior refinement and active disposition identify happiness with honor; for that is, roughly speaking, the end of political life. But it seems too superficial to be what we are looking for, since it is thought to depend on those who bestow honor rather than on him who receives it.... [A]t any rate, virtue is better. And perhaps one might even suppose this to be, rather than honor, the end of political life."[9]

Thus, honor is often perceived to be "the end of political life" by refined and noble people, but it is also a flimsy and contingent thing since, crucially, it depends on others. To be deemed honorable one needs to have honor bestowed on one by others. It serves as a kind of external but thin affirmation—it might be acquired through the work of generations, but it can also be stripped away in a moment as it is fundamentally contingent on others for its function—and for Aristotle it cannot function as a telos, or ultimate end, of political life. Indeed, relying too heavily on honor can lead inexorably to tragedy. This is seen quite clearly in the narrative arc of Ned Stark, for whom a code of honor functions as a regulative idea with destructive consequences.

Ned Stark's sense of honor is closely linked to his duty to his family, his house, and his people. The Stark House motto "Winter is coming," which warns of impending hardship and is a reminder of duty and sacrifice, is a constant refrain in the show, and his ancestral role as the warden of the North is something he takes very seriously. It is worth exploring the conceptual relationship between honor and duty, which is interesting in its convergence and divergence. In contemporary usage, where honor is often thought of as dignity or respect, the terms are often used together (honor and duty, duty and honor), usually in a patriotic context. Conceptually, the difference between the two is less one of kind than of degree. Duty is a close cousin of honor, but it is more directly associated with a sense of obligation to others, which honor does not always contain. Honor can sometimes oblige one to fight in a duel, to stand up for one's family, or to compel a set of actions, in much the same way as duty, and they are similar in that both are constitutive parts of identity and often connected to a greater cause. However, honor has an additional component that duty does not, where it is dependent on the recognition of others. External honor, which is bestowed on one by others, requires titles and ornaments for all to see. Internal honor, usually understood as a code or a sense of integrity, is often seen as closer to duty, but in its subject formation it too is dependent on relations with others. Duty is just as obligatory as honor but perhaps less vulnerable to the recognition of others who can acknowledge its shine.

For Ned Stark, as the head of his house and the warden of the North, his inherited tradition is one of honor and duty, and both are tied to justice, where justice is closely connected to self-sufficiency and the thriving of the community. In the North, it falls on Ned Stark to sentence and punish those who break the laws that must necessarily be obeyed for the community to survive. One such sentence is the penalty of death for any man who deserts the Night's Watch, which is a brotherhood of men who guard the massive icy

Wall that marks the northern border of Westeros. The Starks are tied closely to the Wall—there has always been a member of the Stark family who serves in the Night's Watch, and a member of the Starks, Bran the Builder, was its main architect. When we first meet Ned Stark, he is the picture of familiar happiness as he watches his children play in the courtyard of Winterfell, their ancestral home, when a rider arrives with news that a member of the Night's Watch has deserted and been captured. As warden of the North it falls to Ned to administer the king's justice. He insists on carrying out the sentence himself, a grim duty that he takes no joy in, but he also insists on using the execution as a teaching moment for his youngest son, Bran, over his wife's objections. His wife Catelyn says to him, "Ned, ten is too young to see such things," to which he gruffly responds, "He won't be a boy forever. And Winter is coming."[10] In this harsh climate, he feels the duty of the Stark tradition pressing down on him—its code of honor must be passed down to even his youngest son, despite its brutality. He rides off abruptly with all of his sons to carry out the sentence with his ancestral sword, leaving his wife and daughters behind in Winterfell.

Not only is he rigid in his stance about exposing his young son to death and violence over his wife's objections, but he is also impassive in the face of the deserter's claims of what happened. To him the man is simply an oath breaker, a traitor, a person void of honor, someone whose small part threatens the survival of the whole if his desertion goes unpunished. Thanks to the powerful opening scene of this first episode the audience already knows that the man has witnessed the return of the mythical and threatening White Walkers after centuries of absence and that he has fled the scene of a massacre. Immediately, Ned Stark is faced with competing claims of justice: does he follow the laws of the land and execute the deserter, or does he acknowledge that there might be some truth to these seemingly fantastical claims? "Winter is coming" allows for multiple interpretations—certainly the words are a command to be swift in the lord's justice and carry out the sentence against the deserter to keep the community safe, but they are also a warning about the arrival of the White Walkers and the immense climatic threat they represent, which Ned Stark fails to see.

As the grim scene unfolds, the deserter is hauled up to the Stark party, scared out of his wits and mumbling about the White Walkers even as he is marched up to the block. He says to Ned Stark, "I know I broke my oath. I know I am a deserter. I should have gone back to the Wall and warned them. But I saw what I saw. I saw the White Walkers."[11] Ned listens to him impassively and then nods to his guards to put the man on the block so he can carry out the sentence. Invoking the authority of the king, he says, "I, Eddard, of the House Stark, Lord of Winterfell, and Warden of the North, sentence you to die." Bran looks on, with some encouragement from Ned's bastard son, Jon, who tells him not to look away, that their father will know if he does. Multiple strands are therefore woven into this scene. To Ned, it appears to be relatively uncomplicated: the swift punishment of a deserter, the passing down of an ancestral tradition, the upholding of an ancient code of honor, duty, and justice. In Aristotle's words, he is making "his fellow citizens good and obedient to the laws."[12] But the shifting perspectives in the scene add a deep layer of contingency to the ritual act of execution: the otherworldly threat is real and potentially supersedes the law of the land; the traditional code itself might be more complex than it appears; and the inauguration of his son into the code is a moment that marks the loss of Bran's innocence and passes on to him the confining honor and duty of inherited tradition. The little boy steels himself to watch the execution, and when it is over, Ned rides over to him and asks, "You understand why I did it?" Bran responds, "Jon said he was a deserter." "Yes," Ned says, "but do you understand why I had to kill him?" Bran, who has been raised on Stark tradition, quickly replies, "Our way is the old way" and "The man who passes the sentence should swing the sword." Ned nods. For Ned this settles the matter. For him, this is the way things have always been done in the North, and it demonstrates how closely his code of honor is bound up with tradition and how it clearly regulates his actions. But Bran, like the viewers, is left unsettled about what he has witnessed and asks, "Is it true he saw the White Walkers?" His father explains that the creatures have been gone for thousands of years, but Bran is not yet ready to let it go. "So he was lying?" For a moment, doubt flits across Ned's face before he shuts it out. "A mad man sees what he sees," he replies, and turns and walks away. The scene ends with a lingering shot of Bran's unsettled face.

To further add to the sense of doubt, the very next scene opens with a grisly close-up of a dead direwolf that the execution party stumbles across—a magical creature that, like the White Walkers, has been gone for centuries and vanished into lore, whose living pups the Stark children subsequently adopt as pets. Traces of magic and long buried dangers are everywhere in this opening episode, but Ned misses it all. In that, his actions correspond to the ancient Greek concept of *hamartia*, which arises out "of a misinterpretation of the circumstances in which a person is acting."[13] He carries on with an uncomplicated sense of his own political agency, secure in the honor and the justice of his actions, but with a flawed recognition of the context in which he is acting. His honor binds him and regulates his actions, but it also blinds him to much of what is swirling around him.

The weight of traditional honor and the duty of family are clearly powerful and regulating forces for Ned Stark, and they have kept him securely in the North and away from the political intrigues of the capital for years, but this is quickly called into question. The tight focus on tradition and family pans out to a much wider view later in the same episode when his oldest and dearest friend, King Robert Baratheon, suddenly shows up in Winterfell after a gap of many years and makes an insistent demand on Ned to become the hand of the king. Robert's request is a sovereign command, but it is also grounded in a deep and complex friendship. (Robert and Ned grew up together from boyhood and Ned played a key role in Robert's rebellion and in helping him to win the crown.) "I need you, Ned," Robert says. "I'm not trying to honor you." For Robert it is not a question of bestowing an honorable title on his old friend; he needs someone he can trust to carry out his commands, and so he turns to the man who is much more of a brother to him than those of his own blood. "I'm not worthy of the honor," Ned replies formally, but he is already chafing at Robert's demand that he leave his home and lands and navigate the power politics of King's Landing. When pushed further, Ned reveals the source of his objection: "I'm a Northman.... I belong here... not down South in the rat's nest they call the capital." Following the king's order requires that he leave his home, much of his family, and the security of his identity as a Stark and the warden of the North for a place where none of those aspects of his identity are fully recognized by others. But this is not an order that can be easily ignored as Robert Baratheon is the closest thing to a brother that Ned has. The king is family, but choosing to follow him south requires leaving his own family at a time of crisis, the costs of which are something his wife makes clear to Ned when he makes the decision to leave. In doing so, she begins to untangle some of the tight knots between tradition, family, and honor that Ned has carefully woven.

In a meticulously observed scene that ripples with layers of emotional turmoil, Ned's bastard son, Jon Snow, who serves as a constant reminder of Ned's only act of dishonor to his family, comes to say farewell to his half-brother Bran, who is in a coma after having been thrown from a tower by Jaime Lannister, the queen's brother. A grief-stricken Catelyn sits by Bran's bedside and has an expression of barely concealed loathing on her face as

Jon says goodbye before departing for the Wall, where he is about to take his vows and join the Night's Watch. Ned watches their interaction from the doorway, visibly uncomfortable and strained, able neither to shield his bastard son from his wife's hatred nor to soothe the deep-seated emotional wound in his wife from the seventeen-year-old act of betrayal and dishonor of their marital vows. After Jon leaves, Catelyn says, "The last time you rode off with Robert Baratheon, you came back with another woman's son. Now you are leaving again."[14] Ned protests, "I have no choice." In turn, Catelyn responds, "That's what men always say when honor calls. That's what you tell your families, tell yourselves. You do have a choice. And you've made it."

By reminding Ned of the stain of dishonor he brought home the last time he chose to follow Robert, Catelyn makes clear the limits of Ned's code of honor. Ned needs to follow Robert, as he did once before, and in that "honorable" call lies the possibility of the recurrence of dishonor and the possible abdication of his role in the family. By following "honor's call" to go to King's Landing, Ned must leave behind his grieving wife, his comatose son, and his eldest and youngest sons to somehow manage the command of Winterfell by themselves. For Catelyn, Ned's cloak of honor is a thin covering, a useful principle to disguise a choice that ignores the very real needs of family. Ned wants to externalize the responsibility of his decision, to argue that he has no choice, that he simply must submit to the sovereign power of his king, but Catelyn calls that into question. In doing so, she provides the audience with a more complex perspective of Ned Stark's code of honor, which undercuts the clear and rigid account he provides of himself.

The Journey South: Honor, Displacement, and Subjectivity

When Ned Stark leaves Winterfell and heads south to King's Landing to take up the position of the hand of the king, he inaugurates a larger shift in the story. His move is not simply a spatial shift from the North of the country to the South; it also shifts the political context of the series. His journey takes him from a place where his life is tightly ordered by the bonds of tradition and family to one where those same traditions and values are not recognized easily by the other political actors. Throughout the course of this journey, the links between his honor and his very subjectivity become increasingly apparent precisely because they are called into question by others. The Stark family too is separated. When Ned took his boys to the execution of the Night's Watch fugitive, he left his girls at home. His sons were clearly meant to be steeped in the honor, duty, and tradition of the Starks, while his two daughters were left behind in the domestic sphere. Now his sons are left behind in Winterfell, with his eldest son, Robb, governing in his stead and watching over the rest, while his daughters, Sansa and Arya, are now the ones who are thrown into the outside world and forced to adapt to its shifting cultural and political context. The journey to the South brings with it not just the introduction of the Stark family to the royal court but also experiences of trauma and lessons in vulnerability to sovereign power. The girls learn a different set of lessons about politics than their brothers were taught, not lessons of lordship or the honor of upholding tradition, but rather the precarious and shifting rules of the game of thrones.

The journey south is therefore a journey of displacement and dislocation that underlines the limits of the traditional code of honor but simultaneously accounts for the need to reactively hold on to it more tightly. Honor, particularly chivalric honor, Hegel tells us, is a kind of guiding spiritual faith; it provides "the necessary transition from the principle of religious inwardness to its entry into mundane, spiritual life."[15] But honor, according to Hegel, is also a vulnerable thing that demands recognition from others. In this shifting context, finding that recognition from others becomes increasingly more difficult. Hegel writes, "[H]onor's fight for personal independence is not bravery defending the common weal and the call of the justice in the same or of rectitude in the sphere of private life; on the contrary, honor's struggle is only for the recognition and the abstract inviolability of the individual person."[16] Honor demands recognition, not just for its own validation but precisely to shore up the very subjectivity of the person who holds on to it as a guiding faith. In Hegel's terms, recognition is key to the actualization of the Spirit; one has to recognize the self in order to achieve the Hegelian synthesis: "the eye does not see itself except through its reflection in the mirror."[17] As we have already seen, it is essential to Ned Stark that what is reflected back to him is a paragon of honor, duty, and tradition, but as the royal party travels down the Kingsroad, the mirror starts to get smudged and a bit blurry. For Hegel, the synthesis is one's only hope at redemption and something to strive for, but Ned Stark's story as it unfolds in *Game of Thrones* slowly begins to reveal the errors of such idealism.

The desire for chivalric honor to be recognized by others is complicated within the first few days of the journey with an execution that parallels the one in the opening episode. However, this execution, rather than shoring up the links between tradition and honor, reveals instead the incommensurability between the Stark code and the political intrigues of the royal court. This gap between the two is seen most sharply in the experiences of Ned's older daughter, Sansa, who embodies the naïve romanticism of the traditional and chivalric Stark code of honor. Sansa is introduced to the audience as a girl who lives for romantic tales of knighthood, but her illusions are slowly shattered by violence, betrayal, and abuse. Sansa's first lesson in the incommensurability between the fairytales of honor she has been raised on and the harsh reality of politics comes in the execution of Lady, her pet direwolf, which Queen Cersei demands in the second episode. Her direwolf puppy is innocent, but the Queen, who had previously taken Sansa under her wing, demands her wolf's head in payment for the actions of her sister Arya's direwolf, which bit the prince and is now nowhere to be found. This royal demand is clearly seen as unjust by Ned Stark and both his daughters, but once it is reinforced by the sovereign power of the king, they have no choice but to comply. Sansa cries hysterically as the harsh reality sinks in, Arya turns away in anger, and Ned struggles to come to terms with the blatant injustice of the royal injunction.

The execution that follows clearly underlines the displacement and dislocation that the Starks have experienced along the journey. The shift between the two executions in the first two episodes highlights the displacement in Ned's sense of himself. Back in the North, executing a deserter in a manner that is consistent with the laws that he is convinced are just, he is sure of himself and in command. He even uses the occasion to inaugurate his son into the tradition of the Starks and impress upon him the importance of honor, duty, and justice. In the South, killing an innocent direwolf puppy on the king's orders runs against everything he believes in. He responds the only way he can, by returning to his guiding faith in his code of honor, which compels him to volunteer for this distasteful duty. He insists on killing the direwolf himself rather than allow the royal executioner to do it. "If it must be done, I'll do it myself," he announces. "The wolf is of the North. She deserves better than a butcher."[18] This time the execution occurs under the cover of night in a muddy yard, not in broad daylight on a sweeping plain. There is no accompanying party, no family inauguration into an ancient tradition, no ritual or ceremony, only the same executioner. Ned Stark reluctantly wields his ancestral sword, but in this second iteration the execution is clearly unjust.

There is a clear sense in this second execution that Ned is tied to his code of honor for reasons that go beyond simply the weight of tradition. It is fundamentally tied up with his sense of himself, to his very subjectivity. As Hegel writes, "In honor, therefore, the man has the first affirmative consciousness of his infinite subjectivity.... [T]he measure of honor thus does not depend on what the man actually is but on what this idea of himself is."[19] In this shifting context, removed from the stabilizing forces of family and tradition, Ned struggles to find his footing and entrenches himself further in this idea of himself as fundamentally a man of honor. He cannot fully achieve a redemptive synthesis with his reflection in the mirror, but he tries nevertheless to hold on to his code of honor, even as he is forced into a situation he detests. His code continues to exert its power over his home and shape the very account he gives of himself. In the words of Judith Butler:

> [T]o be dominated by a power external to oneself is a familiar and agonizing form power takes. To find, however, that what "one" is, one's very formation as a subject, is in some way dependent upon that very power is quite another. We are used to thinking of power as what presses on the subject from the outside, as what subordinates, sets underneath, and relegates to a lower order. But if, following Foucault, we understand power as *forming* the subject as well, as providing the very condition of its existence and the trajectory of its desire, the power is not simply what we oppose but also, in a strong sense, what we depend on for our existence and what we harbor and preserve in the beings that we are.[20]

The power of tradition and honor is not merely an external force that impinges on Ned and compels him to comply with its dictates; it forms his very subjectivity and he holds on to it tightly amid his displacement and vulnerability. It is at once a bulwark against the precarity of the game of thrones and a means of preservation, but it is also a source of pride and willfulness that gives him a headstrong and uncomplicated view of his own political agency.

The Hand of the King: The Limits of Honorable Agency and the Politics of Recognition

From the moment Ned Stark arrives in the "rat's nest" of the capital, weary and dusty from the road, he is consistently both othered by the courtiers in the king's council and othering in his dismissal of their schemes and spies, unable to find his balance amid the shifting and contingent political dynamics of the court. He arrives at its first meeting of the king's council disheveled and exhausted from the long journey and is stunned to hear that the king never even attends their meetings. He finds the silky language of veiled threats and subterfuge that Master of Coin Petyr "Littlefinger" Baelish and Master of Spiders Varys are fluent in distasteful and cannot bring himself to learn it. He feels alienated and struggles to find his footing in King's Landing and clings to his code of honor as a compass to steer him through these tricky tides. As he tries to carry out his duties and investigate the suspicious death of the previous hand of the king, he is blunt and open in his questioning of others, dismissive of warnings by potential allies such as Varys, and unsure who to trust.

In one illuminating scene, he walks in the courtyard with Littlefinger, who points out to him all the "little birds" or spies that are eavesdropping on their conversation and reporting back to their many masters, a revelation that shocks Ned. Littlefinger asks him if there is someone in his service he trusts completely and he says yes. Littlefinger responds, "The wiser answer is no."[21] Convinced by his advice and warnings, Ned says, "Lord Baelish, perhaps I was wrong to distrust you," to which Littlefinger responds, "Distrusting me was the wisest thing you have done since you climbed off your horse." It is clear to these skilled courtiers that Ned Stark is making moves in the dark, his honor shrouding him from the limits of his actions, and wholly unaware of the threats that are lurking in the shadows. The queen, Cersei Lannister, offers him a bit of (un)friendly advice in this area: "You're just a soldier, aren't you? You take your orders and you carry on.... [Y]our older brother was trained to lead and you were trained to follow," to which Ned responds bluntly, "I was also trained to kill my enemies, Your Grace," thinking perhaps he has gotten the better of this exchange and issued a warning to the queen.[22] Cersei smoothly responds, "As was I," and tells him that there are two ways to play this game: either by following codes and orders to succeed or by using wits and intrigue and allowing others to do your dirty work for you.

Ned can feel that the political ground is shaky under his feet, which compels him to double down on the Stark code of honor to orient himself in this new vertiginous landscape. Demonstrating his honor therefore becomes even more crucial to him as a way to display power and hide vulnerability, but doing so is no empty gesture either. As Hegel writes, this assertion of honor is essential to the very idea of subjectivity—the "show of honor becomes the real existence of the subject, his supreme actuality."[23] For Ned Stark, every move and every decision he makes in King's Landing consequently become a tussle over his honor; every action is refracted through that prism; every move is a referendum on its value, on its shining. Hegel explains that this happens precisely because it is essential for one's own subjectivity to imbue one's agency with honor so that one can hold on to one's very sense of oneself: "[F]rom the point of view of honor all these relationships, valid and true in themselves, are not already sanctioned and recognized in their own account, but only because I put my personality into them and thereby make them a matter of honor."[24]

While Ned's honor binds him to his actions and his very subjectivity, he is blind to the essential dependence that is at the heart of the politics of honor, which limit his agency and make him vulnerable to the recognition of others. In his insistence on putting his "personality" into all his actions and making everything "a matter of honor," he acts with an astonishingly simplified view of political agency, where he sees himself as an autonomous individual in full control of all of his actions. Charging ahead and making every political decision a litmus test on honor might shore up his account of himself and reinforce his Idea of himself as a subject, but it fundamentally ignores the dependent and constitutive nature of politics. Time and again, he fails to notice that honor at its core requires the recognition of others and is therefore always vulnerable to the actions of others. Hegel pinpoints the essential vulnerability in the politics of honor and how it remains contingent on others, writing, "[S]ince honor is not only a shining in *myself*, but must also be envisaged and recognized by *others* who again on their side may demand equal recognition for *their* honor, honor is something purely vulnerable."[25] In this Hegel comes close to recognizing the inherent vulnerability to others in the formation of political subjectivity.

What Hegel misses and where Judith Butler goes further is in recognizing the constitutive power of relationality in forming the subject. In doing so Butler offers a different way of thinking through dependence and mutual constitution in a manner that is not dialectical and does not need an ideal synthesis. She writes, "[I]t is not simply that one requires the recognition of the other and that a form of recognition is conferred through subordination, but rather that one is dependent on power for one's very formation, that the formation is impossible without dependency, and that the posture of the adult subject consists precisely in the denial and reenactment of this dependency."[26] Subjectivity is much more impacted by power than Hegel acknowledges, and Ned Stark in all his idealism suffers from the same failure of recognition of how his subjectivity and agency are chastened by the power of others or what Patchen Markell calls the "basic condition of intersubjective vulnerability."[27]

Ned Stark's failure to recognize the ontological condition of vulnerability puts him in an increasingly isolated position. He refuses to abdicate his principles, demonstrating what Hegel called the "inflexible singularity which ... is implicit in the principle of honor."[28] All of this comes to a head in an explosive confrontation with King Robert that highlights his reflexive recoil from the dominating power of their friendship. In this scene, Robert has just ordered the assassination of Daenerys Targaryen and her unborn child, who pose a clear, albeit distant, threat to his throne, saying "I want them both dead, mother and child!"[29] Ned can hardly believe what he is hearing from his old friend and says, "You'll dishonor yourself forever if you do this!" Robert's response to Ned's invocation of his code of honor is revealing. To Robert, honor is of little use when faced with the demands of power. "Honor!" he shouts. "I've got seven kingdoms to rule! Do you think it's honor that keeps them in line? Do you think it's honor that keeps the peace? It's fear. Fear and blood." Then he denounces Ned as an "honorable fool." Varys tries to convince Ned of the necessity of the action, arguing that "it's a vile thing, yet we who presume to rule must sometimes do vile things for the good of the realm," but Ned remains wholly unconvinced. The murder of a pregnant 16-year-old is more than he can abide and is wholly inconsistent with his account of himself as an honorable man. Distressed that his old friend Robert would order such a dishonorable thing he says, "I will not follow you now.... I will have no part in it" and throws down the badge of the hand of the king, resigning his post in anger. He says to Robert, "I thought you were a better man" and storms out of the council chamber.

When confronted with the political limits of honor and challenged by a forceful account of the effectiveness of power, Ned finds himself in an impossible position and one that he can't see his way out of. It is a classic example of the ties that bind, of the account that one gives of oneself that quickly becomes a vise and closes off all other options. As Hegel puts it, for the honorable man, "it is not the thing itself but his subjective idea which puts difficulties and complications in his way because it becomes a point of honor to uphold the character he has assumed."[30] In this attempt to break away from Robert Baratheon, which ultimately fails, Ned tries to come to terms with the deep rift in his own account of himself, in his very subjectivity, which Catelyn had bitterly described during his departure from Winterfell. Ned's rigid code of honor that is grounded in the history of the North and the tradition of the Starks is not always commensurable with his deep relationship with the king, as is made clear by this dramatic confrontation.

Robert Baratheon has been an outsize presence in Ned's life since they were boys, and Ned draws much of his reputation as an honorable soldier and an esteemed commander from the role he played in Robert's rebellion. He is the one who put Robert on the throne, inaugurating the games of power in King's Landing, so even as he tries to divorce himself from their machinations, he continues to be interpellated in them. Ned Stark is not someone who is simply subject to the external and sovereign power of King Robert; rather, his very identity is bound up in these relations of domination and the demands of friendship. Robert Baratheon is family to Ned Stark, but theirs is a complex relationship, without an ancestral code of honor to give it meaning and principled clarity. His relationship with Robert is crucial for his own subject formation as a powerful player in King's Landing, but it is also a relationship he recoils from internally as it is hard to reconcile with his account of himself as a Stark and a man of honor. As Butler writes, "[T]he attachment to subjection is produced though the workings of power, and that part of the operation of power is made clear in this psychic effect, one of the most insidious of its productions. If, in a Nietzschean sense, the subject is formed by a will that turns back upon itself, assuming a reflexive form, then the subject is the modality of power that turns on itself; the subject is the effect of power in recoil."[31]

It is this reflexive form of recoil we see clearly in this confrontation between Ned Stark and Robert Baratheon. The internal tension seems impossibly thick, and Ned Stark tries to cut through it by asserting a sovereign sense of agency and attempting to leave the capital and all its dishonorable games of power behind. But he cannot leave. He is now, and to some degree has always been, a player in the game of thrones, and the forces of power that circulate in them continue to constrain and curtail his choices even as they provide him with the productive power to make his own moves. He tries to escape and return to Winterfell, and in this assertion of his own agency, unconditioned by a recognition of the complexity of his own subjectivity and dependence on others, he faces a tremendous challenge. As Butler writes, the "subject pursues its own dissolution, its own unraveling, a pursuit that marks an agency, but not the *subject's* agency—rather, the agency of a desire that aims at the dissolution of the subject, where the subject stands as a bar to that desire."[32] It is Ned himself who stands as an obstacle to his desire to return home. He makes several political mistakes during his time in King's Landing. In his visible role as the hand of the king he angers key players, his investigation of the death of the former hand of the King, Jon Arryn, which he conducts during most of the first season, uncovers some key details but leads to faulty decisions, and his less than prudent handling of his wife's reckless capture of Tyrion Lannister, another key plot point in the season, all arouse the enmity and suspicion of others.

His plans to flee, his illusions of escape, and his desire to achieve the dissolution of his complex subjectivity are all thwarted and his agency firmly limited as he finds himself surrounded in the street by Jaime Lannister and his men, quickly abandoned by Littlefinger, and watching helplessly as his own men are slaughtered in front of him, unable to move to their aid as he is immobilized by a spear through the leg. Tragically, even this fall from grace and dramatic reversal does not fully convince Ned Stark to reassess the limits of his code of honor. When Robert Baratheon refuses to accept his resignation and sends him back to work, he is hobbled and weakened on multiple fronts but still charges ahead with scant recognition of the precariousness of his own position. In Markell's words, he continues to express "the aspiration to a sort of sovereign invulnerability to the open-endedness and contingency of the future we share with others."[33] Ned misses the very ontological condition of vulnerability that renders the political open-ended, multiple, and contingent on others. In the aftermath of Jaime Lannister's brutal attack, Ned persists in his failure to recognize just how dependent he is on the power of others.

He orders the death of Gregor Clegane, one of the key henchmen of the Lannisters, in Robert's absence, a move that is so rash and blind to the realities of power that it visibly shocks the entire court. Littlefinger tries to warn him, saying, "A bold move, my Lord. And admirable. But is it wise to yank the Lion's tail? Tywin Lannister is the richest man in the seven kingdoms. Gold wins wars, not soldiers."[34] Ned ignores the warning about the workings of power, convinced by the honor and justness of his command. In doing so, he confirms Nietzsche's analysis of honor in morality. In *Human, All Too Human*, Nietzsche writes that in the three phases of morality, honor comes in second:

> A still higher state is reached when man acts according to the principle of *honor*, by means of which he finds his place in society, submitting to commonly held feelings.... Now he shows—and wants to be shown—respect; that is, he understands his advantage as dependent on his opinion of others and their opinion of him. Finally, at the highest stage of morality *until now*, he acts according to *his* standard of things and men; he himself determines for himself what is honorable, what is profitable. He has become the lawgiver of opinions, in accordance with the ever more refined concept of usefulness and honor.[35]

Ned Stark is now increasingly aware that his very identity depends on others recognizing him as a man of honor, but, in Nietzschean terms, he refuses to adapt and "refine" his concept of honor as Littlefinger urges him to do. By charging ahead and making a public enemy of the Lannisters and then making the fatal error of confronting the queen with evidence of her incest (what he later calls the error of "mercy"), he appears to seal his own tragic fate.[36] In this context Butler writes that "the subject engages in its own self-thwarting, accomplishes its own subjection, desires and crafts its own shackles."[37]

Even as Ned Stark paints himself into a corner with his belief in the honor of his actions and his sense of unrestrained agency, events start to overcome him. Robert is mortally wounded in a hunting accident and appoints Ned Stark regent on his deathbed, the secret of Cersei and Jaime Lannister's incest is exposed, and the crown and all of the power of the realm are suddenly up for grabs in a vertiginous moment of possibility and danger. But amid the dizziness and the ground that is shifting beneath his feet, all Ned can do is cling to his ancestral code of honor in a futile effort to orient himself. He flatly refuses to recognize political opportunity amid the chaos, and when Littlefinger tells him he could easily seize the power of the throne for himself, Ned's response is to ask in disgust, "Do you have a shred of honor?" Littlefinger tries again: "You are now Hand of the King and Protector of the Realm. All of the power is yours. You need only reach out and take it." He suggests making peace with the Lannisters and using the threat of blackmail over their incest, but Ned only hears treason in this advice and flatly says,

"I won't do it."[38] The farthest Ned will go to secure his own path is to indirectly ask Littlefinger to bribe the city watch guards so they have enough armed men to fight the Lannisters, but he cannot bring himself to say it out loud. Littlefinger can't resist pointing out exactly how constrained Ned is by his politics of honor: "Look at you. You know what you want me to do, you know it has to be done, but it's not honorable, so the words stick in your throat." Ned's insistence on acting honorably, his stubborn belief that his principles will be recognized by others, his failure to acknowledge his dependency on power, and his inability to understand that his agency as a subject is constrained by his attachment to others, all lead him to a tragic loss of power. Cersei Lannister rips apart Robert's will, which Ned had relied on for establishing the truth and justice of his claims, mockingly asking, "Is this meant to be your shield? A piece of paper?" His men are slaughtered, and he is tainted as a traitor and thrown into a dungeon to await the new king's justice. His faith in his honor does not lead to the redemptive synthesis of idealism but to a belated recognition of the power relations that permeate the game of thrones.

In his concluding scenes in *Game of Thrones*, through a series of conversations in the dungeons with Lord Varys, Ned Stark slowly comes to recognize the limits of honor and to accept the necessity of dishonor for political ends. Despite having failed to convince him to swear allegiance to the new king, Varys makes one final attempt to try to convince Ned to actually convert his code of honor into the currency of power. "Cersei knows you as a man of honor," he says. "Give her peace and she'll let you take the black."[39] Varys is asking Ned Stark to give up everything he believes in for a chance of survival. If he publicly repudiates his own actions, admits to treason, and swears allegiance to the king, there is the possibility of life, a chastened life, but a life nevertheless as a member of the Night's Watch. But Ned balks even at this final offer to translate his honor into a political solution, preferring to die an honorable death rather than to give a false confession and live. He says, "You think my life is a precious thing to me? That I'll trade my honor for a few more years of . . . what? . . . I grew up with soldiers. I learned to die a long time ago." He cannot extricate himself from his code of honor, which is so deeply bound up with the tradition of the Starks, and publicly dishonor himself and his family by giving a false confession.

It is only when Varys points out that Ned's daughters' lives are at stake as well that Ned Stark finally confronts the limits of playing the game of thrones with a rigid and unyielding code of honor and recognizes the deep tensions between honor, family, and tradition that he has refused to countenance for so long. Tragically, his final decision to recognize the complexity of his agency and subjectivity by choosing family and compromise over honor and giving Cersei the false confession she needs for peace comes too late, as the sociopathic boy king Joffrey violates the rules of the carefully scripted royal performance and asks for the executioner to bring him Ned's head. In the final execution of the first season, the ancestral sword of the Starks, Ice, swishes through the air again, but this time, it is the public executioner, who decapitates the Lord of Winterfell with his own blade. Ned Stark dies as a convicted traitor, publicly dishonored for all to see, his blood despoiling the holy steps of the sept of Baelor.

The Complex Legacy of Honor

Ned Stark's execution is a tragic echo not only of the execution in the very first episode of *Game of Thrones* that he used as a teaching moment for his family to initiate them into the traditional Stark virtues of honor, duty, and justice, but also of the second and clearly unjust execution of the innocent direwolf puppy that he tried to allay by also adhering to the ancestral code of honor. This time his boys are not physically present to be inaugurated into a family tradition, but instead it is his girls, Arya and Sansa, who both watch their father die and are left in devastatingly precarious conditions. Arya manages to escape King's Landing, but she is shunted into a brutal life of deception and violence, which she survives only by holding on tightly to a burning desire for revenge. Sansa is surrounded by enemies and thrown into a violently abusive situation and has to rely on her own quickly developing political skills to survive. Ned's girls are forced to recognize the limits of honor and its inherent contingency on others in a way that their father never could and in ways he never prepared them for. Arya grows up to be a trained, cold-blooded assassin who is motivated by revenge, not honor, after experiencing so much violence and learning so many hard truths about the brutal world of Westeros. She learns from embittered hard men like the Hound, Tywin Lannister, and the Faceless Men of Braavos, and when she finally returns to Winterfell in the last season, she is lethal, wary of others, and emotionally guarded. Sansa, who in the aftermath of her father's death is beaten and tortured by Joffrey, almost raped by a mob, and controlled like a marionette by Cersei, experiences so much suffering that her girlish dreams of chivalry and honor die a quick death. When she is finally rescued by Littlefinger, she learns even more lessons about the ruthless realpolitik of the game of thrones, but that too comes at the cost of further betrayal and even more torture and trauma. Sansa emerges as the antithesis of her father in the final seasons of the show—a skilled player in the game who can quickly figure out all its tangles and webs of power relations. When she fully steps into her power to order Littlefinger's death, with her sister at her side and acting as her executioner, it is telling that she uses the language of honor for such a ruthless and necessary act. She says, "It's not what I want. It's what honor demands."[40] When Arya asks, "[A]nd what does honor demand?," Sansa replies, "[T]hat I defend my family from those who would harm us, that I defend the North from those who would betray us." The sisters work together to invoke the demands and obligations of honor, but they do so in order to skillfully protect their home and their lands and to defeat those who threaten it. Both sisters have learned that honor is a necessity only when it is used to defend their interests and not a blinding virtue that binds and restricts their actions.

Elsewhere in the show, the aftermath of Ned's execution sets into motion the War of the Five Kings, which takes place over several seasons with multiple contenders for power, most of whom reject his attachment to honor entirely in their ruthless pursuit of the throne. Unsurprisingly, the only one who doesn't is his eldest son, Robb Stark, the newly crowned king in the North, who wants to rescue his sisters and get justice for his family. Robb reveres his father and like him wants to be a leader who protects his people. He does not want the external glory of honor (even as he wins every battle on the field), but he has inherited Ned's powerful sense of internal honor and justice, even as he chafes against the duty of his oaths (and eventually breaks one with tragic consequences). He does his best to be just and honorable, but he makes a series of fatal errors, much like his father, and his arc comes to a brutal end in the show's iconic Red Wedding.[41] Aside from Ned's children, even a sworn enemy of the Starks like Jaime Lannister continues to be marked by Ned Stark's rigid attachment to honor throughout the eight seasons of the show. In a particularly poignant scene in the third season, Jaime, who has been marked throughout the realm as a man of dishonor and is routinely called "the Kingslayer" for his murder of King Aerys, reveals what really happened on that terrible day. He killed the king in an act of defense only when he gave orders to burn down the entire city along with all its inhabitants, but Ned Stark found him in the throne room with blood on his sword and immediately condemned him as an oath breaker without even considering his side of events. Jaime says, "You think honorable Ned Stark wanted to hear my side? He judged me guilty the moment he set eyes on me."[42] In later seasons Jaime tries to reclaim his damaged honor, but he struggles mightily against Ned's condemnation for most of his life and it consistently discolors his relationships with others.

The legacy of Ned Stark's attachment to honor is most clearly seen in the farthest and northernmost corner of Westeros, at the very edge of civilization and governance, where his bastard son, Jon Snow, struggles to come to terms with his inheritance and learns how to become a leader. A full analysis of the relationship between the two is outside the scope of this chapter (suffice it to say that when the show reveals the truth in later seasons, it turns out that Ned was far from dishonorable in raising Jon within the bosom of the Stark family), but it is important to note that prior to Ned's false confession before his untimely execution, Jon was the only embodiment of Ned's one public act of dishonor: his apparent betrayal of his marriage vows 17 years earlier. Ned may have honorably raised Jon among his children by marriage and brought him up with the traditions of the Starks, but the consequence of his choice to do the right thing also resulted in Jon's growing up in a castle he had no claim to, with the constant hatred and anger of Catelyn Stark surrounding him, and a perpetual taint of dishonor following him everywhere. Jon is not a Stark, but a Snow (the traditional last name for bastards in the North), and even though Ned once told him, "[Y]ou are a Stark. You might not have my name, but you have my blood," it is of little comfort or use at the Wall, where he is continually mocked for being a bastard.[43] The stain of Ned's dishonor lingers in and permeates Jon thoroughly, leading to a profound sense of alienation. Being a bastard is "a hard life for a child," he tells his friend Sam.[44]

When Jon learns of his father's imprisonment for treason (and subsequently of his execution), his actions capture the complexity of ambivalence toward and recoil from the politics of honor. He breaks his vows to ride south, but is brought back to the Wall by his friends in the Night's Watch and slowly begins to learn a different set of lessons about the limits of honor, first, from his fellow misfits at the Wall, and second, from the free folk who live beyond the Wall when he infiltrates their army and develops a lingering respect for them. In his struggles to grasp the limits of honor bequeathed to him by Ned and in his emerging recognition of a more humble view of his own agency, Jon Snow begins the process of coming to terms with a more complex view of subjectivity, something that Ned Stark could never fully accomplish. As Butler writes, "[T]he desire to persist in one's own being requires submitting to a world of others that is fundamentally not one's own."[45] Jon learns this lesson many times over as he comes face to face with forces that are well beyond anyone's control. At the Wall, surrounded by criminals, bastards, and other broken things, Jon has to submit to a world of others and craft a new orientation to leadership and struggle to articulate a more complex politics of honor. Beyond the Wall, he learns to get along with people who don't care about Westerosi traditions and norms, but about survival and freedom. These experiences mold him into a different leader than Ned Stark was, one who inherits his sense of duty and his penchant for truth-telling but who also emerges as someone who is able to unite all the warring factions to face the common threat from the North.

Still, Ned's legacy and the hope of fulfilling it never quite leave Jon Snow. When Stannis Baratheon offers to legitimize him and make him a Stark, he rejects his proposal out of a sense of duty to the Night's Watch and a refusal to break his vows, even though his deepest desire is to be recognized as Ned's legitimate heir and return home to Winterfell. In a revealing exchange in the fifth season, Stannis notes the similarity between the two men and tells him, "You're as stubborn as your father. And as honorable," to which Jon responds, "I can imagine no higher praise." But Jon is then brought up short by Stannis, who replies, "I didn't mean it as praise. Honor got your father killed."[46] Jon learns the hardest of lessons when he does what he thinks is right as lord commander of the Night's Watch and again when he is crowned the king in the North. Time and again, following his sense of duty comes with betrayal and tragic consequences, but he still holds on tightly to his ancestral code of honor. Like Ned, Jon accumulates the titles and adornments of external honor that are bestowed on him by others, but he cares little about them. Like Ned, what matters most to him is his internal sense of duty. By first venturing north of the Wall, where few men have dared to go, and then all the way south to the capital, Jon dislocates himself spatially, but unlike Ned, he finally learns some lessons about the limits of honor in the face of great danger. Even though he dismisses himself as "a northern fool" who didn't listen when "everyone told me to learn from my father's mistakes," he does eventually learn.[47] In a candid moment of recognition, he says that Ned Stark was the "most honorable man I ever met. He was good, all the way through, and he died on the executioner's block."[48] Jon Snow at last separates his duty as a shield who guards the realms of men from his inherited code of honor when he commits a final act of treasonous betrayal in order to save Westeros from tyrannical rule. He does the right thing, even as he is bitterly conflicted, and cloaks himself in dishonor for the greater good.

The Limits of Honor

As a key motif that runs through all eight seasons of the show, honor plays a crucial role in the imaginary of *Game of Thrones* and its broader cultural and political impact. The death of Ned Stark ripples through the entire tableau of the show, setting many different chains of events into motion, and plunges Westeros into war as dueling factions seek revenge and power. It clearly undermines traditional tropes of heroism and honor and imbues a deep sense of tragic recognition in both the players themselves and in their audience, orienting them into the contingent and shifting calculations of power that characterize the political. One of the most significant of the show's impacts is that it clearly underlined the limits of honor in the political imagination. It demonstrates that a rigid attachment to honor is both binding and blinding in a ruthless world of power politics. A thousand memes were launched by Ned Stark's shocking execution, many of which made fun of his errors and his inability to see through the layers of the game of thrones. He became an iconic figure who was remembered by the show's audience as an honorable fool.

Ned Stark's faith in the public recognition of his honor and his hope that it would protect him from the dishonorable actions of others ultimately led to his demise. As such, the failure of his politics of honor, untethered from an understanding of the limits of his own agency, clearly underlines what Markell has diagnosed as the problem of recognition, or indeed of misrecognition. Markell writes that the "ideal of mutual recognition, while appealing, is impossible, even incoherent ... [and] in pursuing it we misunderstand certain crucial conditions of social and political life."[49] In aspiring to the mutual recognition of the politics of honor, Ned Stark too easily ignored his vulnerability to others and the structures of power that sustained his interactions. In doing so, he underlined for a broader audience the necessity of recognizing the constraints of power and the tragic nature of the political. Hegel famously wrote that "the content of honor depends for its worth only on the man and does not arise from his own immanent essence, it remains a victim of contingency."[50] *Games of Thrones* demonstrates clearly that honor is not only always dependent on and vulnerable to the recognition of others, but that too often it demands an ideal form of recognition that ignores the intersubjective nature of political life with tragic consequences.

2
Honor among Spies

The Cold War Mom, Family, and Identity in *The Americans*

In the first full day of his presidency, Donald Trump traveled to the headquarters of the CIA, where he delivered a set of remarks that were ostensibly supposed to heal the rift that had developed during his presidential campaign between his administration and the intelligence community. Instead, his remarks turned into a meandering ramble on several topics, during which he accused the media of dishonesty in reporting inaccurately on the crowd size at his inauguration the previous day. The backlash to the speech was swift and overwhelming. It was covered widely by the media, and a range of people from the D.C. foreign policy establishment with ties to the intelligence community took to Twitter to complain. What seemed to upset so many on that occasion was not just the content of the president's remarks but the particular context in which they took place—in this instance, literally the place in which he was standing as he delivered them. Every picture in the news coverage of the event that day showed an unusual backdrop.[1] The president stood at a lectern in front of a grayish-white marble wall covered in five rows of small, dark stars. The picture was framed by an inscription that hit slightly above the president's head which read, "In honor of those members of the Central Intelligence Agency who gave their lives in the service of their country." This is the CIA's Wall of Honor, a memorial of 117 stars to commemorate the lives of all the agency operatives killed in the line of duty. In its report, the *Washington Post* referred to the Wall as the CIA's "most sacred setting" and quoted an unnamed senior U.S. intelligence official as saying that "people are going to think that was offensive."[2] The president only briefly noted the backdrop, saying, "The wall behind me is very, very special," before moving on to talk about media coverage and other topics.[3]

In a post on the *New Yorker*'s website the following day, Robin Wright rounded up a host of sources from the intelligence and the diplomatic communities to report on the anger that delivering such a speech in front of the Wall of Honor had stirred. The very title of the article, "Trump's Vainglorious Affront to the CIA," seemed to draw a contrast between the public recognition of the fallen operatives, an honor earned by sacrifice to the nation, and the excessive vanity of the new commander in chief, whose ego was wounded by the coverage of the small crowds at his inauguration. It suggested that such a juxtaposition was an "affront" in itself, likening it to "going to [the] Tomb of the Unknown Soldier and not mentioning those who died in the Second World War." Wright quoted the former director of the CIA John Brennan, who referred to Trump's speech as a "despicable display of self-aggrandizement in front of CIA's Memorial Wall of Agency heroes."[4] The sharpness of the establishment backlash to the president's remarks was revealing not just in the tight link that many of those who responded drew between espionage and honor but also in the anxiety they betrayed at the disruption of norms of political discourse. To thumb one's nose at such norms as President Trump seemed to have done provoked not just anxiety about the dislodging of established narratives of political discourse but signaled a larger sense of unease about the consequences of doing so in a political present already troubled by a sense of divided or compromised loyalty in the administration as the scandal about Russian interference in the presidential election continued to unfold in the headlines. Clearly the juxtaposition between President Trump's remarks about crowd size and the backdrop of the Wall of Honor stirred a sense of unease and was seen by these same officials as a symbolic affront to ideas of duty, sacrifice, and honor that they held dear.

The deaths of the fallen CIA operatives were clearly meant to be venerated by the public, and the connections between their sacrifice in the line of duty and the necessity of honoring them were apparently obvious enough to require little or no explanation (and certainly needed to avoid the complications of engaging with the CIA's less than rosy history). While the Wall of Honor is the CIA's most visible testament to its fallen operatives, it turned out that the images that drew such a sharp critical response that day did not capture the full scope of the memorial. As Ted Gup notes in his book on the CIA, below the field of stars on the wall is a locked "stainless-steel and glass case.... Inside is a book. The Book of Honor, it was called."[5] Just like the Wall, the book contains mostly "nameless stars, tiny as asterisks, each representing a covert officer killed on a CIA mission. These nameless stars spanned half a century.... [A]ll was veiled in secrecy."[6] There are a couple of things worthy of note in this description of the Book of Honor. First, honor is clearly linked to sacrifice and duty for the covert operatives of the intelligence community.

Second, in marked contrast to the way in which honor is generally portrayed in politics, where public recognition is essential to its operation, in the context of espionage it is shrouded in secrecy. The honor given to the fallen spies is both public in its visibility and hidden in its anonymity. In the realm of espionage there is very little recognition for an extraordinarily demanding job. The KGB honored only one of its spies, Dmitri Yakushkin, for the entire duration of the Cold War, bestowing on him a medal only in 1986, a year before he died, which they referred to as "special award for services to intelligence."[7] He was the "first and only" KGB officer to be so honored.[8] Perhaps this lack of public recognition, which is usually central to depictions of honor in the political imaginary, is why spies so often internalize a code of honor and fuse it to the very core of the identities they construct to embody their lives of subterfuge. As Gup asks in his book, "How, I wondered, could a memorial purport to remember those who are unknown to all but a few? And what sort of person would be willing to make the ultimate sacrifice—the loss not only of life, but of identity as well?"[9] Indeed, such a memorial appears to give rise to subjects that are formed by internalizing a concept of honor that is not just motivated by patriotic duty, but which requires the sacrifice and erasure of identity.

Trump's speech in front of the Wall of Honor and the backlash that followed serve to highlight how tightly the links between espionage and honor are drawn in the political imagination and how uncomplicated this narrative usually is, as it is shrouded easily in the language of duty, sacrifice, and patriotism. However, a much more complex account of the relationship between honor and espionage emerges when its depiction in the political imagination is explored through the lens of popular culture, where the pursuit of honor serves less as a guiding principle for the intrepid spies and more as a kind of anesthetic that dulls their contemplation of the consequences of violence in "the line of duty." This chapter examines this conceptual nexus between honor, espionage, and the formation of identity through a close narrative reading of the FX television drama *The Americans*, set in the early 1980s during the Cold War, which seems more relevant than ever at a time where anxiety over Russian military and nuclear power is heightened after the invasion of Ukraine and evidence of Russian meddling in American electoral processes has been well established.[10] The sense of unease regarding Russian influence resonates with the tense and thorny depiction of espionage in *The Americans*. The uncomplicated conceptual linkage between espionage and honor that is commemorated in the CIA's Wall of Honor may no longer hold so easily (if it truly ever did). Indeed, the anesthetic of patriotism, honor, and duty that often cloaked these narratives may no longer resonate in the political imagination.

The Americans is a show created by Jacob Weisberg (a former CIA officer himself) that examines the lives of two Soviet KGB operatives, Elizabeth and Philip Jennings, who live their lives disguised as Americans (hence the title) and are raising their children in the suburban domesticity of Washington, D.C., during the early years of the Reagan administration. The show's promotional campaign for the Emmy started appearing in newspapers in mid-June 2017 even as newspapers continued to report on the different aspects of the Russia investigation in Congress. The cryptic campaign cleverly played on public anxiety about the unfolding story of Russian interference in the election with a single image of the Washington Monument cloaked boldly in the vivid scarlet of the hammer and sickle flag with a single line of text behind it: "The Russians Are Here."[11] In the image, the beige marble façade of official Washington serves merely as a stage setting in the background, and the takeover by Russian spies no longer lurks in the shadows online but is boldly on display with the Russian flag capping the phallic Washington Monument like a prophylactic and rendering it impotent.

This clever play on the headlines confirmed what the television critic for the *New York Times*, James Poniewozik, had noted earlier in the year, that "this Cold War drama feels newly relevant—but also almost comfortingly small-scale" in the current political climate.[12] On the one hand, the show's depiction of the Cold War of the 1980s with its Reagan-era construction of the "Evil Empire" offers more clarity than our current one does, with its concerns about electoral interference and compromised loyalty. On the other hand, with its complex depiction of family and duty and the intersection of public and private, the show offers a welcome counterpoint to the anesthetizing narratives of patriotism that official Washington consistently returns to as seemingly the only possible corrective to the destabilization of its norms. President Trump might have shown up to the CIA and dishonored its spies in front of their sacred monument, but the reflexive response to both that event and the deeper anxiety about Russian meddling cannot simply be to cloak the Washington Monument in the Stars and Stripes instead of the metaphorical Hammer and Sickle and substitute one form of erasure for another. Rather, such unease calls for a more tragic orientation to contemporary politics that does not eschew complexity for a nostalgic return to the past, but instead tries to reckon with the complexity of compromised loyalty in contemporary politics.

This chapter offers a close reading of *The Americans* as representative of such a tragic approach and attempts to show how it complicates the oft uncontested linkage between honor and espionage. In particular, it examines the show's portrayal of motherhood and how it operates within and against the context of Cold War discourse of mothers as a source of corruption. Honor, in much of literature, and certainly in the context of espionage, is often seen as a heroic, masculine, and gendered characteristic, but *The Americans* subverts this narrative radically by casting Elizabeth Jennings (played by Keri Russell) as the seemingly unquestioning embodiment of this trope. She seems to hold tightly to the notion that her actions are honorable and in the service of a larger goal, whereas Philip (Matthew Rhys) has a much more vexed relationship with the duality of his real and adopted identity and questions his mission constantly. The character of Elizabeth is particularly fascinating as she blends the roles of mother and recruiter in her relationship with her daughter, Paige, and in doing so works to both confirm and subvert traditional Cold War narratives of the mother as a source of contamination. Such a reading of the complex issues of motherhood, identity, and the challenges of family in *The Americans* disrupts the notion of an easy link between honor and espionage in political discourse and, in doing so, reveals a deeper anxiety to sustain such narratives in the political imagination. It further suggests that the outcry about the debasement of the Wall of Honor is reflective of a larger anxiety about facing a political present without the comforting sedation that honor and patriotism can provide.

Honor, Paranoia, and Cold War Rhetoric

In a wide-ranging book on honor, Alexander Welsh lays out the intellectual history of the concept of honor and its seeming fall into disuse in the late modern era. He notes that honor was often historically linked to aristocracy and its codes of chivalry and that it is often suggested that the idea vanished when those structures and norms eroded. It is clear from the reaction to Trump's remarks at the CIA that it is not a defunct concept but still holds some valence today, though perhaps in a different form. Welsh agrees that honor continues to play a role in contemporary society, albeit a transformed role, writing that "if you think of honor as respect, self-respect, and kinds of motivation dependent on respect, then it should be evident that it is not just some relic of the past."[13] Others have argued that honor serves as a powerful, albeit unchastened source of individual agency, as a bulwark against the possibility of tyranny and a source of civic renewal.[14] Honor can therefore be conceived of as a safeguard, a guardrail on the rocky cliffs of democracy, something to imbue the individual with a proper sense of respect, civic virtue, courage, and heroism—all qualities memorialized in the CIA's Wall of Honor.

However, such accounts of honor as inspiring respectful, dutiful, and heroic action too often rely on liberalism's construction of an atomistic individual subject that is lacking in its attention to power relations and the enmeshments of intersubjectivity. These omissions are compounded when honor is cloaked with patriotic duty. During the Cold War, this singular and patriotic construction of identity often fused with the paranoid to construct a binary that demonized its opposition in equally reductive terms. As Richard Hofstadter famously noted, the sense of America during the Cold War was of a country that had been infiltrated thoroughly by Communist agents and where "what is at stake is always a conflict between absolute good and absolute evil."[15] Such a stark construction of group identity, with its multiple acts of erasure, allowed one to see the enemy "as being totally evil and totally unappeasable, [so that] he must be totally eliminated—if not from the world, at least from the theatre of operations to which the paranoid directs his attention."[16]

This paranoid popular discourse of good versus evil is on full display in the early episodes of *The Americans*. In a key bit of stage setting for the entire series, Reagan's "Evil Empire" speech filters in through a TV set and unsettles Elizabeth and Philip Jennings during their dinner preparations. Later, a series of montages shows us not just the Jennings family but also members of the Soviet *rezidentura* and operatives of the FBI all glued to an apocalyptic film, *The Day After*, that depicts a nuclear explosion and its horrific aftermath. The paranoid narrative grips them all, but even in these snapshots the show cannot resist blurring the lines between the different actors, uniting both sides of the Cold War in the private sphere—in the kitchen, in bed, smoking intently in the living room—and making a powerful statement about the complexity of the identities they inhabit as spies, as parents, as lovers. In the paranoid style, "[t]he enemy is clearly delineated: he is a perfect model of malice, a kind of amoral superman—sinister, ubiquitous, powerful, cruel, sensual, luxury-loving," but in *The Americans* not only is such clarity obfuscated; it is actively undermined in favor of a more multifaceted approach to identity.[17]

The show goes out of its way to frame the spies and their adversaries in opposition to patriotic and paranoid narratives, sketching them instead in terms of family and seeming suburban normalcy, even as it makes their political allegiances clear. It collapses the distinction between good and evil, between *The Americans* and the Soviets, to the point of literally placing them adjacent to each other by making the Jenningses' next-door neighbor, Stan Beeman, an FBI counterintelligence officer whose very job it is to track down KGB agents and expose their infiltration. Stan, who often pops over to the Jennings house for a beer, and in later seasons, after his divorce, for meals (including one particularly awkward dinner party with the Jenningses' pastor and his wife), is the stand-in for a familiar model of the patriotic Cold Warrior in popular narratives of the era, a political subject that Suzanne Clark describes as "hyper-male: reasonable, penetrating, vigorous, and healthy."[18] True to the subversive spirit of the show, Stan, even as he shows himself to be a highly skilled FBI operative, does not adhere to the honorable and patriotic Cold War trope, and over the course of the show reveals himself to be vulnerable to temptation, unhappy at home and often at work, and deeply lonely and searching for human connection.

In her essay on literary realism in the Cold War, Clark further notes that in addition to the depiction of the Cold Warrior as hypermasculine, the popular cultural depictions of the era actively worked to erase difference, such that the "identity politics that had portrayed bodies as gendered, colored, sexed, and normed" were emptied out of the rhetorical space entirely.[19] The Cold Warrior was simplified and constructed crudely such that one "who exercises power through force, rather than through persuasion, is gendered male. . . . Using rhetoric instead of force, on the other hand, is gendered as feminine."[20] In *The Americans* it is the character of Elizabeth Jennings who punctures this narrative of Cold War rhetoric as it is she, a KGB spy, not Stan Beeman, who plays the role of the Cold Warrior and relies not just on forceful power (though she is an impressive and brutal fighter) but also on the rhetoric of deception and the practices of seduction.

Elizabeth Jennings operates with a mostly unflinching sense of honor and patriotic duty and only on rare occasions questions her missions and her handlers. Her KGB-arranged husband, Philip (though their deep and authentic attachment to each other makes theirs a much more real marriage than most and is cemented as such on the show in season 5), is also a very experienced operative, but he is much more riven with doubt about their deep undercover mission than Elizabeth is and expresses his frustrations in self-help seminars at EST, where the public confessionals and hotel ballroom workshops help him cope with the heavy burden of living a life of deception. Philip, with his deeply tragic worldview and unease with his assigned missions, offers a counterpoint to the honorable and unquestioning depiction of the patriotic spy. He is dutiful but questioning, a highly skilled and ruthlessly manipulative spy who nevertheless wrestles with the constraints and strictures of his life. Elizabeth, with her strict code of honor and deep commitment to the cause, is much closer to the narrative trope, but she too feels the push and pull between her multiple roles as spy, mother, and wife. In her book on Cold War rhetoric, Clark notes that the era propped up "an illusory coherent subject—of national and individual identity—upon gendered identities that were, in fact, on trial."[21] It is precisely this illusion of coherence that *The Americans* pulls apart for its audience in multiple ways, taking as its space of operation the very "domestic middlebrow" that Clark says was invisible in the Cold War narrative.[22] In its revisiting (but not quite revisionism) of the Cold War trope, *The Americans* renders this domestic terrain visible and even vital, and subverts it even further by using Soviet characters to pose as Americans in 1980s suburbia.

Cold War Moms and the Politicization of the Domestic Realm

In its gendered construction of national identity, Cold War ideology relied heavily on the tropes of masculinity and tried its best to erase women from the narrative. As Clark writes, it was "heavily dependent on denying the significance of gender and projecting the threatening unreality of ideology onto Soviet plots."[23] Women were removed from most constructions of the political by "the gendered distinction between a militarized national civic life and the domestic life of consumers."[24] It is precisely this erasure of gender and of the domestic life of spies that *The Americans* undermines so effectively, by not only introducing the KGB agents as impersonators and practitioners of American identity but by introducing the woman as the key figure in the narrative and collapsing the distinction between the public or political sphere and the private or domestic sphere.

The subversion of this gendered trope is evident in the first episode, which introduces us to these characters in a way that clearly signals the show's revitalized take on Cold War politics. When we first meet Elizabeth, it is at a bar where she plays the classic female role of seductress, the woman as source of corruption and moral decay, laying honey traps for information and blackmail. But soon that image is complicated by a dramatic scene with her and Philip in covert (and crisis) mode: they are in the middle of kidnapping a Russian defector who turns out to have a long and abusive history with Elizabeth (he was a supervisor who raped her during her training in Russia) and handing him over to the KGB when things go awry. An accomplice is stabbed in the gut, and they miss the drop-off for transporting the defector back to Russia because Philip wants to get their injured comrade to the hospital, over Elizabeth's objections, who insists that "the mission comes first."[25] Right away, this establishes Elizabeth as the honorable and patriotic spy, who is much less likely to deviate from her assigned purpose than is her partner and husband, a portrayal that is fleshed out quickly in this dramatic pilot episode.

The next time we see the Jenningses they have pulled into the garage of the neat suburban home they share with their two American-born children, Paige and Henry, the KGB defector now gagged and bound in the trunk of the car. From the beginning, the Jennings home operates as something other than domestic and private; it is shot through with the power of the state, and their basement garage becomes a space in which this first tense plot plays out (do they kill the defector or wait for further instructions from their handler?), inaugurating it as a site of contestation. (In succeeding seasons the garage becomes a place where a deadly biological weapon is stored and one in which Elizabeth trains their daughter in the art of self-defense.) Rather than figuring the home as a site of capture by the state where identity can now be homogenized in the private sphere, from its opening scenes *The Americans* compels us to look at the family in a different way and to rethink gender in the context of espionage. In doing so, it manages to avoid the strict regulation of national identity that Clark identifies as the hallmark of Cold War discourse.

Unlike the traditional Cold War narrative where women and the home are pushed to the margins, in *The Americans* the woman reappears as a central character, and the domestic sphere reappears, but in a new form. This recasting, and perhaps weaponizing, of the domestic sphere is seen once again in the pilot episode, which shows Elizabeth pulling a hot pan of freshly baked brownies from the oven (a housewarming gift for their new FBI agent neighbor) and picking up a long sharp knife to slice them into pieces. The camera lingers on her face for long seconds as she stands in her kitchen, her face an inscrutable mixture of emotions, while the blade of the knife glints over the whole scene. Then, in a moment of sudden decisiveness, she leaves the kitchen and heads down the stairs to the basement garage and the audience is left wondering whether or not she murdered the Russian defector and her former rapist who is still bound in the trunk of the car. She is at once a perfect 1980s wife and mother who bakes brownies from scratch for her new neighbors and also a brutally trained and disciplined KGB operative, and she occupies both roles with dexterity. Philip comes home to see her holding the knife and mirrors the audience's doubt in his face. Later, he is the one who kills the defector, but only after he has flirted with the idea of defecting himself, a possibility that Elizabeth refuses to acknowledge as she holds fast to her allegiance to the "motherland" and says angrily to Philip, "Don't you understand? After all these years? I would die, I would go to jail, I would lose everything before I betray my country."[26] The account Elizabeth gives of herself in this scene is that of the heroic spy, the honorable Cold Warrior whose duty to her homeland is crucial to her very identity construction. She remains wrapped up in an honorable narrative about heroic agency but also dislodges it from its masculine construction. Elizabeth inhabits a complex multiplicity of roles as spy, mother, and lover, but continually tries to ease the friction between their often contradictory attributes by holding on tightly to her code of honor and duty. This code is spelled out explicitly later in the first season, in an episode titled "Duty and Honor," by another female KGB operative, who says to Philip, referring to him by his Russian name, "[O]nly duty and honor are real, Mischa, isn't that what we were told?"[27] The sedative power of this norm doesn't always work for Philip, but Elizabeth rarely questions her ideological training. Her code of honor and patriotic duty remains insistently intact, even as the show compels its audience to uneasily interrogate its value as the cost of operating a life undercover takes a profound toll on the Jennings family and their relationships with each other.

In a famous essay on Cold War depictions of motherhood, Michael Rogin wrote perceptively about the ways in which the films of the era led to "the simultaneous glorification and fear of maternal influence within the family."[28] The mother played a prominent role in these films as the source of subject production, either as the cosseting figure who turned her sons "soft" by smothering them with maternal affection, or as the site of infiltration herself. They introduced the mother as the source of decay and corruption such that "domesticity replaced physical force with loving, maternal influence. She entered the self, formed it, understood its feelings, and thereby at once produced and protected it from corruption."[29] This construction of motherhood is clear in the pilot when Philip angrily accuses Elizabeth of being incapable of accepting how American their unsuspecting children truly are and how they become more and more so every day. She responds to him icily in a manner that echoes *The Manchurian Candidate*: "I'm not finished with them yet. They don't have to be American. They can be socialist."[30]

This particular understanding of the mother figure as the source of subject formation and the construction of the children's identity emerges as central to the plot of *The Americans* over the succeeding seasons as Elizabeth slowly becomes open to the idea of preparing her daughter for potential recruitment as a second-generation KGB spy. Unlike Philip, who is deeply reluctant to reveal their true identities to Paige and bring her into the fold, Elizabeth has been chafing at her daughter's newfound interest in the church and her increasing closeness with her young pastor and his family. Concerned that her daughter, who is already separated from her by the authenticity of her American identity, is moving too close to another family, she expresses her frustration to Philip at the cost of their deception: "I wish I could tell her about the real heroes. People who sacrifice themselves for this world, not some stupid children's tale."[31] She is therefore much more receptive to the idea of recruiting Paige when the Jennings handler, Claudia, tells them that "for the right child, it could give their life a meaning and a purpose they could never find in this country."[32] For Elizabeth, the honor and sense of heroic agency that comes with her covert role imbues her very sense of herself with meaning and is something she wants to share with Paige, both in order to serve the cause and also out of a real desire to be close to her increasingly distant teenage daughter and share an authentic connection with her. A life of honor and patriotic duty is one of sacrifice and meaning and purpose, and Elizabeth very much wants to mold her daughter in that image (and therefore in her own).

In later episodes of the show, the Jenningses turn their home into a recruiting and training ground for Paige. She is told the truth of her parents' identities; is gently encouraged to maintain close friendships with the pastor and his wife, who can potentially blackmail the family; is warned repeatedly against getting too close to Stan Beeman's guitar-playing teenage son (a directive she mostly ignores); and is trained in self-defense in the basement garage by her mom. According to Rogin, "denying the truly private character of the home" makes the family "less a haven for protecting eccentricity than an arena for forming and standardizing personality."[33] *The*

Americans plays on the trope of Momism that Rogin attributes to the writer Philip Wylie (who first coined the term in 1942) and refers to as "the demonic version of domestic ideology."[34] *The Americans* avoids the melodrama of Momism—both parents are engaged in Paige's training, though one is certainly more conflicted than the other—but it doesn't altogether avoid the tension generated by the juxtaposition of mother and trainer in the same role. To echo Rogin's words, "[T]he family is constructed in the name of privacy as a field for social control. State and family interpenetrate in mutually supportive anxiety" in *The Americans*.[35]

Patriotism, Honor, and Tragedy

The Americans is at its best and most complex when it highlights this interpenetration of the state and the family and the multiplicity of anxieties it generates. Over the course of the ensuing episodes we see Paige struggle with the burden of knowledge once her parents tell her their true identity and then with the burden of her guilt when she inevitably slips up and confides in her pastor. The anxiety and mistrust grow in the family until a dramatic and violent encounter at the very end of season 4 that draws mother and daughter closer together in a moment of trauma. Paige and Elizabeth are walking toward their car late one night on their way home from the food pantry, when Paige begins to provide her mother with information that she has gleaned from Stan Beeman's son about the chaos created at the FBI from the recent discovery of a KGB spy in their midst. After all the assessing, the careful disclosure of family history, the quiet training of deception, mother and daughter appear to have found a new plane on which to recalibrate their relationship and are drawing closer. Paige now trusts her mom enough to voluntarily report to her, and Elizabeth's pride in that moment is palpable and touching. But their moment of quiet intimacy is suddenly shattered by a pair of muggers who set upon them with a knife and make lewd remarks about Paige. Elizabeth, in a moment that collapses her roles as both protective mom and spy, springs into action with the full extent of her training on display as she moves swiftly to attack one of the muggers. She stabs him in the neck with his own knife, while his partner flees, and Paige takes in the whole scene in front of her in mute horror.

The next episode shows us the fallout from the violence, with Paige traumatized by the murder, sitting on her bed and asking her mother, "[D]id you have to do that?," to which Elizabeth calmly responds, "Yeah, I did."[36] Later, when the two of them are alone at home Paige observes, "[Y]ou didn't even seem upset. You were calm. How could you be calm? You killed him, Mom." Elizabeth tells her simply, "I didn't want to let him hurt you." She is both mother and protector, and she clings to her ideas of honor and duty to justify her actions, but such narratives are insufficient for a traumatized Paige, who pushes away all her mother's explanations of wanting to make the world a better place or fighting for peace with a curt dismissal: "[I]t's never the whole truth." The gap between mother and daughter is clear. It is also apparent that however much Elizabeth may try to forge Paige in the identity of a spy, her daughter resists the easy erasure offered by honor and duty. Elizabeth's patriotism and the honor she feels in inhabiting her own identity is devoid of a tragic sensibility. She is unable to acknowledge the harm her actions cause as they are readily anesthetized by honor and duty. Patriotism for her becomes a clarifying ideology that is strongly connected to what Rogin diagnosed as the "demonology" of the era, which required a "rigid insistence on difference" but also was derived from the "fears of and forbidden desires for identity with the excluded object. In countersubjective discourse, therefore, the opposition breaks down."[37]

Elizabeth lacks the kind of tragic sensibility that both Paige and Philip, who is always torn between his different allegiances, demonstrate. Elizabeth, whose patriotism is praised by her handlers, who note how "steadfast" she is, bears a different burden as her sense of honor and duty close her off from the complex possibility of the tragic and deprive her of a deeper and more meaningful connection with her daughter.[38] In the final analysis, Elizabeth's sense of patriotism continues to anesthetize, and her code of honor becomes a form of erasure that smooths the more unsettling disruptions to her subject formation into a clear narrative, because the cost of doing otherwise and accepting the splintering of her multiple identities is simply too great. She finds comfort in the clarifying ideology of patriotic duty, but it does not translate to her teenage daughter, who finds such narratives insufficient to cope with the depth of her trauma. As such, Elizabeth's honorable words about making the world a better place and the sacrifices of the postwar generation mean little to Paige. Instead, she copes with her trauma as most teenagers do, by lying on the couch all day and watching soap operas on TV and chatting with the cute boy next door. Eventually she comes to terms with the depth of what her mother has done and what she herself is imbricated in, but she finds no comfort in it, and doubts creep in that persist and grow in the final episodes of the show. To use Rogin's terminology, through the character of Paige, *The Americans* participates in the kind of countersubjective discourse that breaks down the demonology of the Cold War narrative in the political imagination.

The Anesthetic of Honor

In its deeply observed and thrilling dramatization of espionage and family, *The Americans* complicates Cold War narratives of political imagination and subverts their reliance on the heroic figure of the male by casting Elizabeth Jennings in the role instead. Spy, seductress, assassin, and homemaker—Elizabeth inhabits and performs all these roles. In her mothering and recruiting of her daughter, she operates at the very center of subject formation in the show. In many ways, Elizabeth takes on the role of the Cold War mother in altered form—she is a source of infiltration and anxiety, but she is also a source of agency and a figure that Paige grows to trust. Elizabeth, however, continues to hold on tightly to the sense of honor, patriotic duty, and sacrifice that still permeates the idea of espionage in the political imagination, and for the most part she lacks the tragic sensibility that both her daughter and her husband exhibit. Her patriotic and dutiful code of honor serves as an anesthetic—it turns out that honor in the context of espionage is a way to sedate and tranquilize the difficulty of navigating the multiplicity of identities one must assume in this role and requires the erasure of more authentic selves that have to be sacrificed in the name of duty. Unlike her husband, who struggles throughout the show to justify the acts of violence, betrayal, and moral compromises that espionage requires, Elizabeth clings to honor and patriotic duty to erase such doubts and focus on the task at hand. It is only in the penultimate season of the show that her strict attachment to honor and patriotic duty starts to erode and the anesthetic shows signs of wearing off. Both the Jenningses are depicted as exhausted by their missions, mistrustful of their handlers, and ready to end their lives of deception. They ask to be exfiltrated back to Russia, but even Elizabeth is increasingly concerned about the impact of such a dramatic change on their American-born and -raised children. For so long honor, patriotic duty, and love of country were sufficient to smooth over the many fractures in her multiple identities, but they start to lose their enduring power when she is faced with the tragic reality of the choice to stay undercover in America or be sent back to the motherland. It turns out that the center cannot hold after all, and when she finally makes a fateful choice in the series finale, it exacts a tremendous and tragic personal cost.

Over the course of its six seasons *The Americans* immersed its viewers in a simmering tub of unease, showing collusion and compromise at the highest levels of government, laying bare the tragic and complex political identities of its undercover operatives. In doing so, it mounted a deep and sustained critique of honor and patriotic duty, which are often invoked to smooth over the sharp and jagged edges of sacrifice that are required in the name of country. As Steve Johnston notes in his book *American Dionysia*, patriotism can function as "a beguiling alternative" that "obscures tragic necessities and disables tragic possibilities" of political life. In masking the complexity and compromises that are the stuff of politics, patriotism lets its believers "off the tragic hook with a network of ready-made collective narratives, understandings, and attitudes that tell us all is well."[39] *The Americans* resists this impulse and never lets its viewers "off the tragic hook"—it exposes the limits of such justifying narratives of honor and patriotic duty and lays bare the costs of living undercover. In its rejection of the anesthesia of patriotic narratives of honor and duty, it echoes the experience of the show's creator, Jacob Weisberg, a former CIA operative, who fully bought into the Evil Empire rhetoric as a young officer, but "ended up seeing the world in a much more complex way—not so black and white."[40]

The Cold War–era styling of *The Americans* eerily mirrors recent news stories of Russian influence and military conquest; it is easy to imagine Elizabeth and Philip Jennings at the heart of the Russian attempt to influence a presidential election, using their deep knowledge of American culture to infiltrate social media and political culture, or operating behind the scenes to influence lawmakers to curtail American support of Ukrainian resistance to Russian aggression. However, moving beyond the easy logic of such juxtaposition, the dramatic depiction of the anesthetizing effects of honor and patriotic duty among spies in *The Americans* offers a valuable lesson in coming to terms with the tragic complexity of politics, which is not so easily soothed by such narratives. Johnston suggests that "love of country, whether active or dormant," enables one "not only to explain, ignore, deny, rationalize, contextualize, or obfuscate a seemingly endless litany of national shortcomings but also to accept and affirm them."[41]

Time and again, with its complex construction of political identity and its tragic sensibility, *The Americans* reveals that simplifying narratives of honor and patriotic duty are hollow and insufficient for the contemporary political imagination. Indeed, the show remains particularly resonant today because it mirrors the unease of contemporary politics, where democracy appears increasingly vulnerable and where some even invoke such narratives to justify attacks on democratic norms and institutions. Instead, the show underlines the need to reject the demonology of simplifying narratives of honor and patriotic duty that are amplified by cable news cycles and Twitter timelines and insists on reckoning with the tragic complexity of political life.

3

The Ornamental Politics of Honor

Wolf Hall, Machiavelli, and the Art of Power

In the political imagination, honor is usually highlighted in films and television shows, but every now and then a work of fiction breaks through and leaves its mark with a bracing new take on an endlessly regurgitated story that not only becomes a popular phenomenon but offers a fresh perspective on honor itself. Hilary Mantel's Booker Prize–winning novel *Wolf Hall* is one such masterful work, which eschews the soapy narrative tropes of the genre of historical fiction and instead delivers a deeply researched but creatively rewritten account of Henry VIII's most efficient and ruthless counselor, Thomas Cromwell. Mantel's fictional portrayal of Cromwell has proved compelling enough to launch a wholesale revisionism of his role in the Tudor era and has led to two critically recognized sequels (*Bring Up the Bodies*, which won another Booker Prize, and *The Mirror and the Light*, which also received critical acclaim), a BBC and PBS television series, and a West End and Broadway play. The Cromwell of *Wolf Hall* is grounded in the historical record, but he moves through the hallways of the Tudor court in a convincingly modern manner—he is representative of the "new age," a man whose visionary perspective, mysteriously foreign past, and sharp rise from humble origins allow him to craft a new kind of political imagination that is deeply grounded in an understanding of the aesthetics of power.

For Mantel's Cromwell, honor is essentially fungible, a currency to be exchanged and traded, a means to an end, and one of the necessary tools of the art of power. As such, it exists in sharp contrast to the binding codes of honor previously discussed in this book, which often blind its adherent to the costs of its relentless pursuit. An internal code of honor grounded in ancestral tradition or patriotic duty, while inspiring one to action, can nevertheless be rigid and confining and often ignores at its own peril the essential vulnerability and dependency of honor to the recognition of others. By contrast, a realist approach to honor that sees it as a key component of the art of power allows for its skillful deployment in ways that go beyond the rational to the realm of the sensible. Thomas Cromwell, who Mantel masterfully reimagines and brings to life from the historical record, is introduced to the reader of *Wolf Hall* as coming from the humblest of origins (his father was a blacksmith and brewer) and as someone who fits nowhere in the aristocratic hierarchy of the royal court, where birth and rank act as the main signifiers of power. Indeed, it is because of his low station that Cromwell underlines the contingency of the honorable and aristocratic model of power, which is utterly grounded in recognition by others for its continuing potency. However, as a "self-made man" in the Tudor court, he occupies a position of precarity, his low birth and status forever acting as a liability to those whose fortunes have been threatened by his rapid rise. He is always somehow "other" because of his humble origins and his decades mysteriously spent abroad in mainland Europe and is often referred to as "Italian" (even though he hails from the poor working-class area of Putney) to underline his essential foreignness. In *Wolf Hall* and in its sequels, this contingent status means that Cromwell is attentive to the complexity of honor as a tool in the art of power as he rises in Henry VIII's favor to heights that astonish all of his contemporaries. Cromwell recognizes and is careful to mollify the power of chivalric and aristocratic honor that is exemplified by the old guard at the Tudor court, which consistently sees him as an upstart and a threat to its hold on power. However, he is also keenly aware of the increasing obsolescence of honor as aristocratic privilege in the modern era. Honor is one of many tools that he deploys in a flexible and fungible way, not as a rigidly confining code granted by birthright but rather as an ornamental tool of power, cultivated through loyalty, courtesy, and good taste. He never forgets that honor is vulnerable to the recognition of others and that while it is helpful in gaining favor and indeed grows to matter significantly to him as he gains power and influence, it is always a luxury that can be dispensed with if necessary, an ornamental brooch that can always be unpinned from his dark crimson cloak of Italian silk.

Even when Cromwell fails, as he inevitably does, his grasp of the pliability and practical usefulness of honor as a tool in the art of power is notable. Throughout his rise, and even in his downfall, he acknowledges the power of the aristocracy and honor by birthright, even as he works to undermine it. Aristocratic honor is an obstacle to his plans, but also an opportunity. As with his transformation of religion with the dissolution of the monasteries and his modernization of governance in Tudor England, honor too is something he attempts to reshape and refashion. In Mantel's portrayal, Cromwell comes across as a master of the practical arts of power and as someone who is committed to changing the very art of governance itself, a representative of a wave of reform that begins to spread across Europe in the early modern era. As Michel Foucault has written, "*How to govern* was, I believe, one of the fundamental questions about what was happening in the 15th or 16th centuries. It is a fundamental question which was answered by the multiplication of all the arts of governing—the art of pedagogy, the art of politics, the art of economics, if you will—and of all the institutions of government, in the wider sense the term government had at the time."[1]

Cromwell is precisely such a multiplier of the arts of governing, in all its forms, and a particularly sharp observer of what Jacques Rancière has termed the "distribution of the sensible," or the "allocation of ways of doing, ways of being, ways of saying."[2] Mantel describes him in the following way in the beginning of *Wolf Hall*:

> Thomas Cromwell is now a little over forty years old. He is a man of strong build, not tall. Various expressions are available to his face, and one is readable: an expression of stifled amusement. His hair is dark, heavy, and waving, and his small eyes, which are of very strong sight, light up in conversation.... His speech is low and rapid, his manner assured; he is at home in courtroom or waterfront, bishop's palace or inn yard. He can draft a contract, train a falcon, draw a map, stop a street fight, furnish a house and fix a jury. He will quote you a nice point in the old authors, from Plato to Plautus and back again. He knows new poetry, and can say it in Italian. He works all hours, first up and last to bed. He makes money and he spends it. He will take a bet on anything.[3]

Cromwell is the master of a tactile political economy: he is a skilled cook, a deft surveyor of kitchen pantries, a sharp appraiser of jewelry and fine tapestries, well versed in the flows of emerging financial markets, and a brutally precise architect of law—a man particularly well suited to "multiplying" the arts of governance and radically expanding the terrain of power. This chapter focuses primarily on Mantel's *Wolf Hall* in its analysis, the first novel of the award-winning trilogy, but it also discusses key aspects of the two novels that follow it in order to fully explore Mantel's portrayal of Cromwell as alert, tactile, and adept, a man who can refashion not only a dish but the political imagination of a country. It reads Mantel's account of Cromwell alongside Niccolò Machiavelli's *The Prince* to uncover a concept of honor that is instrumental to the art of power and an ornamental representation of its deeply aesthetic nature that is attuned to what Davide Panagia has called "the political life of sensation."[4] In doing so, it excavates an aesthetic politics of honor that is deeply grounded in everyday practice and regimes of perception and that offers fresh insight into the enduring power it has in the political imagination.

Machiavelli and the Ornamental Politics of Honor

In both the historical and fictional record, Cromwell is often referred to as Machiavellian, where the term signifies a cunning and amoral strategist, hell-bent on acquiring power and sweeping away tradition. While the characterization is an apt one in many ways, its crude adjectival rendering does a disservice to both *The Prince* and *Wolf Hall*, which both provide much more nuanced accounts of the art of power. Nevertheless, the connections between Machiavelli and Cromwell exist for a convincing set of reasons, and Mantel offers an intriguing nod to them in her references to Machiavelli's book, which is the talk of Europe at the time and is furtively being passed around the Tudor court. She writes of Cromwell, "He has got Niccolò Machiavelli's book, *Principalities*; it is a Latin edition, shoddily printed in Naples, which seems to have passed through many hands. He thinks of Niccolò on the battlefield; of Niccolò in the torture chamber. He feels he is in the torture chamber but he knows that one day he will find the door out, because it is he who has the key. Someone says to him, what is in your little book? And he says, a few aphorisms, a few truisms, nothing we didn't know before."[5] Initially it might appear that Cromwell is dismissive of the text ("nothing we didn't know before") but his identification with Niccolò is quite apparent. He feels similarly stuck and exiled from the hallways of power, having seen his fortunes decline along with those of his patron Cardinal Wolsey, but he also feels that he might have the key to the door that offers an escape from his current plight. Is the key hidden in *The Prince*, or is it merely a collection of well-worn "truisms"? Perhaps the key lies within Machiavelli, or perhaps it is crafted from his own constellation of skills, but it is possible to at least proffer a reading of similitude on the proximity of the insight; after all, Cromwell's faith in his own resilience comes to him as he's reflecting on Machiavelli's text.

The layered connections between the two are apparent in their accounts of honor. For both Machiavelli and Cromwell, honor remains on the margins of their aesthetic approach to power, but there are enough passing mentions in both texts to signal that it serves as an important tool for both. For Machiavelli, honor serves as an accessory to power, a form of ornamentation, a jeweled brooch to be removed as needed, but also to be noted for its value. Both recognize its value, but both flexibly dispense with it when it no longer suits their purpose. It is a perspective that is echoed throughout the trilogy and one that is brought out most sharply by the deft contrast Mantel draws between Cromwell and his opponents. The contrast is most sharply and vividly drawn in *Wolf Hall*, where the main antagonist is the ascetic and honorable Thomas More, who is unyielding in his refusal to dishonor himself by taking King Henry VIII's Oath of Supremacy, which goes against his fundamental religious beliefs, and who therefore finds himself staring down the perennially flexible, pragmatic, and sharp Cromwell. In the second book, *Bring Up the Bodies*, Cromwell confidently grows into his role as Henry VIII's enforcer, dispenses with honor almost entirely, and is ruthless in dissolving the king's marriage to Anne Boleyn on trumped-up charges and sending her off to the executioner's block. Not only does he get rid of one of the chief threats to his power, but he also takes advantage of this opportunity for political advancement to execute several young men around her at court who are caught up in the dying codes of romantic chivalry and present an easy target for revenge. In the final book of the trilogy, the *Mirror and the Light*, as the adornments of honors and titles pile up as rewards for his prodigious efforts, his comeuppance comes at the hands of the Duke of Norfolk and the old aristocracy, who are so incensed at the astonishing power that the upstart Cromwell has accumulated through his skillful exercise of the art of power that they literally rip his ornamental honors off his robes.

In Mantel's rendering, the issue of Cromwell's honor first becomes visible in its perceived absence by others. In the Tudor court, where honors are bestowed by ancestry and tradition, his low and dishonorable birth stands as an impediment to gaining the king's trust and therefore his access to power.[6] In a sense, the stain of his birth puts him at a similar remove to the halls of power as Machiavelli, who was exiled from the halls of Florentine power and displaced to the countryside, left to gaze longingly at the Palazzo Vecchio from afar. Cromwell's main patron in *Wolf Hall* is Cardinal Wolsey, himself a butcher's son. Wolsey underlines this dishonorable disadvantage for him clearly, and Cromwell can't deny his characterization: "Putney, he means. It is the stark fact. And since he's not a churchman, there are no ecclesiastical titles to soften it, as they have softened the stark fact of Ipswich."[7] Cromwell has no aristocratic lineage and no recognized authority to ease his access to power. (Indeed, the first part of *Wolf Hall* focuses on the loss of the one source of access he did have with the fall of his powerful patron.) He has no titles that are honored and recognized by others, and what he does accomplish has to be painstakingly earned by own virtues.

This is seen clearly in one of his first private conversations with Henry VIII in Wolf Hall. At this point he has impressed the king with his loyalty to and relentless advocacy for his fallen patron, but also with his obvious political and diplomatic skills. Henry is wary of Cromwell's low and dishonorable reputation, but also willing to give him an opening. He asks Cromwell how he came to know as much as he does about European trading, and the ensuing dialogue between them is revealing:

> "I trained in the Florentine banks. And in Venice." The king stares at him in surprise—"Howard said you were a common soldier." "That too." "Anything else?" "What would your Majesty like me to be?" The king looks him full in the face: a rare thing with him. He looks back; it is his habit. "Master Cromwell, your reputation is bad." He inclines his head. "You don't defend yourself?" "Your Majesty is able to form his own opinion." "I can. I will."[8]

Cromwell's reputation may be dishonorable, but rather than be fixed in place by it, he puts his faith in his own skills, or in his *virtùs*, as Machiavelli would characterize it. And in signaling an opening for Cromwell, despite his notably "bad" reputation, Henry follows the advice Machiavelli lays out for the ruler, who "cannot conform to all those rules that men who are thought good are expected to respect, for he is often obliged, in order to hold on to power, to break his word, to be uncharitable, inhumane, and irreligious. So he must be mentally prepared to act as circumstances and changes in fortune require."[9] In this characterization, Machiavelli underlines the inherent contingency of politics, that fortune is never constant and requires a continual shifting and recalibration of strategy, not fixed in place by either tradition or morality, something that Cromwell understands instinctively.

In *The Prince*, Machiavelli notes that it is the nobility who cling most tightly to their inherited traditions and therefore present the greatest challenge to those who unsettle the fixity of the hierarchy of birth. He writes, "[Y]ou will find the nobility, both those who have been your allies and those you have defeated, present you with an infinity of problems."[10] They need to be won over, but their loyalty can never be guaranteed. As much as they deny recognition to those of dishonorable birth, they can be won over with a different approach to honor. Machiavelli articulates an account of honor which can be established despite these difficulties, with tactical skill and the efficient neutralization of enemies, such that "once they have overcome them, and they have begun to be idolized, having got rid of those who were jealous of their superior qualities, they are established, they are powerful, secure, honored, happy."[11] Honor therefore becomes a way to manage one's enemies, to keep them mollified and to remove impediments to one's own power.

In *The Prince* Machiavelli repeatedly refers to honor as something valuable but whose essential value is bestowed on it by the recognition of others. For the Italian nobility, honor retains the vestiges of the chivalric tradition—it is a quest for acknowledgment that one aspires to. He writes of Oliveretto of Fermo that "he said he had only gone to war to acquire honor," and later how important it was to his family that "he was greeted by the people of Fermo with every honor."[12] While reviewing the various rulers of the Roman Empire Machiavelli himself refers to Marcus Aurelius as having alone "lived honorably," suggesting that there is something of inherent value in this concept, even if it primarily functions as a means to an end in the currency of power and is not something to be acquired as a long-term or permanent asset.[13] He advises the ruler to show himself to be "an admirer of skill [*virtù*] and ... honor those who are excellent in any type of work"[14] and that he should carefully pick his adviser and retain him by "heaping honors on him,"[15] thereby "ensuring he receives public recognition ... [and] that he has so many honors he desires no more,"[16] clearly suggesting that honor functions as a form of political ornamentation that is necessary for multiplying the art of governing.

Despite this recognition of the value that is placed on honor, or perhaps precisely because of it, Machiavelli remains sharply attuned to its usefulness as a political tactic and the necessity of dispensing with it as circumstances require. There is often a tension that exists between doing what is honorable and what is harmful, or in other words, being cognizant of its binding and blinding power. He notes, "[O]ne cannot honorably give the elite what they want, and one cannot do it without harming others, for the objectives of the populace are less immoral than those of the elite."[17] Therefore, he continues, "those who tie themselves to you and are not rapacious, you should honor and love."[18] Honor, for Machiavelli, is therefore a reward for good behavior that the ruler bestows on others, a form of adornment or decoration. It is something for individuals who desire political success to acquire tactically;

like a mark or a medal, it is something to be earned and displayed as ornamentation. Since honor is so fundamentally tied to and constrained by public recognition it is necessarily contingent and dependent on *fortuna*: "[Y]ou should therefore know here are two ways to fight: one while respecting the rules, the other with no holds barred.... But because you cannot always win if you respect the rules, you must be prepared to break them."[19] Honor is instrumental to the acquisition and maintenance of power, a useful implement in the toolbox but one to be discarded if circumstances dictate. Clearly it is useful in the acquisition and maintenance of power, but it must be dispensed with when necessary. For Machiavelli, the essential significance of honor is that it is a political virtue dependent on the recognition of others, and as such it is a form of fungible political capital. This is clearly seen when Machiavelli states that honor is fundamentally linked to power, is a means to an end, and that "if a ruler wins wars and holds on to power, the means he has employed will always be judged honorable, and everyone will praise them."[20]

This inherent link between honor and the art of power is intuitive to Cromwell in *Wolf Hall*. He lacks all the recognized forms of ornamentation, and yet his tactical skill gives him a powerful presence that others recognize and are unsettled by. A revealing exchange with the Duke of Norfolk, a brittle and harsh old man with few redeeming qualities, who is the head of the aristocratic Howard family, underlines this. Mantel writes, "The duke scowls. He paces; he rattles a little; at last he bursts out, 'Damn it all, Cromwell, why are you such a ... *person*? It isn't as if you could afford to be.' He waits, smiling. He knows what the duke means. He is a person, he is a presence. He knows how to edge blackly into a room so that you don't see him; but perhaps those days are over."[21] Cromwell can't be honorably recognized by ancient bloodlines and inherited titles, but his presence is nevertheless sensed and demands recognition as a "person." He has crafted for himself an identity; he is a visible subject who the old guard is now forced to acknowledge because of his growing influence. As he rises in the Tudor court, he becomes less constrained by the lowness of his birth and becomes recognized as a person of significance, despite Norfolk's confusion, and begins to accumulate the ornaments of honor from the king in exactly the manner prescribed by Machiavelli. He gains the trust of the king with his indispensable legal, financial, and management skills, and along with that acknowledgment comes an increase in status, wealth, and titles, all of which provide him with the trappings of honor that force the court to recognize him. Still, despite his rapid rise, Cromwell knows not to blindly trust in the recognition of others, and when he speaks to Henry of honor, he is positively Machiavellian in his realist approach to it. In discussing how to deal with the difficult Bishop Gardiner, he plays on the king's chivalric taste for honor: "'It is the more pleasant course, and there is more honour in it.' He watches Henry's face. He is alive to anything that concerns honour. 'Is that the advice you would always give?' He smiles. 'No.'"[22] For Cromwell honor remains a tactic and a tool; there is no need to be constant in it, but it is important to be aware of the effect it has on others. Henry himself warns Cromwell of this, when he says, "Do I retain you for what is easy? Jesus pity my simplicity, I have promoted you to a place in this kingdom that no one, no one of your breeding has ever held in the whole of the history of this realm. . . . I keep you. Master Cromwell, because you are as cunning as a bag of serpents. But do not be a viper in my bosom."[23] His dishonorable status can never be completely wiped away in the eyes of the court and will always be a source of vulnerability, despite the effectiveness of his service to the king. Honor, therefore, remains contingent on recognition. For Cromwell it serves a useful political function, a means to an end that can be bestowed on others carefully in exchange for access and power.

Perspective and the Art of Power

Honor is seen as decorative and dispensable in both *Wolf Hall* and *The Prince*, but what might be the larger significance of this formulation? It is important to recognize that the view of honor as ornamental is part of a larger aesthetic approach to politics, one that sees the art of power as not just tactical but representative of a deeper philosophical shift that expands the political imagination, moving it beyond the confines of the rational to the realm of the sensible. In his book *The Art of Power*, Diego von Vacano highlights this shift by reading in both Machiavelli and Nietzsche an aesthetic approach to power that sees "the human being as one that gets its information about the world through his or her sensory capabilities," such that rather than "imagining beings whose determinations about the nature of the world come from pure reason abstracted from the senses" the human focuses instead on what "is perceived through the senses, or in other words, through sensory cognition."[24] This is an approach exemplified by Machiavelli and also by Cromwell in *Wolf Hall*, who relies consistently on the tactile intelligence of sensation, whether by cooking, assessing the weave of a tapestry, or sniffing out the scent of danger. Such an approach to politics as primarily aesthetic and focused on sensory cognition does not exist in opposition to reason, but rather "the reason that is employed is aesthetic, for it is grounded in [people's] firm belief that perception through the senses is what underlies the human condition."[25] The view of honor as ornamental is representative of this larger aesthetic shift that links the public recognition of honor to sense perception. The decorative use of honor renders it both useful and problematic for politics—it is easy to bestow these medals and marks on others to be recognized through the senses, but the visibility (both literal and figurative) of the ornamentation also allows one to perceive the danger posed by those who wear it too tightly and attach a rigidly abstract sense of value to it.

The aesthetic approach to politics that both Machiavelli and the fictional Cromwell share is clearly seen in the importance each places on perspective, the shifting and fluid point of view of the painter mapping out and capturing a scene, highlighting some aspects with brushstrokes and obscuring others in shadow. In his dedication to the Prince, Machiavelli famously notes this by writing to Lorenzo de' Medici:

> I hope it will not be thought presumptuous for someone of humble and lowly status to discuss the behavior of rulers and to make recommendations regarding policy. Just as those who paint landscapes set up their easels down in the valley in order to portray the nature of the mountains and the peaks, and climb up into the mountains in order to draw the valleys, similarly in order to properly understand the behavior of the lower classes one needs to be a ruler, and in order to properly understand the behavior of rulers one needs to be a member of the lower classes.[26]

In this key paragraph, Machiavelli notes the distinctiveness of perspective that the wise counselor has. Unlike the king or the prince, who are fixed in place by the trappings of power, both Machiavelli and Cromwell as men of "humble and lowly status" are free to move up and down, to shapeshift for a better view, for a keener sense of the machinations of power. Machiavelli recognizes that such a valuable perspective is rightly seen as presumptuous by those who can't move as easily. (Lorenzo, for instance, never granted Machiavelli the audience he hoped for, and the Duke of Norfolk is puzzled by Cromwell, who is only a "person," suddenly having access to power.) But this very notion of perspective is central to the aesthetic view of politics. The ability to truly "see" requires keen sensory perception and literal bodily motion, whether it is to hike up and back down the mountains or to move between the king's royal chambers and the pubs of London. Its power lies in its practical knowledge and tactile experience, in the value of being able to go up and back down, to be mobile in a way the ruler never can be.[27]

It is worth noting that it is also around this time that perspective is literally introduced to Renaissance painting by Filippo Brunelleschi, which led to a shift in regimes of perception in art. In his *Political Life of Sensation*, Panagia notes that with the added "capacity to paint a scene with geometric proportions (by starting from a central point on the canvas that represents the point at which the lines of visuality converge), we arrive at the realization that the source of unity in perception is not the outside world but our own vision of it."[28] Of course, seeing, or vision, has always been central to political theory too. The Greek root of the term *theoria* loosely translates to "vision" or "observation," further underlining how perspective is essential to the very vocation and practice of political theory. Von Vacano argues that "aesthetic political theory begins from the perspectivism of particular experiences. It takes sense perception as its field, and it borrows from aesthetic theory and art criticism not only the ideas of imitation, representation, emotion, and form, but also of imagination, creativity, and originality to explain political phenomena and practices."[29] Political imagination that is rooted in sensory perception and the power of perspective allows for the exercise of creativity and opens up the possibility of entirely new horizons of the future unencumbered by the traditions of the past.

This notion of *theoria* as vision is exemplified by Cromwell when he catches a glimpse of its potentiality, when his shifting perspective allows him to see a moment of political becoming. Mantel writes, "There is a world beyond this black world. There is a world of the possible. A world where Anne can be queen is a world where Cromwell can be Cromwell. He sees it; then he doesn't. The moment is fleeting. But insight cannot be taken back. You cannot return to the moment you were in before."[30] In this moment, Cromwell sees the art of the possible and the potentiality of the future. His shifting perspective leads to a splintering in linear time that allows the glimpse of a future that fundamentally changes his present with the force of its insight. Cromwell's dishonorable birth, while a disadvantage among the ranks of the aristocracy, is actually an advantage that gives him this perspective that is key to the art of power and that allows him to accumulate the ornaments of honor in a different way. He is not restrained by the tradition and trappings of the aristocracy and can therefore sense the possibility of a different future by moving around and observing phenomena from multiple vantage points. As Hannah Pitkin observes in her masterful work on Machiavelli, such a shifting in perspective is "a matter not merely of external observation but of identification, the capacity to put himself in the place of another and regard the world from that location. He must become the other yet remain himself."[31]

Cromwell, More, and the Political Life of Sensation

The central drama of *Wolf Hall* is a taut narrative contrast that Mantel draws between Thomas Cromwell and Sir Thomas More, between the man who can shift his perspective like an artist for his advantage and the man who is fixed in place by his binding code of honor and refusal to take the Oath of Supremacy that his king demands after his break from Rome and installment as the head of the Church of England. This is clear in Cromwell's revealing recollection of his first encounter with More and the way Mantel skillfully crafts their relationship and its reversal as a matter of shifting perspective. In *Wolf Hall* Cromwell first encounters More when Cromwell is only a grubby kitchen boy running errands at the palace in Lambeth and More is already a studious young page, a position reserved for gentlemen's sons, men of recognizable honor. In Cromwell's carefully preserved memory of this first encounter, he takes some bread to More in his chambers to sustain him during his studies and waits. In his recollection, "Master Thomas said, 'Why do you linger?' But he did not throw anything at him. 'What is in that great book?' he asked, and Master Thomas replied, smiling, 'Words, words, just words.'"[32] The encounter is revealing as it highlights Cromwell's curiosity and More's perceived superiority. While More is not cruel to the kitchen boy, he does not deem him worthy of knowledge—he is in no way recognized or honored as an equal. He smilingly dismisses him with a mention of "words" that Cromwell cannot possibly understand, "just words" of no meaning. Cromwell goes up and down the stairs, and his perspective allows him to quickly figure out how to make money off the studious page, whereas More remains ensconced in his study, barely seeing the boy who later becomes one of his greatest threats. The encounter also demarcates the difference in their spaces of experience: Cromwell conveys food and the very bread which goes to More's gut and feeds his mind, but More operates only in the realm of reason and words.

Food—its preparation and its digestion—might seem to belong to some neatly demarcated private and quotidian realm that exists apart from the political, but this is a notion that an aesthetic approach to politics blurs entirely. Panagia argues that much of the devaluing of bodily sensation and its appreciation might well stem from a certain kind of rationalist prejudice that ironically emerges from physiology itself. He notes, "[T]o write about flavor in political reflection requires that I address a normative partition: the mouth cannot eat and speak at the same time."[33] In other words, stemming from the simple physiological division of being unable to talk and eat at the same time, one form of sensation has been valued and the other dismissed. Speech is fundamentally associated with deliberation and therefore the political (indeed, in Aristotle's formulation it is the very quality that makes man a political animal and distinguishes him from other beasts), whereas eating is considered animalistic, too proximate to sensation and bodily function, linked to the visceral and therefore opposed to such rational accounts of the political. Notably, throughout the *Wolf Hall* trilogy, Cromwell continues to attend to food as a source of power, a means to honor guests, and a source of both enjoyment and influence. His kitchen at his home in Austin Friars becomes famous for its dinner parties—there are towering molds of jelly in striped red and white in the shape of a castle, exotic spices are omnipresent in the daily cooking, puddings are scented with elderflower and rosewater, and even the prescribed Lenten food is seasoned as much as possible with citrus and nuts to make it palatable.

This aesthetic approach to politics represents a shift from the past and the multiplication in the forms of governing that Foucault said was symptomatic of this era. What is at the heart of this aesthetic approach is the political life of sensation. Rancière has suggested that "politics is an activity of reconfiguration of that which is given to the sensible."[34] It is this reconfiguration of what is sensed, the self-making and chipping away at one's identity, forever shifting shape and perspective, that Cromwell is particularly adept at. In contrast to More, who was tutored upstairs in the library and chambers of Lambeth Palace, Cromwell "learns to read from the scribbled orders for wheat flour or dried beans, for barley and for duck's eggs, that come out of the steward's pantries."[35] Even at that young age, Cromwell gains a keen appreciation of the wisdom that can be gleaned from the profane rhythms of the mundane, to trust his eyes and his touch such that "at Lambeth he follows the stewards around and when they say a number he remembers it; so people say, if you haven't time to write it down, just tell John's nephew. He will cast an eye on a sack of whatever's been ordered in, then warn his uncle to check if it's short weight."[36] Cardinal Wolsey calls him "the master of practical solutions."[37] As Panagia argues, attending to sensation is simultaneously disruptive and also creative—these "moments of sensation punctuate our everyday existence, and in doing so, they puncture our received wisdoms and common modes of sensing."[38]

The contrast between Cromwell's appreciation of the political life of sensation and More's stubborn rationalism is further emphasized later in *Wolf Hall*, when the former attends a dinner party at the latter's home. Cromwell immediately notes the bland food at More's house and later thinks he should send him a cook to improve the flavors. More thinks the mouth is only for speaking—he is a cool rationalist who doesn't value the political life of sensation. Cromwell is the opposite: he trades in it; it is his currency of power, and he traffics in the political economy of the tactile. For More, the binary between the two functions of the mouth—taste and speech—is starkly apparent in the scant interest he pays to food and drink at his house and the premium he places on the war of words at the dinner table. When invited to dinner at More's house, Cromwell tastes the "gritty" sauce that coats all the various indistinguishable meats at the table. The mouth is solely an organ of speech and lofty expression for More, not to be corrupted with the baseness of flavor and appetite. By contrast, Cromwell's sensory perspective of the tableau at More's dinner party is revealing: "More takes no wine, though he serves it to his guests. There are several dishes, which all taste the same—flesh of some sort, with a gritty sauce like Thames mud—and then junkets, and a cheese, which he says one of his daughters has made—one of those daughters, wards, step-daughters, one of the women of whom the house is full. His eyes are drawn unwillingly to the cheese; it is pitted and wobbling, like the face of a stable boy after a night out."[39] The food is unappealing and lacking in flavor. More's guests leave hungry and disturbed, both by its flavors and by the causal cruelty of the conversation at the dinner table. (Mantel paints a vivid portrait of More's misogyny and authoritarianism, which shades into the emotional and physical abuse of his wards and servants.) It is an ascetic repast, an ugly feast marked by sensory deprivation which plays up the contrast with the life of the mind. More seems to adhere to Plato's view of the danger that lurks in food and the sensations it gives rise to, the moral destabilization that might come from being too attentive to flavor. For Plato and for More, food is necessary only for health, "and the desire which goes beyond this, of more delicate food, or other luxuries . . . is hurtful to the body, and hurtful to the soul, [and] in the pursuit of wisdom and virtue, might rightly be called unnecessary."[40]

By contrast, Cromwell's focus on taste, food, and sensation as essential to the political imagination is captured in detail during the downfall of his powerful patron. At this point in the novel, Cromwell is rising in the king's estimation and has every incentive to abandon his disgraced former patron, who is removed from York Palace and exiled to Esher on the king's orders. But loyalty and something resembling honor bind him to Wolsey's side. Honor is not represented here in words or oaths but rather in an aesthetic shift in perspective and an attendance to sensation as he descends the stairs to a dusty and unkempt kitchen to make a meal for Wolsey and secure him some material comfort. Mantel describes the act of fixing the kitchen as Cromwell's first impulse:

> Make my lord comfortable, he says, and goes straight down to the kitchens. . . . My lord, he says, needs to eat and drink for . . . how long we don't know. The kitchen must be put in order for the winter ahead. He finds someone who can write and dictates his orders. His eyes are fixed on the kitchen clerk. On his left hand he counts off the items: you do this, then this, then thirdly this. With his right hand, he breaks eggs into a basin, each one with a hard professional tap, and between his fingers the white drips, sticky and slow, from the yolk. "How old is this egg? Change your supplier. I want a nutmeg. Nutmeg? Saffron?" They look at him as if he's speaking Greek.[41]

Cromwell's immediate response is to shift his perspective, from lawyer and counselor back to his experience being a serving boy in the kitchens at Lambeth who would bring Thomas More his food. This is not merely a momentary return to his past, though; this is a Cromwell who has chipped away at and refashioned himself and has multiplied his set of skills to commandeer the kitchen in a startling new way. The kitchen becomes a space in which he lays out his siege plans, determining that it must be fortified for the months and years of the cardinal's uncertain exile. At the same time as he orders clerks into position, his hands reach for the familiarity of cooking, the sensation of breaking an egg, the viscous feel on his fingers. But he is changed from the kitchen boy at Lambeth; his travels abroad have rendered him foreign such that he demands spices, not salt and pepper, but a whole nutmeg, and even saffron, rare and exotic items unheard of in the English countryside. He takes command through sensation, through perspective and observation, and he sees things that others don't: "[T]here are weevils in the flour. There are mouse droppings where the pastry should be rolled. It is nearly Martinmas, and they have not even thought about salting their beef."[42] In taking inventory of the kitchen in this practiced fashion he underlines its importance and currency as much more than a place of nourishment. The kitchen becomes a place of fortification and preparation under Cromwell's vision; his gaze renders these omissions perceptible and he wields power with it, by displacing and occupying terrain that people don't expect of him. There is care in it too, and a precise efficiency. He honors Wolsey with his care and skill at preparing the food and sees this act of nourishment as an essential moment of political action.

Ornamental Honor and Political Power

More's and Cromwell's contrasting views of the sensory parallel their approaches to honor in *Wolf Hall*. As the men face off as political foes in adulthood, Mantel portrays More as a man whose rigid sense of honor ties him to his fate. More represents the traditional and honorable forms of valuation, "the political ideals of ancient Athens" onward which are marked by their "'manly' heroism and military glory, and [by] disdain for the household, the private, the personal, and the sensual."[43] He refuses to dishonor himself by signing the Oath of Supremacy—his honor is tied to his duty to God and not the king—he is ideologically rigid, bound tightly by faith, and has a transcendental belief in his moral correctness. More is also pinned in by his place in the constellation of European intellectuals whose recognition is essential for his political identity and honor. He both reasons and prays that his lawyerly intellect and abiding faith will allow him to walk the tightrope between his refusal to take the oath and the scaffold. As such Cromwell "never sees More—a star in another firmament, who acknowledges him with a grim nod—without wanting to ask him, what's wrong with you? Or what's wrong with me? Why does everything you know, and everything you've learned, confirm you in what you believed before? Whereas in my case, what I grew up with, and what I thought I believed, is chipped away a little and a little, a fragment then a piece and then a piece more. With every month that passes, the corners are knocked off the certainties of this world: and the next world too."[44] More is rigid in his faith and in his refusal to compromise. His honor will not allow him to bend and be refashioned for a changing world.

Cromwell combines the spheres of sensation and thought in a way that More never can. From the alleys of Putney to the corridors of power, he can move swiftly back and forth, clothing himself in expensive furs and leathers, efficiently drawing up laws to solve the thorny matter of the king's divorce. As More falls from favor, Cromwell rises swiftly in power, gaining the first of his ornamental titles of honor as master secretary, a position that he uses to insert himself flexibly into all manner of governance. Cromwell's acquisition of external honor in the form of a title grants him visibility and influence to effectively leverage this ornament into political power to make him a "person" that the old nobility is now forced to address and reckon with. He is now an honored subject to which they must attach a predicate. His attendance to the political life of sensation and his capacity for shifting perspective allow him to puncture the received wisdom of the Tudor court and find a solution to the king's divorce when no one else can. Cromwell senses the fear and lust in his monarch; he looks at the matter with a keen and practical eye, sizes up the problem and measures it, and rotates the object until it is no longer stuck in the doorway. Mantel keenly observes that his true political skill lies not just in his ingenious and largely amoral solutions to seemingly intractable problems, but how with his sensory adeptness he is able to transform himself into a presence, one who can "edge blackly into a room" with the stealth of an assassin but also command the attention of nobility who are befuddled to have to take note of a man of his lowly and dishonorable station. As such he relies on perception and sensation, and the work he does "takes place beneath and beyond the discursive register of communicative sense making."[45] In Panagia's terms, this goes beyond the capacity to simply perceive; it is the kind of vision that comes with the artist's perspective, such that "the ability to perceive something is not, in this formulation, an accomplishment that marks a kind of unveiling or illumination; it refers, rather, to the ways in which the postures of attention we occupy—the bendings of the frames of our bodies, the turnings of our heads, the raising of our eyes, the pricking of our ears, and the opening of our mouths—are acts of ethical reconfiguration; they are part of the work we do on ourselves that allows us to live in, and endure, the impact of appearances."[46]

Cromwell's perspective, his attendance to the political life of sensation, and his skillful exercise of the art of power allow him to acquire the ornaments of honor in the form of a growing list of titles and to deploy them to expand his sphere of influence. More, by contrast, is exiled from power as a consequence of his binding honor and his stubborn refusal to swear to Henry's Oath of Supremacy. His monarch wants public recognition of his new wife and future heirs, but More wants to be recognized all over Europe for his dogged adherence to his own internal sense of honor. Their roles now reversed and their perspective now shifted, Cromwell serves as More's principal interrogator, jailer, prosecutor, and would-be executioner. Mantel paints a portrait of a ruthless but somewhat conflicted Cromwell who still feels some empathy for the man he once looked up to as a kitchen boy. He tries to persuade More for hours on end to sign the oath; he tries to trip him up verbally, to trick him into compliance, to threaten him when necessary. He finally turns to More's daughter and son-in-law and hopes they can succeed where he has failed. He tells them that even the king doesn't want to see More imprisoned and is only looking for some sign of support, and then "no honour would be too high."[47] The king and Cromwell both want to let More go home and they both want to adorn him with visible expressions of honor in exchange for his submission.

It is clear, however, that More's sense of honor differs dramatically from theirs. It is internal and binding, not external and ornamental. His son-in-law, Will Roper, tells Cromwell, "I doubt the king can offer the sort of honour he cares for."[48] More has a transcendental and regulative idea of honor that constrains his actions and makes him yearn for the martyrdom of the executioner's block. He cares little for the pragmatic and profane realm of the political, for a world where sensation and reason mix heretically together. One simply does not translate to the other for him, and the realms of sensation and reason remain stubbornly incongruent for the famed author of *Utopia*. He refuses the "words, words, just words" in the oath that Cromwell wants him to sign, refusing to accept that the vow is simply performative. He cannot be flexible and say the words without dishonoring himself, and there is no longer a place for him in a changing world where such codes are increasingly obsolete. More stubbornly clings to his honor and is executed on Tower Green for treason. Cromwell, with a mixture of sadness and pride, thinks, "Words, words, just words. He thinks, I remembered you, Thomas More, but you didn't remember me. You never even saw me coming."[49] Later, More's wife remarks to him, "'My husband used to say,' and he notes the past tense, 'my husband used to say, lock Cromwell in a deep dungeon in the morning, and when you come back that night he'll be sitting on a plush cushion eating lark's tongues, and all the gaolers will owe him money.'"[50] It is a telling fantasy of Cromwell's skillful manipulation of the art of power that More could never match or comprehend because he simply cannot attend to the political life of sensation and partake in the kind of aesthetic politics where honor is instrumental and a bargaining chip for power. *Wolf Hall* draws to a close with More's passing, but Cromwell only grows in power and influence in the sequels and piles up the ornaments of honor that he flexibly deploys to expand his sphere of influence.

The perception of Cromwell as Machiavellian in his approach to the art of power is widespread and one that he favorably accepts, observing that he is both at the center of and surrounded by "a web of favours done and favours received. Those who want access to the king expect to pay for it, and no one has better access than he. And at the same time, the word is out: help Cromwell and he will help you."[51] When he makes a calculated alliance with Anne Boleyn and finally secures her place as Henry's queen, Cromwell rises swiftly in power. He is soon granted additional titles of honor—the adorning power of the master of jewels is soon his, followed by chancellor of the exchequer, then master of the rolls, and soon even vicegerent in spirituals—all honorifics which allow Cromwell to "expand his horizons and his control."[52] He viscerally feels the power he has so artfully acquired: "There's a feeling of power in reserve, a power that drives right through the bone, like the shiver you sense in the shaft of an axe when you take it into your hand."[53] He ripples with the potential energy of his power and the desire to render it kinetic, sensing that at that moment "you can strike, or you can not strike, and if you choose to hold back the blow, you can still feel inside you the resonance of the omitted thing."[54]

His attendance to the political life of sensation continues to allow him to "invent or configure ways of relating the experience it affords" and therefore "interrupt our conventional ways of perceiving the world and giving it value."[55] Indeed, much of the plot of *Bring Up the Bodies*, a tautly written livewire of a novel that dramatically retells the story of Anne Boleyn's downfall and execution, illustrates Cromwell "invent[ing]" and "configur[ing]" a new world when the king demands that she too be set aside. As Henry's fixer he crafts new laws and gets them through the Commons with ease; he invents guilt and treason where these is scant evidence of any; he brings preposterous charges of adultery, and even incest, against his former ally. In one of the book's most telling scenes, he coaxes a confession out of one of the queen's ladies in waiting with cheesecakes covered in primrose petals, because, as Lady Worcester says, "who would not pass time with a man who has cakes?

And Master Secretary is always pleasant and useful."[56] He exchanges cream-covered cakes for crumbs of information, and his efforts are once again rewarded. For his ruthless exercise of the art of power, Henry ornaments him with one of the most sizable honors in the land, making him lord privy seal within days of Anne's execution. Cromwell's ability to skillfully shift perspective and reimagine politics through not just the rational but the sensory leads to his growing power and influence and increasing ornamental honor, which forces the nobility to see him as a force to be reckoned with.

Honor, Contingency, and *Fortuna*

Cromwell's quick ascent up the ladder of power is due to what Rancière has called the "distribution of the sensible," which is the reigning "allocation of ways of doing, ways of being, ways of saying."[57] It makes him a source of destabilization and one who underlines the essential contingency of the political in a manner that makes him a threat to the nobility. In a wide-ranging and thoughtful review of Rancière's writings, Jason Frank asserts that historians "always risk fixing the experiences and actions of historical agents within an unquestioned field of categories and identities and, even when proclaiming the emancipation of these subjects, reify their positions and assign them a proper place and function" within the distribution of the sensible.[58] This has not just been the case for the historical portrayal of Cromwell, but even in the novel itself Mantel examines this desire for fixity on behalf of the nobility who cannot make sense of him. Harry Percy, one of the highest-ranking members of the nobility, calls Cromwell "the lowest man in Christendom" and cannot for the life of him understand how such a low and dishonorable man has risen in power.[59] The king's best friend, the Duke of Suffolk, Charles Brandon, describes the dizzying shift of perspective that Mantel captures so effectively in *Wolf Hall* when he says, "'You do everything, Cromwell. You are everything now. We say, how did it happen? We ask ourselves.' The duke sniffs. 'We ask ourselves, but by the steaming blood of Christ we have no bloody answer.' . . . When did he become the interpreter of dukes, their explainers? He asks himself but he has no bloody answer."[60]

The answer lies in the shifting distribution of the sensible, when ways of seeing, thinking, and perceiving are called into question, when the essential contingency of politics is emphasized by a multiplicity of forces of change.

Cromwell himself notes the shift in sensibility that confuses the nobility and makes his rise possible:

> How can he explain to him? The world is not run from where he thinks. Not from his border fortresses, not even from Whitehall. The world is run from Antwerp, from Florence, from places he has never imagined; from Lisbon, from where the ships with sails of silk drift west and are burned up in the sun. Not from castle walls, but from counting houses, not by the call of the bugle but by the click of the abacus, not by the grate and clock of the mechanism of the gun but by the scrape of the pen on the page of the promissory note that pays for the funds and the gunsmith and the powder and shot.[61]

What Mantel describes here is a rich and vivid account of the political life of sensation—the sharp "click of the abacus" and "the scrape of the pen"—a shift in power that one can hear and feel, that signals a new and emerging political order that is rooted in economic practices and innovation and not in traditional and aristocratic norms of honor. This shift in the distribution of the sensible leads to division and fracture throughout society, but attending to this aesthetic dimension of politics also allows the changes to be perceived. As Frank notes, in Rancière's conceptual framing of this phenomena, "transformative political praxis emerges not from the action of a unitary subject of emancipated consciousness but from the experience of being divided, not from the cohering identifications of class, for example, but from transformative processes of *disidentification*."[62] It is this disidentification that leads both the nobles and Cromwell himself to have "no bloody answer" for his sudden rise in power but also to underline the perceptible change in the distribution of the sensible that has made it possible.

It is this sense of becoming that characterizes both Mantel's fictional portrayal of Cromwell and also much of Machiavelli's writing in *The Prince*, a text that is focused in large part on acquiring and maintaining power amid perennially changing circumstances. Machiavelli's transformative account of the relationship between *virtù* (skills and strength) and *fortuna* (the changing vagaries of fortune) highlights what Miguel Vatter calls the "the radical contingency of all order."[63] No longer grounded in foundational ideas of the Nature of God, "the essence of historical becoming lies in the collision or polemical encounter (*riscontro*) between human action and its circumstances, such that as a result of this meeting the times themselves undergo a change."[64] The radical contingency of *fortuna* appears throughout

The Prince. Machiavelli notes at various instances that men ought to rely on their "strength [*virtù*] and prudence, for in time, anything can happen, and the passage of time brings good mixed with evil, and evil mixed with good,"[65] and that "good will and good fortune are totally unreliable and capricious."[66] He urges the Prince to not inhabit the Utopia that More so strongly believed in, averring that "many authors have constructed imaginary republics and principalities that have never existed in practice and never could; for the gap between how people actually behave and how they ought to behave is so great that anyone who ignores everyday reality in order to live up to an ideal will soon discover he has been taught how to destroy himself, not how to preserve himself."[67] In this world of "practical realities" appearances matter and the art of power relies on understanding the importance of appearances, "for we do not live in an ideal world."[68]

In his most famous account of *fortuna*, which von Vacano calls "a representation of contingency in Machiavelli's vision of the cosmos," he characterizes it as a powerful and rushing river that overflows its banks from time to time and sweeps away those who are unprepared for its rising tides.[69] For Machiavelli, it is those who attend to the building of fortifications and embankments and are best able to shift their perspective and change their appearance who can withstand its onrush. If "one knew how to change one's character as times and circumstances change, one's luck would never change," and "since fortune changes, and men stubbornly continue to behave the same way men flourish when their behavior suits the times and fail when they are out of step."[70] This is precisely the kind of aesthetic politics that the Cromwell of *Wolf Hall* embodies, emphasizing the lively perception of sensation over the transcendent stillness of the rational mind and leaving behind the stain of his dishonorable reputation and making efficient use of the titles and ornaments of honor. As Vatter notes, "Machiavelli's theory of fortuna subverts the primacy of contemplation over practice and provides the conceptual schema for modern revolutionary action. By questioning the derivative role played by contingency in the order of the world, it opens a new horizon for human praxis: instead of making action correspond to the times, action is assigned the task of changing the times."[71]

These are the politics of disidentification that Cromwell embodies in *Wolf Hall* by understanding how sensory moments often operate beneath the surface of rational deliberation and expand the political imagination. It happens not by heroic acts of chivalrous honor, nor is it marked the speeches of great men, but rather it happens in the shifts in regimes of perception, when perspective is slowly, but suddenly, shifted by scent, sound, and feeling. Mantel captures this transformative shift in the art of power when she has Cromwell note the deeply sensory and aesthetic nature of its becoming: "This is how the world changes: a counter pushed across a table, a pen stroke that alters the force of a phrase, a woman's sigh as she passes and leaves on the air a trail of orange flower or rosewater; her hand pulling close the bedcurtain, the discreet sigh of flesh against flesh."[72] The shift in the distribution of the sensible occurs in these profane moments of force and desire, when power is viewed as a constellation of active and reactive forces that even amid their contingency offers a new possibility for political praxis.

In the final book in the trilogy, *The Mirror and the Light*, Mantel paints a Cromwell who is fully attentive to the distribution of the sensible, who has taken full advantage of the possibilities of *fortuna*, and who is at the height of his power. He has been raised to a level at the Tudor court that infuriates and flummoxes the nobility. He is honored beyond his wildest dreams when, a few short weeks before his precipitous downfall, Henry VIII bestows on him the prestigious title of the Earl of Essex. This final ornament of honor hangs heavy on him, piercing through his otherwise thick coat of realpolitik and momentarily obscuring his sensory awareness of himself as a subject. (Mantel begins to address him as "Essex" instead of "Cromwell.") For years, Cromwell has successfully deployed ornamental honor and fungibly exchanged it into ever increasing wealth and power, but now, just for a moment, he relaxes and grows into his ambition and makes the mistake of feeling secure in his newly honored state. In Machiavelli's words, he is momentarily out of step.

He has scaled dizzying heights of success, but *fortuna* turns against him when the king rejects the geopolitical marriage he has arranged to Anne of Cleves. (Henry finds the lady not to his liking.) The increasingly erratic king is finally willing to listen to Cromwell's enemies among the nobility who have been trying for years to drag Cromwell down. The contingency of honor and its vulnerability to *fortuna* (that Cromwell for so long skillfully met with *virtù*) is strikingly clear when the tides turn against him. Even then, he senses danger instinctively, minutes before it presents itself, but overconfidence has dulled his edge, and not only is he outnumbered, but he no longer carries his blade under his shirt to protect himself. His enemies are from both the old aristocracy he supplanted and the new men he trained to seek their own advantage. In a dramatic scene, they attack him in the Privy Council and strip his badges of honor from his robes:

> Like pack animals they yelp and snarl, they grunt and flail. Fitzwilliam is trying to pull his Garter badge from his coat. He bats him away, gives Norfolk a shove that knocks him into the table. But Fitzwilliam comes back. They tug, kick, haul. He is barged and buffeted, his gold chain is off, and he puts his head down, he puts his fists up, he lands a blow, and he is roaring. He is convulsed with rage, he does not know what he says, nor cares: and then it is over. They have taken the chain and the George. Someone has swept his papers from the board.[73]

His foes come at him again and again and he responds with visceral rage, but it is not enough. The badge of St. George that signifies his inclusion in the ancient and chivalric Order of the Garter is the first to be ripped off, clearly accentuating the height of his rise and the depth of his fall. Of course, it is also the badge that most outraged the enemy—that the son of a blacksmith and brewer could be inducted into the most aristocratic and exclusive of brotherhoods. But Cromwell has always understood that honor can be bestowed and honor can be taken away. Unlike those who literally yank the chain of office off his neck, he has always known that one day *fortuna* would turn its face from him, but he hoped that he could accumulate enough wealth for his heirs and create enough systemic change that his legacy would be impossible to undo. Indeed, his success in creating a redistribution of the sensible is precisely what makes his enemies bay for his blood, and it is the contingency of *fortuna* that enables them to finally succeed. Even Cromwell has a moment of forgetting: he lets himself be blinded by the title of Earl of Essex, relaxes into its aristocratic privilege and allows himself to dream of legacy and inheritance, and loses his grip on power. His oldest enemy, Stephen Gardiner, is the one to remind him that even the highest of titles are merely ornamental honors that can be stripped away. Mantel captures this moment starkly and pointedly: "In the doorway, Gardiner says, 'Adieu, Cromwell.' He stops. 'Give me my title.' 'You have no title. It's gone, Cromwell. You are no more than God made you. May he take you to his mercy.'"[74]

The In-Between of Honor

Mantel's richly nuanced portrayal of Thomas Cromwell in *Wolf Hall* gives us a vivid account of a man made for changing times, who shifts his perspective as required by the oscillating tides of *fortuna*, who takes advantage of the contingency of the political because of his very in-betweenness as a man of lowly and dishonorable status who is not hemmed in by the traditional trappings of the aristocracy. His skillful practice of an aesthetic politics of honor, to ornament and gild when necessary for political recognition, as Machiavelli advised, but never to be constrained by honor as an end in itself, allows him to rise rapidly in power. It is only at the very end, when he relaxes into the honorific of his earldom and allows it to blind him, that he missteps and falls from favor. Until the very end of the trilogy (his final moments are a master class in perspective and sensory experience), he is extraordinarily skilled in the art of power. Indeed, if there is a criticism to be made of the final book, it is almost that he is so skilled and his reach is portrayed as so expansive that he starts to become less credible to the reader and his fall appears inevitable.[75]

Wolf Hall remains the most compelling of all of Mantel's books in its portrayal of Cromwell as a man whose perspective on the landscape of power makes him particularly suited to the redistribution of the sensible and the expansion of the political imagination. Mantel evokes this when she has Cromwell observe that "a man's power is in the half-light, in the half-seen movements of his hand and the unguessed-at expression of his face. It is the absence of facts that frightens people: the gap you open, into which they pour their fears, fantasies, and desires."[76] In this space and moment of potentiality, in the shadow of confirmed knowledge, is where the subject is constructed by others through sensation and perception, through fear and desire. As Rancière notes, "The place of a political subject is an interval or a gap; being together to the extent that we are in-between names, identities, cultures, and so on."[77] Those who are always in the in-between at the very border between identities, between titled ornaments of honor and commoner, between the mountain and the valley are those who are more likely to effect change and expand the political imagination.

There is a sense of raw potentiality in the vertiginous shift that Cromwell experiences in *Wolf Hall* and its sequels, a disruption of regimes of sensation that leads to a reconfiguration that makes a new kind of politics possible. Rancière says that "the path of emancipation appears a passing by way of the capacity to become different; not to become conscious, but by dizziness and the loss of identity."[78] Cromwell experiences these moments of disidentification throughout the series: when his wife and beloved daughters die from the sweating sickness, when he finally triumphs over More, and certainly when he is raised to an earl and then precipitously falls from power.

However, the key moment of disidentification comes in *Wolf Hall* when he literally encounters his own portrait, painted for him by Hans Holbein. The man who can skillfully exercise perspective with his deft understanding of the political life of sensation experiences this loss of identity when he sees himself refracted through the painter's eye, unable to distinguish between what is real and what is artifice. What does Holbein's portrait literally paint over, and what does it reveal that Cromwell would much rather have remain hidden? Mantel captures his thoughts beautifully in this moment of disquiet: "He sees his painted hand, resting on the desk before him, holding a paper in a loose fist. It is uncanny, as if he had been pulled apart, to look at himself in sections, digit by digit. Hans has made his skin smooth as the skin of a courtesan, but the motion he has captured, that folding of the fingers, is as sure as that of a slaughterman's when he picks up the killing knife."[79] His household and his friends gather around him, each offering their perspective on the portrait of a Cromwell they recognize from their own vantage point. The Spanish ambassador believes that the painter has "missed his mark," observing that Cromwell's sociability and dexterity for manipulation is missing. The women in his household don't recognize their laughing and friendly uncle and adopted father ("he saves it for men," his ward, Rafe Sadler, says helpfully). But all Cromwell sees reflected in the mirror of the portrait is that he looks like a murderer.[80] His son Gregory says, "Did you not know?"[81]

In this carefully crafted scene of shifting observations, Mantel effectively underlines both Cromwell's security and his vulnerability to the contingency of *fortuna*. He is a man who can change his perspective and his visage for his audience, who leaves behind his lowly and dishonorable beginnings for the highest ornaments of honor of the king's service, but the face he presents to the world is not something he can ever fully control. For all his smoothing, for all his careful calibration of sensation, the maroon silks he now wears instead of basic black, the jewels on his fingers and the spices in his food, the pugnacious Putney boy remains. Beneath the trappings of wealth and taste and power there remains his cunning efficiency, represented in a murderer's visage. As Machiavelli famously explains, appearance is key to the art of power such that one "need not have all the positive qualities I listed earlier, but he must seem to have them."[82] Cromwell ingests this and practices it daily. Mantel writes that he "looks down at [his household] and arranges his face. Erasmus says that you must do this each morning before you leave your house: 'put on a mask, as it were.' He applies that to each place, each castle or inn or nobleman's seat, where he finds himself waking up.... From the day he was sworn into the king's council, he has had his face arranged."[83]

From the lowly beginnings of his political career to his astonishing rise, Cromwell recognizes the essential importance of arranging his face to conform to the shifting needs of power and skillfully wields the ornaments of honor he acquires. He might not always succeed in doing so, as Holbein's portrait reveals. But even the mirror held up by this refracted image underscores how successfully he has altered his appearance to multiple audiences, who either recognize aspects of him in its representation or cannot find him in it at all. That ability to adapt brings to the foreground the importance of appearance and adornment in an aesthetic politics of honor. Unlike aristocratic and chivalrous displays of honor, which are rooted in tradition and trapped in time and space, an aesthetic approach to honor that acquires the ornaments of titles and power but dispenses with the constraints of honor when necessary, fundamentally relies on the ability to change one's perspective and attend to the sensory regimes of perception to expand the political imagination.

4
Honor, Heroism, and Tragedy in *The Iliad*

Honor is a slippery concept that is notoriously tricky to define as it varies widely based on its application. For some, honor is tied tightly to tradition and the formation of political identity (a "code of honor" often figures in these discussions); for others, it functions as an anesthetic that dulls the senses and allows the enchantments of patriotic duty to elide other entanglements. For even others, honor can function as an instrumental, some might say ornamental, tool in the practice of realpolitik that allows for the skillful exertion of power (as seen in *Wolf Hall*). In other words, honor is a multivalent concept that intrigues not because of the fugitive hope that one might finally be able to pin it down with definitional clarity, such that the Hobbesian bird is no longer caught in the twigs of the lime tree, but because of the enduring appeal of reaching for it, whatever form it may take, however be-limed, in discussions of political agency. There is more than a whiff of the heroic in the concept of honor, a lingering smell that goes beyond the mothballs of chivalry, that makes it so appealing to so many as a source of political action. The honorable man or woman is usually cast as someone who goes beyond the confines of the everyday, who transcends the smallness of our politics and escapes the tight restraints of self-interest to accomplish more than what we thought possible. Honor gives agency a certain oomph, a kind of booster power, according to its proponents.

This chapter critically analyzes the heroic capacity for action that honor seems to inspire in its various dimensions. The yearning for this heroic aspect of honor contains a desire for redemption or salvation at its core. Its proponents see it as a bulwark against democracy's tyrannical tendencies or as crucial to moral revolution. While these accounts tap into the "savior" role that the heroic often plays, they ignore other important aspects that are often attached to the heroic, namely the tragic. This chapter takes the concept of the heroic seriously, with all of its complexities, to move beyond the savior narrative to something more complex, unsettling, and destabilizing. In other words, it examines the move toward the honorable hero that saves liberalism from tyranny as a meaning-making practice but tries to strip from it the reductive language of linear progress and ground it instead in the unsettling and "out of joint" contingency of the tragic.[1] Doing so can allow for honor to emerge in its multivalent form—yes, as a powerful source of motivation and meaning, but also as a source of rage and grief that can be deeply unsettling and tragic in politics.

The epic heroes that are discussed in this chapter have a fundamental grasp of the tragic core within the concept of honor. They consistently affirm the importance of honor and the shared meaning it provides, but they also underline its association with rage, grief, and death. Any treatment of honor in the political imagination must take a long look at *The Iliad*, Homer's epic poem whose plot is ignited by the stripping of Achilles's honor, his subsequent withdrawal from the Greek army, and the carnage that ensues. *The Iliad* is a deeply tragic poem whose central dramatic focus is the question of honor and the price that honor exacts. While *The Iliad* is not a classic Greek tragedy but an epic poem, it contains all the key core elements of the tragic. A close reading of the poem reveals that even the epic and heroic pursuit of honor comes at immense cost. By highlighting the exceptional acts honor can give rise to and ignoring the thornier aspects of its heroic capacity, the chapter also makes clear that there are costs to inserting honor into politics as a source of liberal agency. The heroic temper is not the sanitized version that liberal and democratic politics wants to claim for its savior. The Greek hero, of whom Achilles is paradigmatic, is more complex than the heroes that liberalism yearns for to rescue it from tyranny. He is violent, reckless, and dangerous, subject to forces he cannot control, formed by divine power, bound by fate, yet full of human desire. He lives according to a code of honor that is vulnerable to and constructed by power, power that rests on the recognition of others. He is not the atomistic individual at the heart of liberalism. More often than not he is a tragic and deeply flawed character whose pursuit of honor is deeply destructive and yet meaningful.

Is there anything to excavate from honor in this tragic, rage-filled form? Can Achilles give us anything to salvage from this destruction? Perhaps not. And yet the enduring appeal of the heroic aspect of honor in the political imagination suggests something more. There is something meaning-making, perhaps even mythic about honor that is worth thinking about and holding on to, even as it can be both binding and blinding as a political virtue. Honor may not be the solution to the desiccation of political imagination, and urging its adoption in contemporary politics can have adverse consequences. Honor still has currency as a source of meaning and as a motivating force of action, but it is better understood through a tragic lens. This chapter therefore offers a critique of the honorable liberal hero by exploring the linkage between honor, heroic agency, and tragedy. It offers a close reading of the central drama of *The Iliad* through an unabashedly tragic lens, drawing on Nietzsche's work on tragedy and the work of classical scholars of heroism in antiquity, highlighting in particular the links between honor, anger, and grief. It also engages with the fascinating therapeutic work done by Jonathan Shay, who found remarkable parallels between *The Iliad* and his treatment of posttraumatic stress disorder in his Vietnam War veteran patients. By putting this amalgam of texts together, the chapter highlights the tragic dimensions of the heroic agency of honor in political life and underlines both its affirmative appeal and its potential costs.

Honor, Liberalism, and Agency

The contemporary literature on honor that was explored earlier in the book's introduction advocated for its continued presence in politics by emphasizing it as a key aspect of moral revolution and as a potential bulwark against tyranny in liberal democracy. There is an essential component of such arguments that is important to stress here in order to think critically about honor's place in the political imagination, namely that honor is seen as both consistent with and called upon to serve a linear account of time. As detailed in my previous work, such an account of time is quantified and sequential, taking the form of a unidirectional straight line in which the past dissolves into an ephemeral present and is quickly absorbed into an impending future.[2] This concept of time, which is rooted in the Christian theology of salvation (moving from Genesis to Armageddon through grace), is reworked in modernity such that religion is replaced with the core assumption of progress. This is the Enlightenment framework of temporality, which structures much of modern liberal and democratic thought. As much as it has been stripped over time from its religious moorings, it has retained its redemptive impulse, which now manifests through the language of progress. Of course, such a notion of the end of linear time, with all of its teleological purpose, can be seen in Hegel's notion of the end of history and in many of its contemporary versions (for instance, in Francis Fukuyama's work).

But the assumption of linear progress is also seen much more subtly and pervasively throughout the liberal tradition as well. In Sharon Krause's work on liberalism and honor, honor is characterized as having "a certain teleology, if only a partial one."[3] Krause's argument is worth returning to briefly here to underline the redemptive and teleological aspect of honor that has the potential to create a kind of heroic agency because it untethers itself from the past in typical linear form. In a particularly telling formulation, she writes that "honor rests on a boastful self-forgetting of its own conditions and an exaggeration of its independence from the power of circumstance. Still, the boastful exaggeration of human independence is an honorable response to the real power of circumstance, because it makes resistance—therefore agency, and ultimately self-government and individual liberty—conceivable."[4] In this characterization, agency is clearly tied to forgetting and the erasure of the past and firmly focused on the future it believes it can change. The boastful and exaggerated aspects of honor here closely invoke the heroic and are highlighted elsewhere in Krause's work as key to the agentic power that honor can provide in the protection of liberty. Liberal agency that is imbued with honor (which is understood as a desire for self-respect) also remains wedded closely to the atomistic subject who thinks of themselves as free of their embeddedness with and interpellation by others and for whom the redemptive possibility of being the heroic savior is therefore always present. But a closer look at the tragic understanding of the relationship honor has with heroism reveals a form of agency that is much more agonistic and tragic.

What might the nexus of honor and agency look like if it is unshackled from its teleological goal of saving liberal democracy from tyranny and continuing the advance of moral progress? Recently James Martel has shared this critique of liberal redemption, even as he looks for agency in an altogether different place. In the absence of redemptive narratives of progress, where no messiah ever arrives to save us from ourselves, Martel argues that we look for the unlikely, those in the shadows, the seemingly lethargic, who still have the capacity to call into question and challenge the ideologies that seek to interpellate us as subjects.[5] What is intriguing about this alternative is that it also grounds the complex subjectivity of the misinterpellated subject in a deeply tragic recognition of *amor fati*. As Martel writes, "[O]vercoming means the cancellation of our interpellated identities—along with our phantasms of halcyon heights and bright futures—in favor of what emerges once that overcoming takes place."[6] It is this fantasy of a forever brighter future that liberalism cannot escape. Within its linear and sequential temporal frame (which is fueled by the idea of progress) redemption is always possible and the hope for a savior to lead us there remains (though now reworked in rationalist and secular form). Martel's account of the misinterpellated subject is intriguing, but perhaps the desire for heroic agency can still persist if it is recharacterized in less redemptive and more tragic and agonistic form.

Other accounts of agency bring us much closer to an appreciation of the *agon*, or the essential conflict and complexity that political action entails and how it hews more closely to the tragic. For instance, consider Hannah Arendt's account in *The Human Condition* where she writes that "action can be judged only by the criteria of greatness because it is in its nature to break through the commonly accepted and reach into the extraordinary, where whatever is true in common and everyday life no longer applies because everything that exists is unique and sui generis."[7] By emphasizing greatness as a necessary part of action, Arendt plays on the same keys of heroism and honor as extraordinary qualities that agency requires. As such, she "theorizes action not only as essentially nonstrategic and noninstrumental but as essentially *nonsovereign*: the peculiar freedom of action cannot be captured by philosophies of action that place autonomous agency at their center."[8] Dana Villa argues that such an account of political action brings Arendt closer to Nietzsche, the tragic theorist par excellence, as they both "combat the reductionist character of the teleological model of action, exposing the nihilistic consequences of denying meaning or value to the realm of action and appearance."[9] In Villa's terms, Arendt's "desire to preserve the autonomy of action from the incursion of instrumental modes of thought leads her to invoke the analogy of the performing arts, and this analogy—with its emphasis on virtuosity and greatness—yields a conception of political action as *agon*, as heroic."[10] This understanding of political action as heroic and emphasizing virtuosity and greatness is key to conceptualizing the role that honor plays in these discussions. Honor does have the capacity to inspire and motivate action, but the heroic agency that emerges from it is agonistic, as Villa's analysis of Arendt illustrates, when it is not flattened out to fit the redemptive and teleological requirements of liberalism. If there is a criticism to be made of Villa's characterization of Arendt's theory of action, it is the one put forward by Bonnie Honig, that the relationship between Arendt's and Nietzsche's work is too reductive in Villa's "uncritical and approving redeployment of the radically subjectivist, nihilistic Nietzsche," which results in his taming the "Arendtian *agon*."[11] Villa thus diminishes the tragic dimension of heroic agency—its partiality and destructiveness, as well as its affirmative appeal—while retaining its agonistic element.

Taking Nietzsche's account of the tragic aspects of heroic agency seriously also requires understanding the affirmative and meaning-making capacity of honor that approaches the idea of myth. In its boastfulness, its exaggeration, and its ability to inspire courageous action, honor can take on some aspects of the myth that make it difficult to dismiss entirely. Our enduring fascination with and occasional yearning for honor might be understood more productively through this lens. As Joseph Campbell notes in his *Hero with a Thousand Faces*, "Throughout the inhabited world, in all times and under every circumstance, the myths of man have flourished; and they have been the living inspiration of whatever else may have appeared out of the activities of the human body and mind."[12] In its dream-like capacity to "blister sleep," we might begin to think of honor as possessing a faint echo of the "magic ring of myth."[13] Attending to this meaning-making but disruptive and destabilizing aspect of honor crucially requires engaging with a different temporal framework. Instead of rooting honor in a linear and progressive temporality, it is important to consider an unruly, contingent, and "out of joint" concept of time where the tenses flow in and out of each other in disruptive and creative moments that inspire action but also have the spectral capacity to haunt the present with grievous loss.

The heroes of epics are certainly boastful and principled, but they are at once haunted by the past and feel the pressing anxiety of the future closing in on them. In other words, they lack the "self-forgetting" and erasure of the past that liberalism, with its linear notion of time, demands. Their present at once expands and contracts under this temporal flux, and the call of memory and of prophecy imbues their actions with motivation and meaning. As Simon Critchley suggests in his work on tragedy, "The past is not past, the future folds back upon itself, and the present is shot through with fluxions of past and future that destabilize it. Time flexes and twists in tragedy."[14] By contrast with the redemptive agency that liberalism requires for its own salvation, the heroic agency of tragedy is complex in its motivations, its embeddedness in its relationships to others, and its recognition of the regimes of power (whether sovereign, familial, or Olympian) that constrain its capacity to act. To quote Critchley once more, "[T]ragedy gives voice to an experience of agency that is partial and often very painful. It shows the limits of our attempted self-sufficiency and what we might think of as our autonomy. It shows our heteronomy, our profound dependency."[15] It is crucial, then, to turn to Nietzsche to uncover the links between tragedy and honor and to articulate a more tragic and agonistic account of heroic agency to accompany it.

Nietzsche, Tragedy, and the Apollonian Virtue of Honor

The idea of the tragic is one that is periodically invoked in contemporary life, but more often than not, tragedy is presented as a trial to overcome in popular rendering, or more problematically as suffering that must be endured to achieve redemption. Much of our understanding of the tragic in popular culture is tied to these frameworks of understanding. And yet the tragic perspective has much more to offer to the study and understanding of political life. The literature on tragedy is sweeping and encyclopedic—in the Western canon at least, it runs from Aristotle's definition of the tragic to the Shakespearean form of tragedy and to different critical perspectives on it in contemporary work. While this chapter briefly examines the work of some key classical scholars to develop its reading of *The Iliad*, for the most part it circumvents the many debates about the ins and outs of the tragic as a literary genre and its constitution, by focusing instead on the tragic as a theoretical perspective that can add an important critical undertone to discussions of political agency. In order to do so, it turns to an exploration of Nietzsche's work in *The Birth of Tragedy* to more closely analyze the links between honor, heroism, and the tragic.

A tragic thread weaves and winds its way through most of Nietzsche's work and plays a crucial role in the ethical and political theory that develops from his writings. The sweep of Nietzsche's oeuvre is too broad to capture here, but the brushstrokes of his untimely philosophy that emerge through aphorism, riddle, and the occasional song can be marked out quite clearly. The role that *ressentiment* plays in political life and the ascetic morality that emerges from wallowing in it are crucial, as is the critique of sweeping notions of nationalism, rationalism, and idealism and their soporific effects. The need to come to terms with and accept the presence of the past and will its eternal return despite the suffering it might cause is essential, and so too is the notion of overcoming, which in Nietzsche's rendering is rooted in tragic recognition by embracing and acknowledging suffering, loss, and grief, but which evades the pitfalls of narratives of redemption by finding its affirmative capacity through the creative exercise of the will to power. Nietzsche's Zarathustra, as constructed in one of his most complex and layered texts, is not the prophet of redemptive stories or idle mythmaking, but someone who recognizes the failures and pitfalls of the modern age and nevertheless finds creative affirmation and the possibility of joy in it. In his famous text, Zarathustra comes across the small man who is choking on his own spirit of revenge, evocatively rendered as a shepherd choking on the thick coils of a black serpent that is hanging heavily out of his own mouth, and urges decisive action, demanding that the man bite down and kill the snake.[16] The shepherd does so and emerges joyful and giddy, full of strength and triumph through this heroic act of the will to power.[17]

Throughout his writings, Nietzsche develops this particularly tragic account of agency as a creative and decisive act that allows us to overcome the stultifying smallness of a politics rooted in *ressentiment* that is often covered over with a veneer of religious morality or nationalist sentiment. The form of agency that emerges from his writings is deeply tragic, but it also has an important connection to the heroic, emphasizing the nobility of contest and competition and the particular overcoming that emerges from defeating a foe one respects. Nietzsche remained inspired by the Greeks throughout his life, even as his work became increasingly more complex. As Jean-François Drolet has written, "Nietzsche's discourse on tragedy remains to this day one of the most ambitious and challenging attempts at drawing on this distant Greek aesthetic tradition to understand how human propensities towards violence and destruction could be channeled and re-directed towards more creative goals and outcomes."[18]

For Nietzsche, the Greek notion of tragedy was never really distant and it colored many of his writings from the very outset. Drolet notes that "in the agonistic, artistic culture of pre-Socratic Greece, the young Nietzsche believed to have found a more meaningful basis for human agency."[19] This influence is front and center in his first major work, *The Birth of Tragedy*, which he later confessed was at once a tremendous success and also a dismal failure. For Nietzsche, the book succeeding in foregrounding the question of the tragic but missed its mark in not exploring what the tragic meant for life itself, in the here and now (a theme he returned to repeatedly in his later work).[20] Despite some of its limits and perhaps an overreliance on the binary logic of the dialectic, *The Birth of Tragedy* remains an essential text for exploring the tragic underpinnings of Nietzsche's philosophy and his view of heroic agency. As mentioned earlier, the text proceeds by the binary schema (a form Nietzsche later broke from) of the Apollonian and the Dionysian, which come together to create the tragic. The first takes its name from Apollo, the beautiful and powerful god of music, prophecy, and healing, one of the most complex and significant gods of the Olympians. In the text the Apollonian signifies form or representation, and beauty and harmony.

The latter takes its name from Dionysus, the god of wine and ecstasy, and signifies the excess, the unruly, the passionate, and the joyful.

The suffering of the individuals in tragic drama (its Apollonian form) sets the stage for Dionysian ecstasy (often channeled through the chorus) that allows the spectators to experience the joy of existence itself and will its affirmation. Nietzsche describes the Apollonian in the following way: "Apollo, the god of all plastic energies, is at the same time the soothsaying god. He, who (as the etymology of the name indicates) is the 'shining one,' the deity of light, is also ruler over the beautiful illusion of the inner world of fantasy."[21] The Apollonian is the soothing "illusion," the "shining" ornament that makes the tragic condition of life bearable. Given these characteristics, honor, in its anesthetizing and ornamental form and in its capacity to inspire heroic action (but also draw a veil over our many embedded connections with each other), emerges clearly as an Apollonian virtue. Nietzsche says again that the Apollonian is the part that makes "life possible and worth living," but he also notes the dangers of wallowing in this dream image and warns that one should not get too caught up in it or it might have a "pathological effect."[22] Honor, as an Apollonian political virtue, shares many of the same qualities. Honor can serve as a fantasy or a dream image, almost mythic in its appeal and ability to inspire, but there are real dangers to allowing it to be a structuring force in political life. As much as honor has the ability to inspire and supercharge political agency, it is equally dangerous in what it elides through its ability to draw a gauzy veil over the web of power relations that constitute the intersubjective relations of political life. Honor inspires us to heroic action, but it can also achieve the "pathological effect" Nietzsche diagnoses. The Apollonian, however, is not just a beautiful illusion; it exists in its many forms to make the unbearable bearable, to root the idea of tragic recognition in everyday life and to find a way to still affirm and find joy in such an existence.[23] Here is Nietzsche again on this very recognition and the need for art to help navigate it: "The Greeks knew and felt the terror and horror of existence. That he might endure this terror at all, he had to interpose between himself and life the radiant dream-birth of the Olympians.... [I]t was in order to be able to live that the Greeks had to create these gods from a most profound need."[24]

Nietzsche himself turned to the figure of Achilles, whose heroic arc is analyzed in detail later in this chapter, to note this very recognition. This same impulse was used as a "transfiguring mirror" to value life as desirable in itself.[25] He tells his readers to "not forget the lament of the short-lived Achilles, mourning the leaflike change and the vicissitudes of the race of men and the decline of the heroic age. It is not unworthy of the greatest hero to long for a continuation of life, even though he live as a day laborer."[26] This is the Apollonian stage of development, where the will longs for existence and fuses itself with this longing in such a way that the "lamentation itself becomes a song of praise."[27] This is also when the recognition goes deeper that despite the beauty and moderation of the Apollonian, existence rests on the hidden stratum of suffering and knowledge that is the domain of the Dionysian.[28] Eventually the Apollonian is veiled and the Dionysian emerges "as an epic hero, almost in the language of Homer."[29] It is this tragic recognition, which Nietzsche highlights, that contemporary advocates of honor as a political virtue often lack. They find themselves captivated by honor's Apollonian illusion and forget to make the move to root that fantasy in the Dionysian by coming to terms with suffering, loss, and disruption. Nietzsche points out succinctly, "And behold: Apollo could not live without Dionysus!"[30] In his careful exploration of Nietzsche's work on tragedy Drolet notes that this intersection between the two modes is precisely the location of the ennobling power of the tragic, in between the Apollonian representation of fantasy and illusion and the turbulent Dionysian primordial will.[31] It is in this very intersection that the significance of tragic art and drama becomes clear for Nietzsche, who recognized that "in watching these acted rituals of heroic self-destruction we gain existentially pertinent insights into the nature of the human condition."[32]

The key question to now ask is: Can we gain any insights from these tragic and heroic acts of honor, even as we realize how unbound and how reckless they are? It is clear that the idea of honor that permeates heroic accounts of agency does have an important role to play in the political imagination as a repository of meaning and a source of greatness. But honor cannot simply be invoked as the savior of liberalism or as a bulwark against tyranny without folding the tragic recognition of heroic agency back into its midst. Indeed, it is not clear that honor is at all suited for such a redemptive political purpose, or that such redemption is even possible when we fully come to terms with its tragic dimension. The kind of political agency that emerges from the idea of honor, whose heroic appeal is so obvious to its advocates, is necessarily partial, agonistic, and tragic. It is not the redemptive savior who pushes us relentlessly and linearly forward into a bright future marked by progress, but the out-of-joint and disruptive agency of the untimely. Nietzsche makes this clear when he links Dionysus to Hamlet, the prototype for the Shakespearean tragic hero, who occupies the very moment of time's splintering, when his past rushes into his present in vertiginous form and destabilizes his future. Nietzsche writes evocatively about this partial and tragic kind of agency in a paragraph that is worth quoting in its entirety as an untimely reminder to not seek salvation or redemption in heroic political acts:

> In this sense, the Dionysian man resembles Hamlet: both have once looked truly into the essence of things, they have *gained knowledge,* and nausea inhibits action: for their action could not change anything in the eternal nature of things; they feel it to be ridiculous or humiliating that they should be asked to set right a world that is out of joint. Knowledge kills action; action requires the veils of illusion: that is the doctrine of Hamlet, not that cheap wisdom of Jack the Dreamer who reflects too much, and, as it were, from an excess of possibilities does not get around to action. Not reflection, no—true knowledge, an insight into the horrible truth, outweighs any motive for action, both in Hamlet and the Dionysian man.[33]

Nietzsche makes clear in this evocative passage that a full immersion in the Dionysian stratum of suffering is paralyzing and overwhelming. It can impart knowledge, but it can also lead to a loss of agency. Without the Apollonian to help attenuate its impact, it is all too easy to lose oneself in Dionysian pessimism and be resigned to the meaninglessness of one's actions to make a difference.[34] The Apollonian therefore provides the necessary illusion to moor oneself amid the out-of-joint eddies of time and gives rise to the heroic impulse for action. Neither works without the other, and to divorce the Apollonian virtue of honor from its Dionysian primordial essence is to retain its capacity to inspire and move, but to strip away its tragic core. The move toward the beautiful fantasy of the Apollonian illusion of honor is understandable if the project attached to it is one of political redemption—the heroic quest to save liberalism from its tyrannical tendencies—or to the desire to usher in moral revolution. But this is a naïve and simplistic view of political agency that can be dangerous and reckless if it is untethered to tragic recognition. Clearly, there is a place for honor in political life, but we must come to terms with all its dimensions and accept its capacity for disruption and destabilization too.

The Homeric Contest and Heroic Action

Nietzsche's early writings on tragedy allow us to see its twin components, the Apollonian illusion of fantasy that inspires action and the Dionysian substratum of suffering and pessimism whose overcoming allows for the possibility of joy. In another essay on the Homeric contest, Nietzsche explores this notion of action in more detail, emphasizing that the kind of agency that was valued in Homeric epic was indeed disruptive, unsettling, and often violent. He writes that the modern opposition between nature and the human is a fallacy, that the very humanity of man has the natural intertwined in it, and that "those of his abilities which are terrifying and considered inhuman may even be the fertile soil out of which alone all humanity can grow in impulse, deed, and work."[35] He talks about the "trait of cruelty" and "tigerish lust to annihilate" that the Greeks had and goes so far as to call them the most "humane."[36] He wonders if it is perhaps our modern perspective that is skewed (at times he calls it flabby) and argues that it is the contest itself, the competition among the best of the Greeks, that was necessary for the health of the state as it allowed the unruly and violent impulses of humanity to work themselves out in the agonistic challenge. The gore-splattering Homeric hero is celebrated, and indeed worshiped, by the ancient Greeks, not because of some sadistic streak but because they valued the contest itself and understood the pursuit of honor as a trophy to be earned through competition and conquest (on the battlefield or in games of archery or in races and wrestling matches). In other words, for the ancient Greeks, honor is understood to be an integral part of the body politic.

In a similar vein, contemporary theorists of honor such as Robert Oprisko have observed that "the emphasis of excellence as meriting honor fills the text of the *Iliad*" and that such an idea of honor is clearly linked to prestige.[37] Oprisko further notes that "Homer places emphasis on excellence being honored not only with social value, but with tokens that symbolize that honor."[38] In *The Iliad*, honor is clearly seen as ornamental. It takes on the Apollonian representative form and is swathed in heroic myth and is therefore considered crucial to preserving the vital force of the state itself. Further, as Ari Kohen notes, for the Homeric battlefield hero there is "a connection between an appreciation of the necessity of death and the decision to take heroic action," and it is the very recognition of the finitude of life that opens up the possibility of heroism.[39] Achilles makes the tragic choice of the short but honorable life of a hero, who is covered in glory for all eternity, over a long mortal life shorn of such heroic recognition. However, it is also crucial to acknowledge the full dimensions of unleashing this heroic capacity for action—its cruelty, its blood-letting rage, its lust for annihilation—and the need to filter these destabilizing aspects through codes of competition and through cultural norms of respect for one's enemy. It is such filtering through society, culture, and art that provided the Greek political imagination with an understanding of tragedy as crucial to life itself.

The contest and the norms that surround heroic agency in ancient Greek culture are crucial to consider when undertaking a close reading of *The Iliad*, a text that is entirely about honor spurned, the rage that its scorning unleashes, and the bloody triumphs and grievous losses on the battlefield that result from its effluence.

In order to understand Homeric heroes like Achilles and Hector, one has to appreciate the norms that circulated during the Trojan War, the shared understanding that the soldiers and the commanders had of them, and the sense of unmooring and disorientation they could feel if these norms were violated. As Nietzsche points out, the entire Greek world exulted over the combat scenes of *The Iliad*, and it is important for the modern reader, who is often far removed from its tragic perspective and insulated from those embedded norms, to understand why.[40] To that end, Nietzsche notes that the contest itself was crucial and that the struggle itself and the victory were also significant. Envy "spurs men to acticity: not to the activity of a fight of annihilation but to the activity of fights which are *contests*. The Greek is envious, and he does not consider this quality a blemish but the gift of a *beneficent* godhead. What a gulf of ethical judgment lies between us and him!"[41] There is something about competition itself that inspires heroic agency, for competitors to match their strengths against each either, that is the Dionysian primordial urge to express itself. For Nietzsche, the contest was "necessary to preserve the health of the state," and it was important that no one person would be allowed to be the best "because then the contest would come to an end and the eternal source of life for the Hellenic state could be endangered."[42]

Nietzsche therefore provides a framework for understanding the agonistic contest as essential for the ancient Greek polis as a source of health and vitality. However, it is also important to explore the notion of heroic agency itself, or what the classical scholar Bernard Knox calls the "heroic temper," in more depth before we turn to a close reading of Homeric heroes and their attachment to honor in *The Iliad*. Knox's text focuses on the later Sophoclean dramatic hero and not the Homeric epic hero, but it is useful for tracing how the former developed out of, and indeed was inspired by, the latter in detailing key aspects of the heroic in tragic art. Knox starts by explaining that the tragic hero is "a single central character whose action and suffering are the focal point of the play" and then proceeds to outline certain characteristics the hero almost always possesses.[43] The central plot of tragedy always begins with heroic agency, when the hero (or heroine) resolves to act and announces this decision in emphatic and uncompromising terms. Others try in vain to persuade the hero from the action, and soon enough the heroic resolve is put to the test. The assault on the hero's will is usually an argument designed to persuade them from his path that appeals to reason, not emotion, and is often couched as advice or admonition. The hero is then asked to yield and refuses to do so. Even though they cannot be dissuaded from their path (and responds with anger if anyone tries), the hero recognizes they are under attack and responds violently and swiftly. To everyone else the hero's angry and stubborn temper seems thoughtless and ill-considered (usually conveyed to the play's audience through the Greek chorus), and the impossible hope persists that the hero will change their mind and realize the truth.[44] Knox notes that there is a stubborn defiance in the heroic temper, not only in the hero's defiance of the counsel of others but that the hero, to bring Nietzsche's tragic insight back into it, faced with the vertiginous and pessimistic insight that time itself is out of joint, chooses to defy time itself. Knox states that the hero is defiant of "time and its imperative of change . . . [and] it is through this refusal to accept human limitations that humanity achieves its true greatness."[45]

The heroic agency, or what Nietzsche calls its "acticity," seems to contain all the unruly aspects of the Dionysian primordial urge, even as it is wrapped up in the Apollonian form of tragic drama and understood within the honorable norms of the contest. Knox writes of the hero that "to those who face him, friends and enemies alike, the hero seems unreasonable almost to the point of madness, suicidally bold, impervious to argument, intransigent, angry; an impossible person whom only time can cure. But to the hero himself the opinion of others is irrelevant. His loyalty to his conception of himself, and the necessity to perform the actions that conception imposes, prevail over all other considerations."[46] Knox unpacks the importance of self-esteem and respect for the hero, and while his take on honor is reductive (he thinks of it in terms of extra achievement in our contemporary understanding), it is important to note that the heroic urge to relentlessly pursue the loss of esteem, respect, and honor is a core motivating force. Although Knox focuses on the Sophoclean hero, he makes it clear that the concept of the tragic hero is firmly based in Homer, and particularly rooted in the *Iliad*.[47] Indeed, he goes even further here to point to Achilles himself as the ground for the heroic temper in Greek tragedy, writing that "in the baleful wrath of Achilles, his self-absorbed brooding on the affront to his self-esteem ... is to be found the model and even the formulas of the Sophoclean tragic situation. Sophocles might have taken for himself the Aeschylean claim that his tragedies were 'slices from the banquets of Homer.'"[48] It is to a close exploration of Achilles himself, his scorned honor and his unrelenting rage, his conflict not just with the Trojans but with the leadership of the Greek army itself, his utter disregard of norms of competition amid his blinding grief, and his heroic agency that this essay now turns.

The Honor, Rage, and Grief of Achilles

The Iliad is one of those enduring texts that continues to find ways to speak to us, even in its male-dominated and bloodthirsty perspective. One could easily read it as a text of toxic masculinity, of heroes scorned, of women objectified in the lust for power and conquest, as a text that glorifies the use of violence as the primary means to address conflict. Such a reading would not be wrong. Women (or at least mortal women; the goddesses are at the center of the action) and the family make very few appearances in *The Iliad*, and when they do appear they are ornamental to the male hero's honor, such as Briseis, Achilles's slave trophy who is taken from him at the start. Helen, the wife of the king of Sparta whose abduction kicks off the entire Trojan War, is consistently mentioned only in terms of her legendary beauty and the honor she brings to men who possess her and the dishonor and shame to those who lose her. Clearly, this is a deeply patriarchal text and one that in many ways is uncomfortable and alien to modern readers, focusing as it does on a Bronze Age conflict in the Mediterranean. It tells the tale of the last year of the decade-long Trojan War, and that covers only a mere 52-day period in its 24 books. In all these ways it is a narrow and narrowing text, but it is also one that is rightfully termed an epic because of its sweeping heroic scope.

The Iliad gets deep into the tragedy of war, the tremendous appeal and the crushing costs of heroic action in battle, and the primordial essence of conflict itself. As filtered as it is in its narrow cast, it is unfiltered in its portrayal of the cruelty and the glory of war and in its depiction of human agency straining against all the norms and ties that bind it. *The Iliad* depicts a kind of gritty realist mythic world of its own, one that was very familiar to the Greek audience that heard it recited. It is a text full of complex and flawed heroes who chafe against both mortal and immortal authority and bemoan the restrictions of fate. But as Simone Weil notes, "[T]he true hero, the true subject, the center of the *Iliad* is force. Force as man's instrument, force as man's master, force before which human flesh shrinks back. The human soul, in this poem, is always shown in its relation to force: swept away, blinded by the force it thinks it can direct, bent under the pressure of the force to which it is subjected."[49] In other words, *The Iliad* depicts the human subject, and indeed heroic action, as formed by and embedded in power relations of multiple kinds. The heroic subjects of *The Iliad* find themselves both subject to and produced by power relations at all times, whether those of family, the command structure of the army, or Olympian imperative. They struggle constantly against power, are formed by power, and produce immense power themselves. As Weil notes, in a manner that anticipates Foucault, the "force is what makes the person subjected to it a thing."[50] It is a poem that continues to resonate because of its visceral depiction of power and its deep undertones of tragedy. For an epic poem with unforgettable heroes like Achilles, Hector, Odysseus, and others, there are clearly no winners, no redemptive purpose, no arc of moral progress that bends unfailingly toward justice. As Knox avers in his introduction to the Fagles translation, at the conclusion of the poem "we are left with a sense of waste, which is not adequately balanced even by the greatness of the heroic figures and the action; the scale descends towards loss. The *Iliad* remains not only the greatest epic poem in literature but also the most tragic."[51]

The opening line of the poem is an evocative one that sets the dramatic plot into motion and provides the interpretive framework for understanding this deeply tragic text: "Rage—Goddess, sing the rage of Peleus' son Achilles, / murderous, doomed, that cost the Achaeans countless losses."[52] We enter the conflict in medias res, in the middle of things, and with the first word of the poem are given an unusual pathway for entering it. Rage, or *mênis*, is nothing if not a destabilizing and disruptive force. It is clear right away that Homer wants us to approach the text as a study of the hero's rage and the tragic consequences that unfold from it. Achilles is described as violent and "murderous," his mortal end is already fated or "doomed" by the gods, and his stubborn heroic temper is unrelenting and will cost his fellow soldiers "countless losses." *The Iliad* unfolds from these opening lines, following the course of Achilles's rage and its effects on both the Trojan War and the Olympians themselves. Gregory Nagy suggest that "complex as it is in its ramifications, the plot is simple in its essence. The *tīmé* 'honor' of Achilles has been slighted... [and] he becomes angry and withdraws from the war."[53] In the very first book, indeed in its opening lines, all these threads come together: the Apollonian virtue of honor, the Dionysian primordial urge that Achilles's rage unleashes, the slighting of honor as the fulcrum of the plot, and the tragic consequences of heroic action.

Given the invocation of unrelenting and tragic rage in its opening line, it is interesting to note that the poem actually starts by presenting a powerful portrait of Achilles as a skilled military commander and a respected leader of men. He is honored by his troops for his actions, not just his preeminent fighting skills in combat (we are told time and time again that Achilles is far and away the best fighter the Greeks have, almost superheroic in his skills) but how he treats his fellow men. Achilles, the royal prince of the Myrmidons, is not someone who leads from the rear. He is at the forefront of every raid, of every skirmish and contest in battle. He disdains politics and the scheming it requires and values the labor of combat itself. As Oprisko has observed, he clearly views honor as external and linked to prestige; for him honor is earned through heroic deeds and the bloody work of battle. The trophies of war are ornaments that symbolize this hard-earned honor achieved through heroic excellence, not merely decorative medals that one is entitled to because of one's political or aristocratic position. As such, the contrast between Achilles and Agamemnon, the commander of the Greek army, is established from the outset. Agamemnon is known for his political status and not his battlefield prowess and is introduced to the audience as a petty and grasping figure who always takes more than his share of plunder and who demands obedience to his authority. The contrast between the two as leaders is all too evident in the opening pages. Achilles is depicted as a natural leader of men; in response to the plague sweeping through camp, he gathers the troops together and speaks to them, and even suggests to Agamemnon that it is time to turn to a prophet as the plague seems to be caused by the gods. (It is in fact caused by the wrath of Apollo, who is angered by Agamemnon's treatment of his priest.) There is nothing petulant or selfish about Achilles in these early pages, nor is he the crazed killing machine he becomes in the latter stages of *The Iliad*. Instead he is portrayed as in command of his troops and respected by his fellow Greeks. The prophet Calchas, who is summoned to diagnose the plague sweeping through the Greek ranks, calls him "dear to Zeus" and begs him for protection from Agamemnon's certain wrath, underlining his stature among the men.[54]

Calchas's words, which point the finger at Agamemnon as the cause of the plague, set off the quarrel about honor that spurs into motion the tragic plot of *The Iliad*. Told by the prophet that he must give up his captured slave, Chryseis, the daughter of Apollo's priest, Agamemnon erupts in righteous anger. Chryseis is his war trophy, an ornament of his honor, and he clearly considers giving her up to be an affront to his reputation and authority. He wants to be compensated by taking the slave trophy of another, and in his indignation he turns his focus on Achilles. Agamemnon says, "But fetch me another prize, and straight off too, / else I alone of the Argives go without honor. / That would be a disgrace."[55] He ties his honor to his war trophy and suggests that her loss is equivalent to the loss of his honor. Achilles is stunned by his pettiness and calls him the "most grasping man alive," and Agamemnon counters by accusing him of trying to cheat his commander and again demands someone else's prize, "equal to what I have lost."[56] The opposite of honor is shame, which is underlined here. The shameless greed of Agamemnon leads to the dishonor of Achilles, the greatest warrior of the Greeks. Even before he takes away Briseis, Achilles's slave, as compensation for his loss, Agamemnon's expressed desire to be recompensed for giving up Chryseis is intolerable to Achilles. Agamemnon always takes the most from the war loot at the end of every battle even though he does little of the fighting. For Achilles, this grasping demand from their leader is too much to bear. He sees it as stripping away his own hard-earned honor and a form of public shaming in front of his troops.

There are dueling concepts of honor at work here: for Agamemnon, his sovereignty and political authority entitle him to the gilding ornamentation of honor, whereas for Achilles, honor is earned through actions and is a form of recognition by others as recompense for the heroic and laborious work of battle. Achilles describes it in the following way:

> No, you colossal, shameless—we all followed you,
> to please you, to fight for you,
> to win your honor
> back from the Trojans—Menelaus and you, you dog-face!
> What do *you* care? Nothing. You don't look right or left.
> And now you threaten to strip me of my prize in person—
> the one I fought for long and hard, and sons of Achaea
> handed her to me.[57]

Achilles is fighting far from home in another man's war, to earn back Menelaus's honor from the Trojans. He has been the bulwark of the Greek army for nine years, the force that the Trojans can never seem to break, and now he feels deeply shamed and scorned by a man he clearly does not view as honorable. "My honors never equal yours," he tells Agamemnon; when they sack a Trojan city, Agamemnon gets the "lion's share" when the loot is divided, whereas Achilles bears the brunt of the fighting and goes back to his ships "clutching some scrap, some pittance that I love, when I have fought to exhaustion."[58] Honor here is a ranking of value and worth; it is not about the material possessions but rather the sense that an already greedy commander wants to snatch away a token of hardwon respect earned in battle. Of course, this only amplifies the stakes because not only is Achilles accusing Agamemnon of shameless dishonor, but in doing so he is also questioning his leadership and his political authority. Agamemnon certainly perceives it that way and uses this moment to assert his sovereign authority over Achilles and in turn shame and reduce him. He dismisses Achilles by saying, "you *are* nothing to me—you and your overweening anger!" and that he will take Briseis as recompense

> so you can learn how much greater I am than you
> and the next man up may shrink from matching words with me,
> from hoping to rival Agamemnon strength from strength![59]

Homer tells us that "anguish gripped Achilles" at these words and he debates whether to draw his sword and kill Agamemnon, the insult to his honor is so great.[60] Achilles's rage at this public shaming is so intense that even the gods on Mt. Olympus worry that bloodshed will ensue, and they send Athena down to calm him with the promise that he will one day be rewarded "three times over" to pay for the outrageous insult to his honor.[61]

As the quarrel between the two men deepens and Achilles's rage intensifies, there is a clear sense that this has devolved into a contest over forms of power that are irreconcilable and incommensurable with each other. At the core of the conflict is the competing ideas of honor that each man holds dear and the extent to which he is willing to go to defend it. Honor and leadership are therefore fused together in these opening pages. A war that has been relentlessly waged for years to win back honor, to avenge the dishonor of Paris abducting Helen, is now about to be derailed because of a question of honor.

The tragic dimension of Achilles's honor being scorned is further underlined after he storms off to his tent, where his immortal mother comes to comfort her weeping son. Achilles's tragic fate is the same as that of all mortals, no matter how heroic their actions: he will die. It is what separates mortals from Olympians, the fact of mortality, and it is what lends beauty and terror to tragedy. In Achilles's case, it is even more pronounced by a prophecy that has long been foretold: that if he stays and fights in Troy, his death will quickly follow Hector's. He knows this. But in exchange for a short life he gets a shot at everlasting glory and honor. The insult to his honor from Agamemnon strikes much more deeply, then, because it seems to tip the scales even further and strikes at the one thing that has made this tragic fate bearable for Achilles and the other Greeks soldiers: the promise of the glory and eternal honor of the epic hero. But now that Agamemnon has stripped Achilles of his honor in front of the entire army, he refuses to fight any longer for him and refuses to let his men fight for him either. Yet in withdrawing from the battlefield he is also abandoning his opportunity to earn honor and glory. Achilles is therefore constrained and restrained by his sense of honor in multiple ways, and the loss of honor has tragic consequences for his heroic ambition as well. Not only is he furious at Agamemnon, but he is also enraged that Zeus, the king of the gods, would allow something like this to happen to him. He weeps with fury and calls out to his mother, Thetis:

> Mother!
> You gave me life, short as that life will be,
>   so at least Olympian Zeus, thundering up on high,
>   should give me honor—but now he gives me nothing.[62]

As Nietzsche wrote in *Homer's Contest*, "[E]very talent must unfold itself in fighting: that is the command of Hellenic popular pedagogy." For Achilles this is truer than for most Greek heroes. His talent is fighting, and fighting is his only path to becoming an epic hero, but he now feels bound by his honor to withdraw.[63]

He stays in his tent and refuses to return until the Greeks are truly desperate for him to do so. Thus he shows the key flashes of the heroic temper—the scorned hero who stubbornly persists in his refusal and who turns a deaf ear to the reasoned pleas of his friends and advisors. The sheer amount of carnage that unfolds over the next several books of *The Iliad* only serves to underline this tragic nexus between honor and heroism. The Trojans take full advantage of the Greeks having lost their best warrior and wreak havoc within their ranks, sweeping them off the battlefield and pinning them against their ships on the water's edge. The entire years-long campaign seems doomed to certain failure without Achilles, who shows no sign of relenting. Agamemnon, on the other hand, forced to come to terms with his army collapsing and his entire mission on the verge of defeat, finally relents and admits he was mad and blind. When the rout is imminent, he finally sees the paralyzing cost of his fixation on his honor and says of Achilles, "[T]hat man is worth an entire army."[64]

He returns Briseis to Achilles, along with several chests of treasure, and sends an embassy of the best commanders of the Greek army to deliver his apology and coax Achilles out of his tent. This section of *The Iliad* is fascinating as it underscores all the key elements of the heroic temper that Sophocles later made a crucial part of Greek tragic drama. The stubborn hero who stands firm in the face of all manner of persuasive arguments and refuses to relent ushers in the most devastatingly tragic outcome with his all-consuming rage. Ironically, the agentic power of honor or its capacity to inspire heroic action can also fuel the hero to *not* act. The stubborn adherence to his honor, which is crucial to Achilles's subject formation and his heroic hopes, holds him in a paralyzing grip that he cannot allow himself to break out of. He is bound and limited by his honor in a way that is immune to any kind of persuasion and that clearly underlines the danger that honor can pose to the political. Even Odysseus, the smartest and most politically shrewd of the Greeks, cannot pierce the wall that Achilles has built around himself with his scorned honor. Odysseus tries in vain to shift the terms of the argument from Agamemnon to the army, reminding Achilles of the troops who respect and honor him and trying to invoke his sense of duty toward them, at least so that he will agree to return to protect them from slaughter. Referring to Agamemnon, he tells Achilles:

> But if you hate the son of Atreus all the more,
> him and his trove of gifts, at least take pity
> on all our united forces mauled in battle here—
> they will honor you, honor you like a god.[65]

But neither this appeal to pity for the men who are being mercilessly cut down by the Trojans nor promises of god-like honor are sufficient to move Achilles, who responds:

> But now that he's torn my honor from my hands,
> robbed me, lied to me—don't let him try me now.
> I know *him* too well—he'll never win me over.[66]

He tells the embassy of commanders that he has "no desire to battle glorious Hector" and notes that while he was on the battlefield Hector "had little lust to charge beyond his walls."[67] The men are stunned into silence by Achilles's unrelenting rage, his expressed desire to sail home, and his utter refusal to help his fellow soldiers. They try one last tack, begging:

> But now, Achilles, beat down your mounting fury!
> It's wrong to have such an iron, ruthless heart.
> Even the gods themselves can bend and change,
> and theirs is the greater power, honor, strength.[68]

But even this is not enough, not even the invocation of the gods and their willingness to change their minds. Achilles's rage is beyond even immortal scope. He refuses to relent and says he will move only when Zeus himself decrees it, but for now he will stay in place by his ships and avoid the fray.[69] Ajax speaks for much of the audience with his disgust when he says in response:

> Achilles—
> he's made his own spirit so wild in his chest,
> so savage, not a thought for his comrade's love—
> we honored him past all others by the ships.
> Hard, ruthless man.[70]

Achilles's refusal of the most generous of apologies, his rejection of his duty to his fellow soldiers, and his stubborn adherence to his idea of honor usher in the most devastating tragic sequence of *The Iliad*. Clearly, even for the ancient Greeks who valued the notion of honor and its capacity to inspire action and create mythic sources of meaning, the stubborn pursuit of honor has its limits. We are meant to sympathize with Ajax and his fellow commanders who are fighting a losing battle on the edge of the beach with their backs to the very ships they once hoped to sail home in glory (and which Hector will soon set aflame), all while their best fighter and his rested troops are sitting idle and will not come to their defense.

It is worth noting the etymology of Achilles's name at this juncture, which Nagy explains is already interlaced with tragedy. The name can be broken down into its component parts: *ákhos*, which translates to "host of fighting men," and *lāós*, which simply means "grief."[71] And the stage is now set for him to suffer traumatic loss. When the ships are set on fire and the final hour seems upon the Greeks, Achilles agrees to let his dearest and closest friend (some speculate his lover), Patroclus, to wear Achilles's own famous gleaming gold armor and lead the Myrmidons into battle, hoping that just the glinting image of the most fearsome of the Greek warriors will be enough to force the Trojans back. Nagy calls Patroclus Achilles's *therápōn*, or "ritual substitute," and says that in wearing Achilles's armor into battle "he became the actual surrogate of Achilles, his alter ego."[72] Achilles warns Patroclus to only push the Trojans back to their city walls and not dare to go further as he is no match for them in combat and they will soon realize that he is not who the armor proclaims him to be. But Patroclus, crazed by the beguiling promise of victory and spurred on by the meddling gods, doesn't heed this advice and is cut down by Hector, the heroic commander of the Trojan forces, right in front of the city walls.

Achilles's grief as he watches the rout is shattering. He truly occupies the vertiginous moment when time is out of joint—he does not know yet that Patroclus is dead, but he can already feel the fingers of this devastating future reaching into the present, a present that is also fully haunted by the prophecy of his own death. (As Nagy notes, the death of Patroclus the *therápōn* foreshadows the death of Achilles himself.)[73]

There is a creeping sense of the immensity of the loss Achilles is about to suffer (is already suffering?). For now, it is only a premonition, but he is already haunted by it. He cries out:

> Dear gods, don't bring to pass the grief that haunts my heart—
> the prophecy that mother revealed to me one time...
> she said the best of the Myrmidons—while I lived—
> would fall at Trojan hands and leave the light of day.
> And now he's dead, I know it.[74]

He cries out hopelessly against the cruel fate that is ripping his closest companion away from him—he starts by begging the gods to not let the prophecy happen, and by the end of his proclamation he is already beset by tragic recognition. The heaviness of the loss breaks like a wave over Achilles, and in his trauma he is completely unmoored from his heroic desire and detached from his relentless attachment to his scorned honor. He laments:

> All those burning desires
> Olympian Zeus has brought to pass for me—but what joy to me now?
> My dear comrade's dead—
> Patroclus—the man I loved beyond all other comrades,
> loved as my own life—I've lost him.[75]

Achilles is true to his name in his devastating grief—the *laós* that pours out of him after the loss of his beloved Patroclus is even more intense than the rage that spilled out of him at the loss of his honor. Even as it sweeps him under Achilles knows that the loss of Patroclus is his undoing. In a moment of profound tragic recognition, he cries out, "I'm sick with longing for you! / There is no more shattering blow I could suffer."[76]

The grief is so traumatic it *does* shatter him into what Jonathan Shay, who applied the lessons of *The Iliad* to his therapeutic treatment of Vietnam War veterans, calls the "berserk" state, which comes from the Norse word for "the frenzied warriors who went into battle naked, or at least without armor in a godlike or god-possessed—but also beastlike—fury."[77] Shay sees Achilles's character as being ruined by Agamemnon's initial betrayal and then undone by grief at the loss of Patroclus, writing that "the *Iliad* is the tragedy of Achilles' noble character brought to ruins."[78] For Shay, who treated numerous Vietnam veterans for posttraumatic stress disorder, the parallels between the epic tale of *The Iliad* and the accounts he hears daily in his therapeutic practice are both fascinating and numerous. Not only does it make sense to Shay that Achilles is shattered by the death of Patroclus, but even his rage at Agamemnon makes sense in the context of military codes of honor. Agamemnon taking away the prize that the troops had voted to give Achilles for his valor can be understood as a profound betrayal of the norms of the military that caused him to detach from the group in a way that is difficult for even Odysseus and Ajax to understand. Shay does a close reading of Homer's term *mênis* (rage) to describe this phenomenon, noting that "it is the kind of rage arising from social betrayal that impairs a person's dignity through violation of 'what's right.' Apart from its use as word for divine rage, Homer uses *mênis* only as the word for the rage that ruptures social attachments."[79] By the time of Patroclus's death Achilles is shorn of his attachments to others. He wears his scorned honor like he once wore his glittering armor, except rather than defending them with it, he uses it to separate himself from the army and his duties to them and tries to ignore or reject the very conditions of his subject formation as a respected leader among his soldiers. Shay notes that prior to the death of Patroclus, "Achilles possessed a highly developed social morality. This was reflected in his care for the welfare of other Greek soldiers, respect for enemies living and dead, and a reluctance to kill prisoners."[80] But in this traumatic moment of loss, betrayed first by the initial loss of honor and then tragically undone by the loss of his beloved companion, Achilles snaps. The initial quarrel with Agamemnon is about much more than ego—the high price placed on honor and the blinding attachment to it once again creates an anesthetizing effect where the scorned individual can hardly see how vulnerable he is to others and the power relations that form him and his relationships to others. To borrow a word from Judith Butler, the "precarity" of the entire arrangement is exposed, and the mythic but unexpectedly fragile nexus of forces that bind together honor, heroic agency, and the Homeric contest is laid bare. Shay describes Achilles's undoing in an evocative way, writing that "we can never fathom the soldier's grief if we do not know the human attachment which battle nourishes and then amputates."[81] The profound grief that Achilles feels at the loss of Patroclus is multiplied by his earlier betrayal and alienation and quite quickly transforms into rage. Shay relates that in his clinical practice many veterans who suffered the traumatic loss of a friend in combat with inadequate opportunity for grieving reacted similarly, and the replacement of grief by rage became an enduring and entrenched way of being for many of them.[82] It is no surprise to Shay after his years of clinical practice that Achilles shatters at that moment. For him it is clear that "the *Iliad* charts the ambiguous borderline between heroism and a blood-crazed, berserk state in which abuse after abuse is committed."[83]

Achilles's bloodlust after Patroclus's death is truly legendary, but it is no longer the heroic golden valor of epic but a seemingly unending and numbing tale of gore-spattered butchery of such detached cruelty that even the gods recoil from its savagery. This description from Homer captures Achilles's initial onslaught, when he is in his chariot literally riding across the wave of bodies he has cut down in his berserk state:

> so as the great Achilles rampaged on, his sharp-hoofed stallions
> trampled shields and corpses, axle under his chariot splashed
> with blood, blood on the handrails sweeping round the car,
> sprays of blood shooting up from the stallions' hoofs

> and churning, whirling rims—and the son of Peleus
> charioteering on to seize his glory, bloody filth
> splattering both strong arms, Achilles' invincible arms.[84]

This is a terrifying sight, beyond argument, beyond persuasion, the epitome of the unrestrained primordial Dionysian urge, detached from all norms of contest and competition. Shay's diagnosis of Achilles in this state is convincing: "[D]uring berserk rage, the friend is constantly alive; letting go of the rage lets him die."[85] Achilles's paralyzing grief turned rapidly into violent rage has devastating political consequences both for him and for everyone else. It detaches him from the norms that bind him and leads him to commit one war crime after the other. At his worst, Achilles ruthlessly kills Hector in front of the city gates of Troy in a contest that is devoid of the Apollonian structures of honor and, in a particularly nauseating sequence, defiles and desecrates the Trojan commander's body.

Hector, the eldest of King Priam's sons, the commander of the Trojan forces, and the prince of Troy, represents quite the contrast to Achilles throughout the poem. He is the other equally compelling side of this tragedy, the heroic and honorable leader of the Trojans, the fiercest of their fighters and an excellent commander (far surpassing Agamemnon), who clearly has the respect and devotion of his soldiers. Hector is the dutiful son, husband, and commander who is trapped between all these roles. Knox writes that "on him falls the whole burden of the war.... [U]nlike Achilles, he is clearly a man made for peace, for those relationships between man and man, and man and woman, which demand sympathy, persuasion, kindness and, where firmness is necessary, a firmness expressed in forms of law and resting on granted authority. He is a man who appears most himself in his relationships with others."[86] He is honored above all by the Trojans, but he also draws honor and respect in a different, more intimate way. Hector is the only one of the many characters in *The Iliad* who is framed via the *oikos*, the home. We get the most private and intimate portrait of him as the much beloved family man who finds his happiness with his wife and child, who puts aside his fierce-looking helmet because it scares his baby, and who is loved deeply by his wife and parents.

This rare and fugitive domestic portrait of Hector complicates in a productive and compelling way the formal sense of him as a martial hero. Here we see a Hector who is kind and empathic (to Helen too, who all the other Trojans loathe for bringing an army to their gates) and grounded in family.

He is deeply loved and respected by all, which makes the horribly tragic fate that is to befall him and his wife and child that much harder to bear. The twin figures of Achilles and Hector are braided together with a deep sense of the tragic in this poem, offering different glimpses into the complexity of honor. Hector is fixed in his resolve; he knows he cannot get out of this tragic bind, but he too is bound by pride, reputation, and, yes, honor. In that terrible moment, Knox writes, when Hector finally turns to face Achilles in a hopeless last stand, knowing he is about to die, and Achilles hears his horse prophesy his death soon after Hector's, "the true tragic note is struck."[87] Hector is fixed in his resolve, he knows he cannot get out of this tragic bind, but he too is bound by pride, reputation, and yes, honor, to flee inside the city gates. He turns to face Achilles in a heroic last stand that Homer juxtaposes with the heaviness of fate. On the very next page, Zeus raises his golden scale on which both names have been placed, and Hector's side dips down, doomed by tragic fate.

All that is left for Hector is to appeal to the battlefield code of honor and beg Achilles to respect his body if he falls. But Achilles is beyond all restraint and appeal and murders him mercilessly in front of his parents' eyes. He then proceeds to desecrate Hector's body by dragging it behind his chariot, first around the walls of Troy and then around Patroclus's funeral pyre—a circle he repeats with numbing regularity until the gods finally take pity and intervene to make him stop. As Shay notes of his work with veterans, "The crucial trait that emerged from this analysis is the absence of restraint—apparently *any* restraint—when berserk."[88] Achilles, in his state of traumatic grief transfigured into rage, is beyond any kind of social attachment; he is a beast or superhuman, to use Aristotle's terms—someone who is no longer a political animal but a figure who is outside the norms and the binds of political community and who is destructive to the very idea of the political in his berserk state. He is pulled out of this state only by the Olympian intervention that allows Hector's father, King Priam, to visit his tent in the dead of night and beg for his son's body. The old man's grief somehow pierces through Achilles's rage—he remembers his own father, Peleus, who is aging and lonely and who he will never see again, who will also grieve for a son whose death is imminent. Finally Achilles relents. Something pulls him back with Priam, a touch of humanity, a recognition of his own subjectivity, the love for his father and the deep sense of loss that Peleus will also suffer. He has a moment, in other words, of recognition of his attachment to others. In Kohen's words, "he is ultimately returned to community by his sympathy for Priam" and therefore rehabilitated as a hero.[89] This return to the values of the community leads him to honor Priam as a guest and to honor Hector's body by releasing it for a proper burial.

Kohen observes that in this pivotal moment, Achilles returns from the "nihilistic void" to finally emerge "as a model of heroic behavior, because, irrespective of his savagery, he is a doer of impressive, courageous deeds."[90] *The Iliad*, which begins with the assault on the honor of Achilles and its devastating effect on the Greek army, ends with a resolution of sorts with the dutiful Hector, the son of Troy, being fully honored and mourned by his people. The last line of *The Iliad* is from the funeral of Hector, a moment of profound civic honor made legible by ritual and lamentation. This final tragic scene demonstrates the linkage between honor, mourning, and grievability in the political imagination and further underlines honor's mythic capacity to create meaning.

The Tragedy of Honor

This analysis of Achilles's fixation on his honor in *The Iliad* clearly demonstrates the complex relationship between honor and heroic agency. Honor has the capacity to create heroic action and plays a crucial role in the heroic temper. It has the ability to inspire an individual to perform the most difficult of tasks, and as such it is easy to see what its appeal might be for those who look for it to play a redemptive role for liberal democracy today—to safeguard its cherished principles of freedom and equality and serve as a bulwark against tyranny. However, as this analysis has shown, despite the "acticity" and agentic power of honor that gives it its heroic potential, it remains a thorny concept that also contains within it the capacity for destruction and tragedy. Attending to this tragic capacity of honor allows us to see not just its sparkling and structured Apollonian outlines, but also the primordial Dionysian urge it can unleash, which, while creative at its best, also has the ability to cause immense destruction.

In *The Iliad* this tragic fallout from the scorning and betrayal of Achilles's honor threatens to pull apart all the rules of engagement with its violation of the very ideas of respect for one's enemy. Achilles seems beyond human in his berserk rage and poses a threat to the very idea of politics itself with his sheer destructive power. And yet, as Shay pointedly observes, the lesson that many American military commanders have learned from the text is the value of dishonoring and desecrating one's enemy because Hector's death turns the tide and allows the Greeks to win the Trojan War. What is emphasized more often than not is the success engendered by the superhuman destructive capacity of the war hero, and not the anesthetizing fog that honor (and the betrayal of honor) brings to the attachments between soldiers and their units, their families, and, yes, their enemies. Emphasizing only the agentic power of honor and ignoring its tragic consequences comes at a tremendous cost. Much of the Vietnam veteran experience Shay outlines in his book shows that the U.S. military strategy explicitly dishonors the enemy—through systemic racism and dehumanization, by refusing to respect them and their skills in combat (which created a sharp tactical disadvantage as American soldiers were often taken by surprise when their enemy fought bravely), as the Americans had little understanding of the notion of honoring your enemy and valuing the idea of contest itself.

That demonization and dehumanization of the adversary also strips the conflict of complexity—it is reduced to biblical good and evil. And when that paradigm is quickly exhausted by the messiness of war there is nothing to replace it. The U.S. army in Vietnam had no sense of Homeric contest, no inherent concept of the tragic, no sense that honor and respect could be found in the very act of facing a formidable opponent. To return to Nietzsche one last time, the value of the Homeric contest lies precisely in its celebration and recognition and in affirming the norms that sustain it. Such an idea of the contest, which relies heavily on honor and its capacity to inspire heroic action, could have real value for political life, but as Nietzsche himself noted, if we "remove the contest from Greek life we immediately look into that pre-Homeric abyss of a terrifying savagery of hatred and the lust to annihilate."[91] This primordial urge stripped of its Apollonian structure is evident in Achilles as his grief and rage remove him from the ennobling and honorable codes that structure the contest and place him outside of it—outside both the contest and the polis. Hector tries in vain to wage their fight on the terrain of the contest, to give it the restraint of the accepted code of honor, to give it meaning in terms that are legible and understood by the audience, but Achilles refuses. He dishonors Hector and defiles his body in terms that stand in stark contrast to the rest of the poem.

A poem that is about the tragic costs of the betrayal of honor is also in some ways a testament to the restraining value of the code of honor that holds the army together and requires that its combatants respect the norms or the *themis* of the contest. That structuring idea of honor is one that awards prizes for the gory and glory of labor on the battlefield and allows for moments of true respect between opponents (for instance, the wonderful scene during Diomedes's *aristeía* when he recognizes his opponent as an honored guest and they stop mid-combat and exchange gifts). But it also shows how clearly that code of honor is structured by power, or force, as Simone Weil called it. The other side of honor is the destructive force that is unleashed by its betrayal that can rupture all attachments and fray all the norms that tie the idea of the contest together. Patroclus's death ruptures that notion for Achilles and makes the idea of honor on the battlefield meaningless and irrelevant in his blinding rage and grief. Achilles, whose tragic insistence on honor, which is at once understandable in the context of the army but also comes at immense cost to it, throws off the binds of that code of honor in a terribly destructive moment, and we see the wave of blood and carnage that follows, that spatters him and even the wheels of his chariot as he drives it forward in relentless rage. In Nietzsche's terms, he is driven by the lust to annihilate, unbound by codes of honor, and undone by his unfathomable grief. Honor therefore works in a complex and tragic way in *The Iliad*: it is the code that ties together the Homeric contest and gives it its capacity for meaning, but its betrayal extracts a tremendous price and is profoundly destructive. Honor, understood in terms of the contest, of ambition and envy, of labor and skill, makes battle legible and heroic. Stripped of that honor and burned by its loss, there is only savagery, emptiness, and tragedy. Thankfully for *The Iliad*'s audience, Achilles recovers his humanity and honors Priam as a guest and gives Hector the full honors of death. The funeral of Hector is a moment of profound civic honor that shows the continuing significance of a code of honor for the polis—as a way of making meaning and inspiring heroic acts of valor even as it recognizes the tragedy of honor itself.

If *The Iliad* tells us anything about honor it is that honor is shot through and through with tragedy. As such, the hero of the epic, with his mythic capacity for action, is not the best fit for the political, and we should be careful about the consequences of extolling the agentic power of his honor. As Knox writes beautifully:

> The hero offered the ancient Greeks the assurance that in some chosen vessels humanity is capable of superhuman greatness, that there are some human beings who can imperiously deny the imperatives which others obey in order to love. It is not that the hero is worshipped as an example of human conduct; he is no guide to life in the real city man made or the ideal city he dreams of. But he is a reminder that [a] human being may at times magnificently defy the limits imposed on our will by the fear of public opinion, of community action, even of death, may refuse to accept

humiliation and indifference and impose his will no matter what the consequences to others and himself.[92]

This quote encapsulates the pitfalls and the possibilities of a politics of honor. The kind of agency that honor can engender can certainly rise to the level of the heroic. But heroic agency itself is an agonistic and tragic concept, capable of inspiring great acts in defense of liberty but also petulant and stubborn and with a capacity for immense destruction. Honor can at once inspire and restrain, create and destroy. This tragic dimension of honor cannot be ignored when we look to it for inspiration in contemporary political life.

5
Honor, Nostalgia, and Democratic Anxiety in the Marvel Cinematic Universe's *Captain America*

The idea of honor clearly continues to resonate in the present, where it remains a fixture in both political discourse and popular culture and shapes the political imagination. In particular, the concept of honor is often fused with its close cousin, duty, and reworked into the discourse of patriotism, militarism, and heroism. In recent years, the Marvel Cinematic Universe (MCU) has revived and created a tremendous appetite for superheroes. There have been several blockbuster films; a new subscription channel (Disney Plus), whose primary appeal is its MCU catalog; and a genuine sense of the "event" around the release of these films. This suggests something significant is at work in the myth-making role that superheroes play in contemporary life and the outsize role they exert on the popular imagination. This chapter looks at the genre of superheroes in film by focusing on the most ostensibly honorable and patriotic superhero of them all, the supersoldier who is literally armored in the red, white, and blue: Captain America. It analyzes the iconic superhero through selected films and television series in the MCU to explore the interstices of honor and democracy. Democracy needs consistent imaginary investments in itself, and the aesthetics of democracy are a crucial part of its renewal. Democracy too requires myths and heroes—indeed it is an open question as to whether or not the mythic world of the MCU, with its focus on personal honor grounded in character and duty, is a help for or a hindrance to democratic endeavors that should be rooted in equality. This chapter argues that as a central figure in the American democratic imaginary, Captain America also sits uncomfortably within it. He is a singular figure who has to embody the virtues of an imagined community—an individual who is meant to represent the collective idea of "the people" and provide inspiration during times of democratic anxiety and satisfy its longing for a simpler, more idealized (and whitewashed) past. As a superhero who has a deep sense of internal honor rooted in ideas of goodness, loyalty, and sacrifice, Captain America fits uneasily within the very premise of democratic equality and institutional restraint, often working to undermine it with his (super)heroic actions. This chapter underlines that honor and democracy operate in tension with each other in the political imagination.

This chapter explores the connections between honor, nostalgia, and democratic anxiety along a few different lines of inquiry. It begins by exploring the generative mythic world of the MCU and its impact on contemporary politics and popular culture. It then turns to an analysis of Steve Rogers as Captain America in his stand-alone MCU films: *The First Avenger*, *The Winter Soldier*, and *Civil War*. From his origin story in the MCU as the First Avenger during World War II until his character arc reaches its conclusion in *Avengers: Endgame*, Steve Rogers operates consistently throughout these films as a patriotic superhero with an entrenched sense of honor and duty. His journey embodies democratic struggle, appearing when democracy faces threats both external and internal but also containing the tension between democratic equality and a lingering attachment to heroic agency. The chapter analyzes these moments of struggle and tension by reading these visual texts alongside Carey McWilliam's work on democracy and honor and Jason Frank's analysis of the aesthetics of democracy to highlight the appeal of "grandeur" in democracy. The chapter closes with an examination of the links between honor, nostalgia, and democracy through an analysis of the latest iteration of MCU's Captain America story in the Disney Plus television series *The Falcon and the Winter Soldier*. In this series, Sam Wilson's Falcon, as a Black man in America, struggles with the legacy of the shield he has inherited from Steve Rogers, and in doing so draws attention to the silences of American democracy and how its nostalgic fantasies of heroism can both conceal and perpetuate racial injustice. This chapter therefore argues that the MCU's Captain America, in his many forms, embodies the unsettled relationship between democracy and honor itself: he is a figure who is, on the one hand, essential to the mythic imaginary of American democracy but who, on the other hand, threatens its very stability with his unyielding attachment to honor. As the stories we tell ourselves to rewrite and reinvest and renew democratic belonging change, so too does Captain America. As an essential figure in the democratic imaginary, the nostalgic appeal of a heroic Captain America is at once a necessity in a time of fracture and contestation and a fantasy of displacement that conceals unjust silences and what Elisabeth Anker has called its "ugly freedoms."[1]

Superheroes and Mythic Meaning

The MCU has become a juggernaut at the box office, with highly anticipated film releases drawn from a seemingly inexhaustible set of comic book sources and a subscription channel, Disney Plus, that explores the world of superheroes in live-action and animated form. It is therefore worth examining what the appetite for superheroes in the contemporary imaginary signifies and how it might shape our political desires and perspectives. Much ink has been spilled about Hollywood and its influence on politics, going all the way back to the notorious blacklist during the McCarthy era, to debates about censorship of violent and sexual content, to concerns about both pro- and antiwar messaging in films during the heyday of the War on Terror. What is it, though, about superheroes in our present moment that stokes the popular appetite? At a time of democratic erosion and rising authoritarianism across the globe (the 2021 Democracy Index showed that the percentage of people living in a democracy had fallen well below 50%),[2] the appeal of superheroes in increasingly stylish spandex battling enemies lends credence to the notion that we need characters who are honorable and dutiful and do the right thing, even though they are sometimes compromised and conflicted, to help us make sense of an increasingly fractured and disenchanted world. In all of these films and shows, the superhero eventually does the right thing against all odds, despite the political machinations and corruption that regularly show up to stymie them. Increasingly, even the villains make a compelling political and ethical case for their actions. (See, for example, Michael B. Jordan's scene-stealing turn as Killmonger in the first *Black Panther* film.) As such, the MCU storylines in their own way increasingly resemble some of the contours of ancient epic and play on some of the same keys of tragedy, loss, duty, and honor. Some contemporary scholars, such as Ari Kohen, have even explicitly linked superheroes such as Tony Stark's Iron Man to classical heroes like Achilles, whose tragic relationship to honor was explored in depth in the previous chapter.[3]

For some, like the *New York Times* film critic A. O. Scott, blockbuster Hollywood studio films making bank at the box office speak to a desire for consensus. He writes that they tell many different stories: "About the grit and glory of the American military; about the heroic, essential work of law enforcement; about the centrality of revenge to any serious conception of justice; about the superiority of common sense over credentialed expertise; about the lessons ordinary small-town folks can teach fancy city slickers;

about individual striving as the answer to most social problems; about the need for heroes."[4] Scott is correct about the "need for heroes" and the liberal emphasis on the need for individuals (and not collective action) to solve sociopolitical problems, and he makes an essential and compelling point about some of the conservative values that are part of many recent blockbusters. (His essay is a response to the recent *Top Gun* remake, which is a nostalgic and thrilling celebration of the U.S. Air Force.) Though Scott makes a strong case about the appeal of consensus, his argument is a little too optimistic. While consensus might be a standard to aspire to in democratic deliberation, there is some slippage between a desire for heroes and a desire for democratic reinvigoration. Indeed, the two are seemingly at odds, as shall be explored later in this chapter. Rather than consensus, the MCU films, in particular, appeal to the mythic imagination. As Neal Curtis notes, "In comics scholarship it is common to talk about superheroes in terms of myth. In broad terms, myths are about the origin of life and the founding of a specific community. They speak of beginnings and ends, order and rank, victory and defeat, virtue and vice. In this sense, they bind and regulate a community through the explanation of spiritual, natural and social forces."[5] Curtis's argument about the ways in which mythic imagination can help "bind" and order a community and shape the virtues it endorses and the vices it avows brings us much closer to understanding the popular appeal of the MCU.

In their volume on the politics of the MCU, Lilly Goren and Nicholas Carnes write that "one of the most powerful effects of popular culture, and fiction in particular, is that it can encourage audiences to contemplate ideas that depart sharply from the status quo, to engage in what scholars call *social or political imagination*. Scholars refer to fiction that does so as *speculative fiction*."[6] For Goren and Carnes, the MCU actively engages its audience through multiple forms of speculative storytelling "threaded together across dozens of films and shows, connecting characters and ideas temporally, commercially, and artistically. . . . Above and beyond the normal effects of speculative fiction, the expansive nature of the MCU encourages audiences and fans to engage with the narratives, the character arcs, and the imaginary space created by these interwoven stories in a way that is unique in media history."[7] As such, the superheroes of the MCU help inspire the political imaginary in ways that resemble myth (and indeed often draw deeply on Greek, Roman, and Norse mythology).[8] As Curtis explains, superheroes "deal with mythological themes such as creation and destruction, life and death, structure and entropy, friend and enemy that have captured our imagination for millennia. Peel back the façade of the contemporary telling and you will find age-old, metaphysical quandaries.... They offer a template for behavior and guide readers on the adjudication of issues pertaining to good and evil and right and wrong, and offer ideological representations of gender, race, sexuality and nation."[9] Captain America tries to hold on to his sense of honor and duty as he battles Nazis and emerges in a moment of temporal dislocation decades later to battle shadowy nongovernmental actors; Thor takes on enemies across the planets while engaging in delightful moments of sibling rivalry with the mischievous Loki; Black Widow actively works to recover from her abusive and traumatic past and becomes a key member of the Avengers in their fight to save the universe from Thanos.

In its latest incarnations the MCU has been pushing further in the direction of racial, cultural, and gender representation with films and series that feature non-White superheroes, such as Chadwick Boseman's iconic *Black Panther*, the recent *Shang Chi and the Legend of the Ten Rings* with its predominantly Asian cast, and the wonderful *Ms. Marvel*, which features a young female Pakistani American lead. This welcome move toward diversifying its predominantly White and male roster of superheroes has had mixed results, as a portion of the fanbase has chafed against these necessary changes and the move toward a more equitable and pluralist worldview that they exemplify.[10] Curtis emphasizes this point by pointing out that superheroes can also provide an adaptable version of myth and that, beyond simply reproducing and reifying existing cultural and political values, they can also function as sources of social change and adaptation in what he calls the *generative* role of myth-making.[11] Seen as generative and adaptive sense-making of an emerging and always changing world, "myth does not simply provide an explanation for and make sense of a world that already exists but brings that world into being. The world in this sense is an interpretation of the things, forces, and relations that we encounter around us. Here, myth can also be said to realize a world; it both substantiates and legitimizes a particular worldview, giving it a sense of reality and naturalness."[12] The MCU consistently does both. On the one hand it reifies and legitimizes a patriotic and military worldview that is grounded in notions of honor and duty, and, on the other hand, it introduces disruptive elements of nostalgia and democratic anxiety that make a compelling case for grappling with the silences of America's past in the present in order to generate a more pluralist and equitable world in the future. In Curtis's words, "the world is nothing but an interpretation realized and made substantial by the stories that underpin it. Our sense of place, value and purpose is consequently dependent on the stories that substantiate our world and secure an identity for us. This means that telling different stories is directly connected to the political project of bringing another world into being."[13] In its telling and retelling of stories, the MCU both secures certain narratives in the political imagination and participates in the political project of remaking it in the present.

Captain America might seem like an odd choice in this context of increasing representation and generative myth-making; what could be more fossilized in some ways than the man with the star-spangled shield who became an iconic figure during the Second World War? But it is precisely the mix of honor, duty, and militarism that is an essential part of the myth of Captain America that is fascinating. The iconic version of Captain America is Steve Rogers famously wearing the red, white, and blue and carrying the star-spangled shield, but the depiction has changed multiple times over the past 70 years in comic books and film, with different characters at times taking on different roles to match the political needs of the time. Despite all these changes, however, he has never strayed too far from his mythic importance in popular culture. The figure of Captain America becomes even more compelling as he changes over the decades and generates a new era that allows for a deeper exploration of how nostalgia functions in politics and how it colors the relationship between democracy and honor.

For some, Captain America is the very depiction of an unchanging American monomyth which, as articulated by Robert Jewett and John Shelton Lawrence, is rooted in the desire for redemption and requires a selfless, dutiful, and honorable servant who sacrifices himself for others and crusades against evil.[14] In their account the "monomythic superhero is distinguished by disguised origins, pure motivations, a redemptive task, and extraordinary powers. He originates outside the community he is called to save, and in those exceptional instances when he is resident therein, the superhero plays the role of the idealistic loner."[15] However, others point out that once he emerges from the ice decades later, when the moral landscape is foggier, politicians are increasingly corrupt, and the government is no longer fighting a singular enemy, he makes choices that often undermine democratic institutions and eschew deliberation. Captain America never hesitates to go it alone and hold on tightly to his sense of honor and duty, but his choices are ethically and politically complex and at times significantly conflicted about democratic politics. While Cap fits many of the criteria of the American monomyth he also complicates and fragments it in both destructive and productive ways that exemplify the generative form of myth that Curtis outlines.

Captain America begins his journey in the MCU as Steve Rogers, a scrawny young man living in Brooklyn during the Second World War in *The First Avenger*. Steve has lost both his parents and has only one real friend. He is a loner who lives on the margins of community, but he is motivated by a burning desire to serve his country and a clear sense of duty. He has a strict code of honor that makes him unswervingly loyal to his best friend, Bucky Barnes, and a patriotic duty to protect and preserve freedom no matter the cost. Over the ensuing decades, Steve Rogers as Cap functions as a mythic hero out of time, from another time, acting in the present to redeem it from its errors and save it from the mistakes it is yet to make, as seen in the subsequent films *The Winter Soldier* and *Civil War*.

Frozen and preserved in ice for decades, Cap is literally a symbolic representation of pastness in the present, an honorable and dutiful hero who still rises to the chivalrous challenge of the duel—not out of deference to a long-lost aristocratic tradition, but out of the assemblage of honor, patriotism, and militarism that constructs him as a mythic superhero. But in these latter films, his core sense of honor and duty are stained with nostalgia (perhaps both his and ours), a yearning for a simpler past (for some), and a clearer ethical and political landscape. His sense of honor puts him at odds with democratic processes, even as it opens up space to critically interrogate the relationship between the two concepts. In *The Falcon and the Winter Solider*, Sam Wilson's Cap searchingly examines this nationalist monomyth and finds it severely lacking in its erasures of racial violence and suggests a different path forward. However, through all of these changes, the mythic imaginary of Captain America endures because it is at once reifying and generative— he "represents the ultimate American story: permanent enough to survive more than seventy years of continuity but with a history hazy enough to be constantly reinterpreted to meet the needs of the contemporary culture through which he walks from decade to decade."[16]

Honor, Patriotic Duty, and the Military: The First Avenger

One of the most striking things about Captain America is his strict adherence to an internal code of honor and its close cousin, duty—a theme that consistently appears in the first MCU film in the series, *The First Avenger*.

In their book *Honor in the Modern World*, Laurie M. Johnson and Dan Demetriou echo much of the contemporary literature on honor and politics by describing how it gradually faded from the center of political theorizing. They write that "the idea that honor can be a legitimate moral or political motive was an ideological casualty of the First World War. It took decades for modern social science to take honor seriously again, the interval having rendered honor so quaint that it could be discussed with detachment."[17] Indeed, much of their book is spent exploring the question of "whether honor has a place in a modern, democratic, and/or liberal society."[18] Johnson and Demetriou trace this gradual disappearance of the study of honor in social science to the period following World War I, whereas the first superheroes, including Captain America (who was created by Jack Kirby and Joe Simon in 1941), emerged shortly after the start of World War II in 1939. This juxtaposition lends credence to the central thesis of this book: that the concept of honor did not consign itself to the dustbin of chivalric history but has endured in the popular imaginary and continues to play a significant role in contemporary political and cultural life. Clearly the mythic world of superheroes provided necessary grounding during wartime, with Captain America helping to sell war bonds and inspire support for the military.

Some conservative treatments of honor have openly bemoaned this purportedly shrinking role of honor in modern life, tracing its erosion to such varied origins as the collapse of the aristocracy (which took away its emphasis on traditional codes and forms of identity), the rise modern feminism (which, in their view, undermined the masculinity at the heart of honor), and the Vietnam War and its enduring legacy in American foreign policy (which underlined the futility of war). Even the challenges of military recruiting today have been traced to "the cultural consensus of the last thirty years" and its "continuing project of discrediting and disgracing cultural honor."[19] In James Bowman's characterization, militarism, patriotic duty, and honor were always fused together historically in warfare as the consequence of an "honor culture inherited from the Victorians," which began to erode with the modernization of the army.[20] He argues that even during World War II, the army began to ignore honorable and patriotic justifications of war and increasingly relied on moral reasons.[21] This was made worse, in his view, by the Vietnam War, which increased the sense that "honor, like the ruffles and flourishes, was worth nothing in comparison."[22] While Bowman is clearly nostalgic for and bemoans the loss of honor as an overt justification for warfare and the aristocratic codes that accompany it, he still argues that "military honor—which is at the very foundation of the idea ... must be something more than a mere relic of a primitive and long-outmoded order of society."[23] Even though the conservative cultural critique that he launches about the loss of traditional forms of honor and the need for its revival never quite manages to make its way to superheroes in the MCU, he gets adjacent to the connection, noting that "heroes were becoming by definition fantasy figures" when most people discounted the idea "that there could be, or perhaps should be, any heroism at all in the real world."[24] Bowman, however, ignores the notion that honor might have been remade in the contemporary world in new and productive ways. There is a myopia in this conservative longing for a lost past, ignoring how honor has been highlighted in popular culture in renewed mythic form in blockbuster superhero films. Honor, patriotism, and militarism merged together at a moment where America emerged as a superpower on the global stage. In this reading, "superheroes are not reflections of, but are instead (along with many other elements) co-constitutive of, the discourse popularly known as American exceptionalism."[25]

Nationalist superheroes were created during "the crucible of World War II, which began in Europe even as superheroes were rolling off their freelance assembly lines in New York City."[26] Richard Reynolds writes in *Superheroes: A Modern Mythology* that this was the key period when both Superman and Captain America were created as "solitary but socialized heroes, who battle from time to time as proxies of US foreign policy."[27] Superheroes emerged during the Second World War as codes of aristocratic honor were fraying to form a new mythic discourse that fused together patriotic duty and American exceptionalism with military power. In a perceptive article on the practice of dueling and its relation to masculine identity, Mika LaVaque-Manty writes, "One history of Western politics has it that under modernity, equal dignity has replaced positional honor as the ground on which individuals' political status rests.... In rough outline, the story is correct, but there are important complications to it. One of the most important of them is that aristocratic social practices and values themselves get used to ground and shape modernity."[28] In other words, the pastness of honor remains present, but it gets reinscribed and remade, and in the MCU it grounds a mythic retelling of a superhero who is honorable and dutiful and who, perhaps precisely because of that profound sense of internal honor, has a complex and anxious relationship with democracy.

This patriotic recasting of a traditional honor code, where it is linked to the duty to one's country and the discourse of American exceptionalism, has since become a powerful feature of American militarism and has gained mythic force in popular culture. Carl Boggs and Tom Pollard argue that "following the pattern of great imperial powers throughout history, the United States has produced a culture of militarism in which the themes of warfare, combat, and patriotism have resonated across the entire society."[29] In their work on honor and the military, Joe Thomas and Shannon French note the particular role that honor plays in the culture of the military, writing that "the concept of honor rarely takes on a pejorative connotation or produces pernicious outcomes within the military. Understanding how to embody honor and, more specifically, display consistent honorable conduct, is an explicit learning outcome set for professional military education."[30] They find that honor serves a grounding function in the sense that it is the "one thing that remains within [soldiers'] control, even in the chaos of the so-called 'fog of war'"[31] and that it "has taken up an exalted place in military culture."[32] The mythic force of patriotism and the honor and value attached to it are enmeshed. Not only is bravery on the battlefield decorated with ornamental forms of honor, such as with bronze stars and purple hearts, but the most elite officer training school in the United States, West Point Military Academy, places adherence to its code of honor at the heart of its formation of the military subject, calling it the bedrock of its character development.[33]

This mixture of honor, patriotic duty, and militarism is seen throughout the MCU and is at the forefront of all of its *Captain America* films, in particular. Boggs and Pollard call this assemblage of popular cinema, militarism, and patriotism the "Hollywood War Machine" and use this term to refer to the "production of studio films that depict and glorify the heroic exploits of US military power, either directly or indirectly."[34] In their argument, the depiction and perpetuation of this culture of militarism through mass-market films not only creates popular support for imperialist foreign policy, but it relies closely on generating intense feelings of patriotic duty in its audience such that "ultrapatriotism is one of the great mythologies embedded in American political culture."[35] These connections are then amplified in popular culture, where "militarism appears as a form of *ideology*, a rationality that deeply influences the structures and practices of general society through storytelling, mythology, media images, political messages, academic discourses, and simple patriotic indoctrination."[36] Others have termed this assemblage of militarism, honor, and popular culture "militainment" and argued that it goes beyond translating state violence into an object of pleasurable consumption.[37] The MCU plays a key role in this assemblage, and, in particular, "militarized films like *The Avengers* both play into and sustain the system of military fervor within the United States."[38] It is unsurprising, then, that a film like MCU's *Captain America: The First Avenger*, which charts the origins of Steve Rogers taking on the role of Cap amid the patriotic backdrop of World War II, received support from the U.S. Army as well as the British Ministry of Defense. They subsequently dropped their support for the Avengers movie with the introduction of S.H.I.E.L.D. but later came back on board for *Captain America: The Winter Soldier*, which depicted Steve Rogers and Sam Wilson (as The Falcon) as military veterans seeking to preserve freedom at all costs amid a shadowy conspiracy to overthrow the global world order.[39]

This assemblage of the (super)heroic agency that honor can provide, along with the centrality of patriotic duty, and the ideology of militarism all came together in the depiction of Captain America. Yann Roblou writes, "What makes Captain America such an interesting subject is contained in his superhero identity and his status as a soldier and a national icon."[40] As a supersoldier with origins in World War II and as a patriotic superhero whose very mission was to sell military bonds and gin up support for the war effort while armored in the red, white, and blue, Cap was constructed to personify the assemblage of honor, patriotic duty, and militarism and its mythic role in popular culture—a role that he has successfully played for generations.

The MCU's introduction of Captain America very much continued his depiction from the World War II era, even as it adjusted to the needs of its time. The very first MCU *Captain America* film, *The First Avenger*, which retells Steve Rogers's origin story as Cap, was released during the Obama presidency, at a moment when America was hoping to reclaim its role on the global stage and change the impression of its military power abroad after almost a decade of the War on Terror together with its dark underbelly of torture, rendition, human rights violations abroad, and restrictions of freedom at home. The president of Marvel Studios, Kevin Feige, said of the shift at the time of Obama's election while *The First Avenger* was in development, "The idea of change and hope has permeated the country, regardless of politics, and that includes Hollywood. Discussions in all our development meetings include the zeitgeist and how it's changed in the last two weeks. Things are being adjusted."[41] The movie, when it was finally released in 2011, downplayed the nationalism of its comic book source material and instead emphasized Steve Rogers's core attributes of honor, duty, and loyalty. Richard Stevens notes, "The film version of Captain America drew heavily from both the mainstream and Ultimate versions of the comic character but also added new elements.... Rather than jingoistic patriotism, the movie Cap's motivation is that he simply doesn't like bullies.... It is difficult not to see even the movie version of Captain America as representative of the American monomyth, if a gentler one."[42] While the MCU shifted to match a slightly more humbled and honorable America on the global stage (if only in its adherence to some international norms, like banning torture), it clearly represented a continuation of the Captain America mythology, even as it actively worked to adapt it to a new era.

Steve Rogers is introduced to the audience in *The First Avenger* as a scrawny kid from Brooklyn, sitting in a waiting room at a recruitment office and trying for the hundredth time to enlist in the army. He is reading a newspaper report about Nazis retaking a town, a piece of news that makes a fellow recruit think twice about enlisting. Of course, Steve is denied once again because of his slight build and his asthma and other health conditions, and he leaves the recruitment office disappointed but still determined to find a way to enlist. Not only does Steve want to honorably and dutifully fight for his country, but he wants to fill his father's shoes and carry on a family tradition of serving in the 107th Infantry. The film then cuts to a scene in a movie theater where a war propaganda film is being screened before the main feature; intoning that the "price of freedom is never too high," it firmly establishes at the outset the connections between honor, patriotism, and the military.[43] A man in the theater yells for the main attraction to start already, and Steve repeatedly asks him to stop. The film then cuts to a scene of Steve fighting the man, who we are clearly supposed to see as a bully through our modern eyes, in a back alley. Steve gets the stuffing knocked out of him but repeatedly staggers back to his feet to take yet another round of beatings, until his friend, the newly enlisted Sergeant James Buchanan "Bucky" Barnes, shows up and rescues him. In these opening scenes all the facets of Steve's identity are forged: his adherence to a traditional code of honor that forces him to duel with the obnoxious man; his strong sense of patriotic duty and faith in freedom that extends all the way to the movie theater; his adherence to the ideology of militarism, cast here as America using its power to fight a different kind of bully in Europe; and the loyalty of his friendship with Bucky. Bucky ships off to fight in the war the very next day, leaving Steve alone and friendless in Brooklyn, trying one more time to enlist.

He finally succeeds when he encounters the esteemed Jewish scientist Abraham Erskine, who fled the Nazis and the Teutonic-myth- and occult-loving HYDRA led by Johann Schmidt (later known as Red Skull) with a super serum that he invented. Erskine seems impressed by Rogers's honorable and dutiful character and his persistence and dedication to his country. He ignores the boy's obvious physical limitations and approves him for training. Of course, Rogers excels at training because of his courage and strong sense of moral purpose—he is terrible at climbing ropes and running drills, but he is the only one to jump on what seems to be a live grenade when it is thrown into the midst of the pack of trainees to test their bravery. The training officer, Colonel Chester Philips, clearly articulates the monomyth of the superhero as savior, saying, "[O]ur goal is to create the best army in history. But every army starts with one man. And this week we will choose that man. He will be the first in a new breed of super soldiers. That man will personally escort Adolf Hitler to the gates of hell." When Erskine chooses the 90-pound asthmatic Steve to be that supersoldier it is not just the military brass who have doubts. The night before he is to be injected with the serum that will transform his body, Steve himself asks Erskine why he was chosen. Erskine tells him that "a weak man knows the value of strength and knows compassion" and that the serum amplifies a person's best and worst qualities and that is why Steve was chosen: "[Y]ou must promise me you will stay who you are—not a perfect soldier, but a good man." Captain America's mythic origins are therefore firmly established in *The First Avenger*, not as an ultranationalist who cares most about fighting Nazis but as a man of honorable character and patriotic duty for whom the price of freedom is never too high.

The film then follows Steve as he dutifully takes on the role of Cap. One particularly striking montage is a veritable smorgasbord of World War II propaganda that shows him reading speeches with a troupe of female dancers to sell military bonds; shooting ads in which he proclaims that each bond bought "is a bullet in the barrel of your best guy's gun"; and a sold-out national tour, complete with fake punching Nazis on stage and a spirited musical rendition of "The Star-Spangled Man." The contemporary MCU audience is obviously supposed to see this as empty symbolism and to agree with Peggy Carter, one of the founders of S.H.I.E.L.D. and Cap's love interest, when they meet again on the muddy battlefields of Italy and she tells him that he was meant for more than these ridiculous performances. Cap finally gets to leave behind the USO stage and his dancing shoes when he hears that the 107th Infantry, including his best friend, Bucky, have been captured behind enemy lines. Disobeying the commander's orders not to attempt a rescue mission, Cap swings into full superhero mode, a swirling blur of red, white, and blue, destroying HYDRA's base and defeating its leaders and rescuing the unit and his friend. The MCU underlines that his internal code of honor, grounded in his patriotic duty to his country and deep loyalty to his friend, is paramount and even more valuable than his superheroic identity as it pulls back to show him dressed in military fatigues, not his star-spangled costume, leading the 107th Infantry back to base, with Bucky marching next to him. To emphasize his commitment to military hierarchy and his desire to first and foremost be a soldier, the first words out of Cap's mouth are "I'd like to surrender myself for disciplinary action" for disobeying orders.

His attachment to his honor is again emphasized in a later scene when Cap is absent from a ceremony where a senator wants to present him with a medal for valor—clearly Cap cares more about his internal code of honor, his character, his patriotic duty, and his loyalty to his friend than empty decorations and emblems. He rejects the ornamental honors of political life for the mythology of the American superhero who selflessly puts his mission above all else. The film concludes with Cap fully integrating his superheroic capacity, his sense of honor, his patriotic duty, and his militarism as he goes on one successful mission after the next, until, on a final tragic mission, he seems to lose Bucky forever when his friend tumbles off a train in the Alps and plummets thousands of feet below into the snowy depths. Cap too ends up in a frozen interregnum when his plane crashes into the Arctic ice. The film ends with him waking up in a recovery room in New York City. He panics and runs into Times Square, a man out of time and place, after Nick Fury from S.H.I.E.L.D. tells him he's been asleep for almost 70 years.

Nostalgia and Democratic Anxiety in *The Winter Soldier* and *Civil War*

While *The First Avenger* introduced Captain America to the MCU in a reframed version of the original comic book, it still hewed to the main outlines of his World War II origins, while toning down his most jingoistic and Nazi-fighting elements to instead emphasize Steve Rogers's main attributes as a man of honor, duty, and loyalty. Anthony and Joe Russo, who directed the second and third *Captain America* films for the MCU, announced that their version would shift Captain America even further from his comic book origins: "To be honest with you, that golden age Captain America never really appealed to us. . . . [W]e were like, 'This is going to be the movie where we fully bring Captain America into the modern world. He's going to be a different person in this new world.'"[44] *The Winter Soldier* operates in a different time, 70 years forward into a new present, when the simple binaries of good and evil in World War II have shifted to a cloudy and uncertain future and a present marked by shifting loyalties. The temporal setting of the second film is a time when democracy is under threat at home and from shadowy global forces. This film cleverly intertwines themes from both the Nixon Watergate scandal and the War on Terror to put Cap in a contested democratic space. In doing so, it moves the audience beyond "both a Golden Age comic book hero and the golden age of American foreign intervention in terms of how both can be mobilized to generate consent for political or military action. These films go a step further and examine the ways in which nostalgia can be used subversively."[45] In this film, Cap is a man out of time, operating in a shadowy world where he can trust no one, where even the highest levels of American government and global order have been infiltrated by HYDRA, where the enemy has shifted from killing Americans on the battlefield to gunning them down as they go about their everyday lives because an algorithm has determined they might pose a threat in the future. The threat is at once nowhere and everywhere, and Cap is surrounded on all sides by constant reminders that his new present is a bankrupt one marked by the erosion of norms of honor and duty. The film repeatedly underlines how this fractured and fallen present is nostalgic for its honorable and heroic past and posits Cap as the one man who can redeem it. After all, who better represents that past than the star-spangled superhero who has emerged out of the ice perfectly preserved and with his core values intact, a mythic hero who is ready to be reshaped once again for a post-9/11 reality in order to redeem American democracy?

It is important to explore in greater depth both the consistent theme of nostalgia in *The Winter Soldier* (which focuses on both individual and collective memory) and what it says about democratic anxiety in the contemporary era. Norman Austin writes in an excellent article on Homeric nostalgia, "Nostalgia is not an ancient word. Webster's dictionary informs us that it was coined in 1688 by a certain Swiss scholar, J. Hofer, to translate the German *heimweh*, 'homesickness.' The word is built from two Greek words, *nostos* (homecoming) and *alga* (pain). But if the word is modern, the idea is as ancient as poetry itself" (italics mine).[46] As such nostalgia represents a kind of aching and longing for a distant and now seemingly lost past, when the lines between enemy and country were more clearly drawn, when the government was not seen as fundamentally corrupt, when society at large was honorable and dutiful. In other words, nostalgia represents a turning away from the thorny problems of the present and an unwillingness to engage with the messiness of democratic politics and instead to muddle through its thickets and do the hard work of forging new offshoots of possibility. It is essential to note that the nostalgic longing for home is often for an illusion, such as the fantasy of 1950s white picket fence America, which easily obscures the systemic racism, widespread sexism, and rampant consumerism that also characterized that era. Even at the height of the Cold War, though, it was a time of optimistic possibility. So it is understandable that in times of democratic erosion and increasing anxiety and frustration about contemporary policy, one's gaze shifts wistfully toward a past that one wants to tug into the present. As Austin writes, "At its simplest, nostalgia is homesickness (the desire to return home), but usage over time has expanded its semantic field to mean any kind of longing for the past.... But survival too has its cost, which is the loss of the past, Proust's *temps perdu*" (italics mine).[47] *The Winter Soldier* is rife with nostalgia for Steve Rogers and his *temps perdu*, or decades of lost time; he finds himself unmoored and uncertain in his out-of-joint present, where everything has changed around him. The film traces the contours of layers of pastness—Cap's own past, America's collective past, HYDRA's violent past—which come together in a pastiche of nostalgic longing that leans heavily on the honor of the superhero to ground itself in the present and paper over the tragic complexity of political life in the 21st century.

Nowhere is this nostalgia clearer than in the Smithsonian exhibit that Steve Rogers wanders into as he tries to find his bearings in this uncertain present at the start of the film. A repository of collective memory and a clear attempt to articulate the official monomythic version of Captain America for a new generation, the exhibit pulls together pictures and artifacts from Steve Rogers's life. He is at once in the exhibit and outside it, othered from the nostalgic pull of the past by the intervening 70 years and the loss of connection that now separates him from his World War II days, but still feeling a duty to carry the mantle forward in the new order for the American government. The narrator in the exhibit describes him: "A symbol to the nation. A hero to the world. The Story of Captain American is one of honor, bravery, and sacrifice."[48] Steve sees pictures of himself and his best friend, Bucky, and the love of his life, Peggy Carter. All of the strands come together here for Steve: the fragmentation of his memory, a deep sense of loss, an overwhelming sense of a past that is at once present but vanishing. Trying to maintain the attachment to his own identity by connecting with the one person who at least partially remembers his past self, he visits a dying Peggy in the hospital, who is suffering from memory loss herself. "For as long as I can remember," he tells her, "I just wanted to do what was right. Guess I'm not quite sure what that is anymore. I guess I thought I could just throw myself back in, follow orders, serve. It's just not the same." Operating amid this temporal dislocation, Steve finds it hard to ground himself and spends much of the film searching for an internal code of honor that can ground him, because serving orders is no longer enough, particularly when the politicians who give them are corrupt. Austin, in writing about Virgil's *Aeneid*, describes this struggle succinctly. Just as Aeneas comes across a statue of himself in a foreign land, Steve Rogers finds himself enshrined in American collective memory in the Smithsonian in ways that are insufficient and even discomfiting. Austin writes of Aeneas, "How strange to find himself preceding himself, himself already an icon but in an alien land.... Our dictionaries define nostalgia as a bittersweet feeling, and certainly that is the feeling here."[49] Like Aeneas, Cap too precedes himself as an icon in a land that is increasingly alien to him.

Clearly the world has changed, and Cap must adjust, struggling in a present where political leadership and global institutions are compromised and the restraints of norms, rules, and codes are eroded. The underlying message as the film unfolds, first directly from Nick Fury, and later as S.H.I.E.L.D. is compromised, from all angles, is to "trust no one." Cap himself becomes a fugitive from S.H.I.E.L.D. and is on the run for much of the film as HYDRA reemerges from its World War II casing, showing that they have been there all along in the shadows, embedded in and thriving at the highest levels of government and have created so much chaos that "humanity will sacrifice freedom for security." Captain America is once again cast as the defender of freedom in this new post-9/11 era. The undertones of the War on Terror and the Patriot Act that was pushed through Congress in the immediate aftermath of the 9/11 attack (and that sacrificed individual rights for homeland security and ushered in an era of warrantless wiretapping and privacy violations) are made evident to the audience. The theme of democratic erosion is further underlined by the cinematic echoes of Watergate and the Nixon era. The corrupt senator in the film is played by Robert Redford in a callback to his role as journalist Bob Woodward in Alan Pakula's film *All the President's Men*, and when Cap is attacked in a glass elevator by security forces, the Watergate building itself is framed in the background. Cap survives the attack after crashing to the ground, his star-spangled shield breaking his fall, in a symbolic reminder that he must reorder and restore this fallen America with the soothing blanket of nostalgia. But Cap himself finds that he needs to be reoriented to become the symbol of honor, bravery, and duty once again.

This nostalgic longing and the need for a redemptive Captain America to help overcome democratic anxiety is at once disorienting and generative in the kind of politics it can shape. As Lilly Goren observes:

> The contemporary Marvel Cinematic universe establishes an internal nostalgic narrative, integrating presentations of an American past, from World War II or the early Cold War period or the post–Cold War period, and threading those images and ideas into many of the films. . . . Captain America's successes during WWII or Captain Marvel's heroism in post–Cold War America present a dimension of our thinking about how we see our political and social environments in previous periods, as well as projecting a concept of how we may see ourselves today. . . . This layered nostalgia is directly connected to a form or kind of American nationalism, and that the nostalgia and nationalism are braided together, which we also see in our contemporary politics.[50]

This is precisely the adaptation of the mythological imaginary of Captain America that is at the forefront of *The Winter Soldier*—the collective nostalgia for him and his nostalgia for his own past are both used to reforge his code of honor and nationalist identity in a way that makes sense in contemporary politics. As such, it is unsurprising that Cap rediscovers his mission once the patriotic duty to fight for freedom becomes clear after HYDRA's reemergence from the shadows, and even more so when Bucky Barnes as the Winter Soldier comes back as a supersoldier whose identity and memory have repeatedly been erased and who has been turned into a ruthless killing machine by HYDRA. When Bucky doesn't recognize him, Cap is disoriented yet again but is also reminded of his own status as an outsider in his youth who had one true friend who was always loyal to him. He tells Natasha Romanoff (Black Widow), "[E]ven when I had nothing, I had Bucky." Cap needs to find Bucky and save him, to rescue both his friend and himself, to restore his own fraying code of honor and duty in this uncertain present. The rest of the film and its sequel, the Avengers-heavy *Civil War*, trace this journey of return and redemption for him. With his new lieutenant, Sam Wilson (The Falcon), the veteran air force special ops pararescue airman, by his side, Cap sets out on his new mission and tries to reorient his world and make sense of the strands of the past that have tumbled into his present.

In a key flashback scene in *The Winter Soldier*, a dashing young Bucky tells a lonely Steve after they have returned from Steve's mother's funeral, "I'm with you until the end of the line," and offers him a place to stay along with his enduring support. This message is underlined in the closing scenes of the film as Cap now finds his footing in this new present by reclaiming his code of honor marked by the duty to preserve freedom and his undying loyalty to his friend, no matter how muddled or compromised the world has become, no matter if his friend's brain has been reprogrammed and weaponized by an evil organization bent on world domination through mass murder. In a speech to the few remaining S.H.I.E.L.D. officers near the climax of the film, clarity has returned to Cap and his code of honor is renewed and reforged as he intones over the loudspeaker in an echo of the first film, "[The] price of freedom is high. Always has been. But it's a price I'm willing to pay. If I'm the only one, then so be it. But I'm willing to bet I'm not." The past is remade once more in the present in a final confrontation he has with the still murderous Bucky. Bucky remembers Steve in fugitive flashes of memory, but that memory is distorted and fractured after continually being wiped by HYDRA. Steve, however, refuses to kill him and repeatedly reminds him that he is his friend. The Winter Soldier responds, "You're my mission" to which Cap says, in yet another echo that reorients him in the present, "Then finish it. Because I'm with you till the end of the line." The film ends with Cap falling into the water and drowning but with his code of honor intact. The gamble he takes on his adherence to that code of honor—his faith in freedom and his loyalty to his best friend—finally pays off. Bucky drags him out of the water and saves his life and stumbles away into an uncertain future. The post-credits scene shows Bucky at the Smithsonian exhibit looking at his own poster enshrined in collective memory and trying to find his own fragmented memory within it.

At the end of *The Winter Soldier*, Cap finds his grounding in his code of honor, but in the next film, *Civil War*, it becomes increasingly clear that adherence to that code is an uneasy fit with democracy and the checks and balances of institutional restraint. If anything, Captain America's struggles cast light on the conceptual relationship between honor and democracy, as his uneasiness with democratic processes mirrors some of the ways in which honor itself remains an uneasy fit within it. Laurie Johnson writes, "There is some confusion surrounding the definition of honor because it has internal and external expressions. In its internal expression, honor has to do with self-image, and can be distinguished from modern morality, virtue, and ethics, which have more to do with self-interest. Honor is about self-image because it literally has to do with how I view myself, in fact, with who I am. If an honor code is internalized by members of a group, the external expression comes forth, and we can speak of an honor code, and honoring and shaming."[51] Cap's code of honor is deeply internal and individual, in keeping with the liberal tradition, even as it leads him in illiberal directions in the name of freedom. As he gathers superheroes around him in *Civil War*, Cap shows how a strong attachment to personal honor, which he understands to be personal loyalty to his friends, can lead to antidemocratic actions and vigilantism. His internal view of honor as linked to his image of himself brings him into conflict with international institutions and democratic processes.

Civil War pits Steve Rogers's Captain America against Tony Stark's Iron Man and splits the superhero team into two as they clash over whether or not to submit to international regulation. Christopher Galdieri notes that "MCU films routinely wrestle with difficult questions about how mortal governments and militaries can exercise oversight of superbeings.... No character engages with these debates more than Captain America.... Across these films, Cap presents a sustained consideration of what might restrain and control individuals with superhuman abilities. Somewhat remarkably, that consideration puts Captain America directly at odds with some of the best-known theoretical underpinnings of the American form of government, most notably articulated by James Madison in key sections of *The Federalist Papers*."[52] For Galdieri, Captain America's insistence on going his own way and holding fast to his honor and his sense of what is right run counter to the Madisonian argument that institutional restraints can keep "government from exercising its power in ways that endanger Americans' liberties, even when individuals with less than pure motives hold office. The cinematic Captain America, by contrast, is wary of institutions precisely because they may be populated by people with hidden or sinister motives, and instead argues that the only way to ensure power will not be abused is to ensure those who wield it are of good character."[53] This is a running thread through *Civil War*: only those with internal honor and good character are fit to exercise power, which can exist in tension with the deliberative processes and the norms of international regimes. Captain America refuses to be regulated by an international governing body and is steadfast in his internal code honor, which pits him against the wishes of his own government. It puts him directly at odds with the norms of global democracy, which argue that the proper way to resist vigilantism by superheroes is for all of the Avengers to sign the Sokovia Accords and submit to oversight. As Galdieri writes, "Captain America argues, in deed and occasional word, that external controls and regulations on super-powered individuals are doomed to be ineffective at best and destructive at worst. Instead, Captain America argues that the only check on those who wield extraordinary abilities with any chance of being effective is the character of those individuals themselves."[54]

The message is clear in *Civil War*: Cap will fight to preserve freedom and stay loyal to his falsely accused and long-suffering friend Bucky, no matter the cost, even if it puts him on the other side of the law and turns him into a criminal. His resolve is fixed at Peggy Carter's funeral, where her niece Sharon delivers the eulogy, quoting her aunt: "[C]ompromise when you can, but if you can't, don't, even if everyone is telling you something wrong is something right, it's your duty to plant yourself like a tree and tell them, 'Your move.'"[55] Cap is fully restored in his internal code of honor and his sense of duty and loyalty, and he is unflinching in his course, even when it results in his fighting his own team and, in the climax of the film, taking on Iron Man in a pitched duel that results in his famous shield bending and breaking. His loyalty to Bucky and desire to protect him from wrongful prosecution puts him on the other side of the law and on the other side of global governance. But Cap reasserts his mythic status at the conclusion as the outsider always there to save others and redeem them not just from the mistakes of the past but from the errors of the future. He says he has never had family, that he didn't even fit in with the army, and that his "faith is in the people." This last point speaks powerfully to his ambivalent and conflicted relationship to democracy. On the one hand, Captain America puts his faith in the people, the *demos* itself, and this is a constant in his life, even as he feels like an outsider everywhere else. He might occupy a temporal space that is out of joint and have a serum running through his veins that differentiates him from most, but he believes in the people themselves. On the other hand, the institutions and practices of democracy, its deliberative processes and its corrupt practitioners, are easily discarded when they conflict with his internal sense of honor and duty.

This disjuncture between a patriotic and nationalist superhero and his ambivalence and anxiety about democracy can be attributed to Steve Rogers's deep attachment to his internal code of honor, which sheds light on the conceptual relationship between the two concepts themselves. Honor and democracy *are* an uneasy fit. At first glance, a concept like honor, which is often linked to chivalric tradition and aristocracy, might seem antithetical to democracy. On the other hand, it can generate a set of virtues like courage and loyalty that are compatible with democracy's highest ideals. Much of the literature on the relationship between democracy and honor tends to break down into opposite positions, between those who argue that honor is obsolete in contemporary democratic times, and those who wish to refashion it and make a case for its enduring importance to liberalism and democracy. But there is a more complex relationship to explore here than mere opposition or compatibility when one looks closely at the aesthetics of democracy and pays attention to the importance of grandeur in it.

In his writing on honor and contemporary politics, Carey McWilliams outlines the oft-noted disjuncture between the two concepts: "Honor is associated with rank and inequality, so that it is somewhat paradoxical to speak of democratic honor at all. A democracy can aspire to 'an aristocracy of everyone' in the sense of making excellent things available to all its citizens. But inevitably, increasing the number of those honored decreases the value and significance of honor."[56] Clearly an aristocratic virtue often associated with nobility and tradition is less than compatible with the equality at the heart of democracy. McWilliams notes that "democratic practice especially... works to erode and undermine honor. In one sense, honor is a code or standard by reference to which we can be said to deserve respect or acclaim. In principle, such a rule asks us to uphold, for the edification of others, something truly fine or admirable.... So understood, honor is largely indifferent to opinion. However, the term honor also refers to esteem, a measure that is resolutely social and subjective, and to that extent, concerned not with what is, but with what is seen."[57] In this understanding, honor is at once both dependent on and vulnerable to public recognition, as discussed elsewhere in this book. The visibility of honor, often seen in contemporary times in the heroic individual (or in this case, the superheroic figure) with an abiding internal sense of honor, can still fit into democratic politics. McWilliams quotes Tocqueville to outline this desire for recognition: "In democratic politics, Tocqueville wrote, the public is 'the natural and supreme arbiter of the laws of honor.'"[58] Of course, the problem, as the *Captain America* films clearly underline, is that democratic honor in this sense becomes deinstitutionalized and "the self secedes, and institutions—laws, parties, churches, families, even language—cease to be the 'home' of the self and instead become oppressive realities"; then, once they are "separated from institutions and forms and authorities, honor and dignity are exposed to the temptations and dangers that are inherent when human beings are judges in their own cases."[59] This is precisely the danger outlined in *Civil War*, where the blinding attachment to internal honor separates Steve Rogers from institutional authority and oversight altogether and exposes his lingering anxiety and unease about democracy itself.

It may be that this is an irreconcilable tension between honor and democracy, where the adherence to the former always risks undermining the latter. Indeed, this book has emphasized throughout the political dangers of holding too tightly to a concept of honor and how it is at once binding and blinding to its most loyal adherents. But it has also demonstrated how it endures in the contemporary political imaginary in significant ways. So what is it about honor that persists in democracy today, despite the anxiety and unease it engenders? The answer lies not in the institutions and electoral practices of democracy but in its aesthetics. In his brilliant work on the democratic sublime, Jason Frank fills in this hole in the democratic theory literature by turning his attention to "the enchantments of democracy, the sustaining fictions that enable it and give it life, as well as the collective phenomena that point beyond those fictions while never fully dispelling their allure."[60] Frank seeks instead to explore the idea that "entirely new forms of political enchantment are required by democratic politics. Democracy places new pressures on the collective imagination, unprecedented environments of collective fantasy."[61]

The *Captain America* films in the MCU proffer their own source of collective fantasy, and perhaps even enchantment, in the generative mythology they create and propagate. The popular imaginary of the superhero as a central part of the American imagined community is fascinating in this regard. There is obvious tension in the idea of Captain America, one person symbolizing a people, or a *demos*, but such evocation is necessary for the notion of democracy itself, because, as Frank asserts, "imaginary investments of peoplehood mediate the people's relationship to their own political empowerment. . . . [F]ar from being a barren site of disenchantment and demystification, democracy engenders new fantasies of collective belonging and transformative agency. Democratic citizenship is inseparable from this unending elicitation of the popular imagination."[62] Read in this context, Steve Rogers as Captain America is a significant figure in the aesthetics of democracy as someone who sits uneasily in it, who acts in undemocratic ways, but who nevertheless remains important to its enchantment and mystification.

Even his internal code of honor can be seen as part of this imagining, much as the notion of grandeur was characterized by Tocqueville as central to democracy itself. Frank writes that "without a sense of elevated grandeur, Tocqueville argued, political life would be overwhelmed by social interest, individuals would be drawn into the increasingly narrow purview of their material needs, and people ... would become a mere population."[63] In his analysis of democracy in America, Tocqueville parted ways with liberals of his time in his emphasis on heroic action and grandeur as necessary, and not simply as chivalrous relics of a bygone age. Tocqueville's "affirmation of political grandeur is linked to his understanding of political freedom and to the threats posed to freedom in the democratic age," and, in Frank's terms, grandeur has been "too quickly dismissed by some admiring liberal readers as unfortunate inconsistencies or anachronistic commitments to the values of a lost aristocratic age."[64] Grandeur, honor, heroism, and myth are therefore seen as essential to democracy. Ignoring the aesthetics of democracy and the powerful role that speculative fiction, fantasy, and myth play in shaping the collective imagination, and instead relying only on desiccated notions of utility and reason, lead to a partial and myopic understanding of contemporary politics. Indeed, "one of the central ironies animating Tocqueville's social and political thought was that the very age that promised to finally empower the people as makers of their own history, and to bring the vicissitudes of social life under democratic control, ultimately engendered pervasive anxiety about the weakness, isolation, and political incapacity of human beings."[65] Seen in this light, as unlikely and fantastical as it might seem, the star-spangled superhero with his righteous sense of honor and patriotic duty is a necessary ingredient in the democratic imaginary at a time of increasing democratic anxiety and erosion, as the people feel increasingly powerless to effect change amid the challenges of economic decline, global health disparities, and rising inequality.

"Honor"ing the Past in the Present: *The Falcon and the Winter Soldier*

Steve Rogers as Captain America comes to the end of his character arc in *Avengers: Endgame*. What is most important in terms of the analysis of honor and nostalgia and democracy is the ending of this film. Steve Rogers as Captain America departs the stage in epic form, fighting Thanos alongside the superteam of the Avengers, with Bucky and Sam by his side, wielding not only his remade shield but Thor's legendary hammer. He leaves the MCU swathed in a soothing blanket of nostalgia when he gets to travel back in time to finally make good on his promise to dance with Peggy Carter and live a full life with her. He hands his shield to Sam and departs the stage, but we are not done with Captain America just yet. The myths of democracy always need to be made and remade, however uneasily, and sometimes the silences exposed by their adaptation can be heard loudly in a new era that is perhaps more willing to listen to them. Steve Rogers as Captain America underlined the ambivalent relationship between honor and democracy, toggling between an idealistic faith in the *demos* to always do the right thing and anxiety about democratic leaders, processes, and institutions. By contrast, the new Disney Plus television series *The Falcon and the Winter Soldier*, holds up the nostalgic and mythic imaginary of Steve Rogers's Captain America to critical scrutiny and finds it lacking in its smooth and homogeneous rendering of America's past. By calling attention to past and present silences on race and equality, this recent MCU installment complicates the democratic imaginary of the MCU, even as it reinscribes some of its core tenets.

The Falcon and the Winter Soldier picks up in the aftermath of *Avengers: Endgame* with Steve Rogers gone and Sam Wilson's Falcon reluctant to fill the void and assume the responsibility for the shield he has inherited from his old friend. The first episode opens with Sam looking at the iconic shield and a voice-over of Steve that brings the past once again into the present. Steve asks, "How's it feel?," to which Sam responds, "Like it's someone else's," to which Steve insists, "It isn't."[66] In these first few minutes, the miniseries adds a different layer to the soothing nostalgia that Steve Rogers's character often provided and sometimes displaced. For Sam, the *nostos*, or the home, of the shield is somewhat alien and at a distance, and the *algia*, or longing, that many feel for that home is much more complex and fraught for him. This is underlined later in the episode, at the official ceremony at the Smithsonian to honor Steve Rogers's legacy when he says, "Steve represented the best of us." Sam gives up the shield and the role of Captain America and later makes his way to the Smithsonian exhibit, the shrine of collective memory to Captain America's contributions, with one of his fellow Avengers, War Machine, who asks why he won't accept the shield. The scene is framed in a deeply compelling way: the two Black Avengers stand in front of a wall of militaristic nostalgia that displays all of the Captain America World War II posters, the USO shows, and the war bonds, with Steve Rogers's visage looming everywhere. The two Black men in the foreground are in shadow, whereas the wall of honor is brightly lit up and gleaming white. War Machine tries one more time to change Falcon's mind, arguing that the need for Captain America endures in a world that is less stable and more dangerous after the "blip." He says, "The world's broken: everybody's just looking for somebody to fix it." Sam stops in front of the shield, which lights up his face for a minute, but his expression remains enigmatic and the audience is left to ponder what seems to be both his attachment to and alienation from the iconic object.

The significance of Sam Wilson's agonistic relationship to the role of Captain America is perhaps best captured by the novelist Zadie Smith in her reflections on historic nostalgia in the fall of 2022 in the leadup to the U.S. presidential election. In an interview on NPR's *Fresh Air*, Smith said:

> I would say we're in a process of radical—a radical desire for time travel, which is something different. You know, there was a survey really fascinating to me done of Republican voters in this last election. But at times, 7 out of 10 of them report wishing America could go back to how it was in the 1950s. This is a very interesting point for me because that kind of historical nostalgia is only available to a certain kind of person.... I can't go back to the '50s, because life in the '50s for me is not pretty, nor is it pretty in 1320 or 1460 or 1580 or 1820 or even 1960 in this country, very frankly. So that's what interests me—the historical nostalgia that is available or not available to others.[67]

In her comments on time-travel, or a nostalgic desire some voters express to return to the 1950s, Smith makes clear that such nostalgia is not equally available to all and that the silences of American democracy, particularly with respect to race, make the prospect of such a return or "homecoming" one of alienation and displacement. Sam Wilson is a superhero, as the ass-kicking Falcon as the first episode shows us, someone who Steve thought of as honorable and as a worthy successor. But Sam is still a Black man in America, who still faces structural racism in his everyday life. The nationalist and patriotic collective memory of Captain America that is displayed in the Smithsonian is not only partial in its glossing over of Steve Rogers's illiberal tendencies and rejection of institutional restraint; it also whitewashes America's racial past in a way that makes his era feel far from home for Sam Wilson. Lilly Goren argues that "nostalgia is particularly key in considering the successful integration of the politics of anxiety. And it may be even more important to consider the nostalgic impulses that surround us in our cultural milieu, since it is possible that the toggling between the actual historical events and the narrative recreation of those events contribute to a cleaned version of both the events of the past that may contribute to this nostalgic longing while also creating the heroic narrative that is overtly embedded within these historical events that press on long-standing cultural understandings of the nation itself."[68]

The Falcon and the Winter Soldier "toggl[es]" back and forth between the reality of life in America as a Black man, even a Black superhero, while trying to come to terms with the country's nostalgic longing for Steve Rogers's Captain America. Indeed, the whiteness of the mythology is front and center when the shield is quickly passed to John Walker, a highly decorated army ranger, who has the requisite blond hair and blue eyes but who, it is quickly evident, lacks Steve's (and Sam's) abiding sense of honor. As Goren notes, "The images and narratives that work into our collective understanding of 'the past' construct an understanding of that past, and build on nostalgic longing in such a way that we should interrogate those narratives and images ... to understand if there are embedded connections that may lead more fully to the way that the past is recollected and how that impacts the nationalistic understandings of self and nation."[69] The series compels its audience to confront the whiteness at the core of the nostalgic longing for Captain America and at the very least grapple with its silences and erasures.

It does so in multiple ways, first by demonstrating the marginalization and micro-aggressions that even Sam Wilson encounters in everyday life in contemporary America, and then by its focus on the brutal silencing of Isaiah Bradley, a Black supersoldier who was lost to history and erased from the collective memory of the nation. The reality of racial prejudice and antiblackness is made clear in the next episode, when Sam returns to Louisiana and sees his family boat in disrepair and his sister unable to secure funding to restore it and her livelihood. With his superhero status and faith in his country and its institutions, Sam thinks he can solve her problems. But the scene that follows lays out all of the daily humiliations of blackness in America. The White loan officer wants a selfie with The Falcon but denies him and his sister the loan. Not even half an episode away from an epic aerial action scene that shows him fighting brilliantly for his country and its military, he is shut out by it. The "color-line," as W. E. B. Du Bois called it, may not be as starkly marked as in the Jim Crow era, but Sam clearly still feels its effects. As Du Bois put it brilliantly, "It is a peculiar sensation, this double consciousness.... [O]ne ever feels his two-ness."[70] Sam is marked and shaped by this double consciousness, and it makes the requisite mythic attachment to the promises of American democracy that the Captain America role requires that much more difficult for him.

However, it is not until Bucky Barnes (the newly deprogrammed Winter Soldier, who is the other half of this "buddy" series) introduces him to the former Black American supersoldier, Isaiah Bradley, that Sam fully confronts the violence and brutality behind the official Captain America myth. It is a moment not just of democratic anxiety but of the erasure of a troubling racist past that persists in the present, and of a nation that demanded silence about its sins in order to maintain its heroic sense of itself. Bradley was one of an elite group that was injected with super serum during the Korean War, a Black man whose body was experimented on by the American government in much the same way as the Tuskegee experiment, then brutally discarded and left out of the nation's mythology when he dared to stand up for his own humanity and that of his comrades. Bradley tells Sam bitterly, "Do you know what they did to me for being a hero? They put my ass in jail for thirty years. People were running tests, taking my blood, coming into my cell. Even your people weren't done with me."[71] Sam is shocked by these revelations and asks Bucky, "How could nobody bring him up?" Once he finds out that not even Steve Rogers knew about Bradley, he yells, "You're telling me there was a Black supersoldier for decades and nobody knew about him?"

As soon as Sam and Bucky leave Bradley's house in inner-city Baltimore, the presence of America's racial past is felt clearly as a cop car pulls up, once again underscoring how complex homecoming (*nostos*) is for Sam. Indicating he means Sam, the police officer asks Bucky, "Is this guy bothering you?," to which Bucky responds, "No he's not bothering me. Do you know who he is?" Immediately the cop replies, "Sorry Mr. Wilson ... didn't recognize you without the costume." In that moment of humiliation and recognition lies the ugliness of American democracy and its failures to live up to its grandest ideals, even in the mythic stories it tells about itself. James Baldwin evocatively writes about this profound alienation and the collective culpability of America in *The Fire Next Time*, "I know what this world has done to my brother and how narrowly he has survived it. And I know, which is much worse, and this is the crime of which I accuse my country and my countrymen ... that they have destroyed and are destroying hundreds of thousands of lives and do not know it and do not want to know it."[72]

These are the crimes that Sam Wilson must now grapple with and come to terms with if he is to remake the myth of Captain America for a new era, one where such silences cannot be left unheard. As Baldwin advised his nephew, "One can be, indeed one must strive to become, tough and philosophical concerning destruction and death, for that is what most of mankind has been best at since we have heard of man.... But it is not permissible that the authors of devastation should also be innocent. It is the innocence which constitutes the crime."[73]

The subsequent episodes follow Sam and Bucky through a series of twists and turns and conflicts with the nonstate actor group the Flag-Smashers, who engage in violent acts of terrorism in the name of equality and recognition for the stateless. Its leader tells Sam that the Captain America shield "is a monument to a bygone era" and should be destroyed.[74] When John Walker is disgraced and Sam Wilson finally picks up the shield (though he is still uncertain whether he wants to wield it), his first stop when he returns to America is Isaiah Bradley's Baltimore home. Sam asks Isaiah to help him understand, and which Isaiah replies, "You understand. Every Black man does. Whether you want to deny it or not.... You want to believe jail was my fault, because you got that White man's shield. They were worried my story might get out. So, they erased me. My history. But they have been doing that for five hundred years. Pledge allegiance to that, my brother." Thus Isaiah directly ties his erasure to the silences of America's racism. Isaiah's diagnosis echoes Baldwin in that moment, who poignantly wrote, "You were born where you were born and faced the future that you faced because you were black and *for no other reason*.... You were born into a society which spelled out with brutal clarity, and in as many ways as possible, that you were a worthless human being. You were not expected to aspire to excellence: you were expected to make peace with mediocrity."[75] Isaiah makes Baldwin's point explicit when he says, "They will never let a Black man be Captain America. Even if they did, no self-respecting Black man would ever want to be."[76] Sam is left grappling with these truths; he too needs the balm of nostalgia in that painful moment. He leaves Isaiah's house once more, this time with the shield, and calling his sister, tells her, "I'm coming home."

In her book on nostalgia, Svetlana Boym describes it as "a sentiment of loss and displacement, but it is also a romance with one's own fantasy."[77] The final two episodes of *The Falcon and the Winter Soldier* are an attempt to reforge the Captain America fantasy for Sam Wilson in ways that are not altogether satisfying. The storytelling in the final installment seeks to redeem American democracy and atone for its sins in ways that are partial and, for some, set the ambitions for its democratic reimagining too low.[78] Sam returns home to Louisiana, where the whole community pulls together and helps him repair his family's boat (along with a bionic assist from Bucky Barnes), and the now familiar mythic story of honor, duty, and patriotism is remade and tries to smooth over the ruptures the series has exposed about American democracy and the stories it tells and retells itself. The enduring need for a hero is once again front and center as the show works to create the iconography of the first Black Captain America by acknowledging the sins of the country's past and offering a redemption narrative in ways that are compelling yet also anodyne. Sam explicitly points to this ambivalence when he acknowledges that Isaiah has been to "hell and back" but then asks, "What would be the point of all the pain and sacrifice" if he didn't stand up and fight now?[79] An inspirational training montage follows, in which Sam finally picks up the iconic shield in his backyard and begins to wield it. In the final episode Sam tells Isaiah that they all bled for this country and adds, "I'm not going to let anyone tell me I can't fight for it."[80]

The Captain America myth is remade in this series by its acknowledgment of the silences of history, and indeed, acknowledging and redeeming those exclusions becomes an explicit reason for it to endure. It is no surprise, then, that the show returns once again to the Smithsonian and the official repository of America's collective memory of Captain America. Sam takes Isaiah and his grandson to the new exhibit that honors Isaiah and features his statue in brass, with a plaque of recognition and photos of his mission. Sam says, "Now they will never forget what you did for this country. Never."[81] He compels the country and the audience to acknowledge the presence of the past and to work together to overcome it, and in constructing himself as a superheroic representation of a new America, he paints an optimistic picture of its ability to overcome its democratic anxieties and erasures.

Honor and Collective Memory in the Political Imagination

The MCU's retelling of the Captain America story in *The Falcon and the Winter Soldier* provides a feel-good ending to an otherwise complicated story of racial exclusion and alienation, which is compelling yet insufficient in ways that echo the previous iterations of its democratic imaginary.

Boym notes that "modern nostalgia is a mourning for the impossibility of mythical return, for the loss of an enchanted world with clear borders and values."[82] *The Falcon and the Winter Soldier* continues to sustain this longing for enchantment and grandeur, even as it reshapes the mythology of Captain America for contemporary times. Boym writes that nostalgia often takes two forms, one that is restorative in its evocation of the past and future of a nation, and one that is reflective in its focus on individual and collective memory, but still both overlap in their frames of reference.[83] The Smithsonian exhibit at the close of the MCU's retelling of the Captain America story traffics in both forms of nostalgia, restorative and reflective. As noted in my previous work, the politics of collective memory are a necessary, but always partial, response to the presence of the past, and in this instance, the narrative retelling of Captain America's story and that of American democracy too remains incomplete.[84] The work of collective memory and of constructing democratic imagination is an ongoing process that must be made and remade over time.

The mythic imagining and continued reimagining of Captain America, the original star-spangled hero, in the MCU remains a compelling example of the enduring need for honor and (super)heroic agency in contemporary times, even as it also illustrates the uneasy and anxious relationship honor has with democracy. The aesthetics of democracy also require imaginative retelling to allow for a sense of "grandeur" that moves beyond thin notions of rationalism and utility. Clearly the desire for heroes with abiding codes of honor endures, even if their attachment to their honor at times compels them to eschew institutional restraint and oversight and to act in ways that demonstrate they are less than enamored with democratic practices. There is still a need for superheroes in the popular imaginary to inspire us and to redeem the silences and exclusions of American democracy, from Steve Rogers to Sam Wilson, as well as an enduring need for honor to generate heroic and superheroic action and remake democratic myths for contemporary times. In times of increasing democratic anxiety and erosion, the generative world of myth continues to adapt, and not always in wholly satisfying ways, and yet it still helps shape the sense of a people that has an appetite for heroes and a lingering appreciation for honor in the political imagination, no matter how binding and blinding it remains as a political virtue.

Conclusion
The Agonism of Honor

This book has explored how honor persists in the present and endures in the political imagination, even though it is often dismissed as obsolete, old-fashioned, and too closely tied to a chivalric past marred by inequality and prejudice. It has examined the multivalence of the concept of honor, which can be external and tied to tradition and a code of honor, internal and linked intimately to subject construction, and ornamental and displayed in medals and titles that represent the accumulation of power. It is the very multiplicity of honor, its fundamental conceptual slipperiness, which allows it to mean different things to different people at different times and which accounts for its persistence today. Honor is an inherently agonistic concept, and its place in the political imagination remains both complex and contested.

The concept of agonism is derived from the ancient Greek term *agōn*, which exemplified the idea of the contest. *Agōn* in Greek culture was "much more than a game. In antiquity, the term could refer to a gathering, a war, a court trial, a rhetorical debate, dramatic action, or almost any kind of struggle."[1] Agonism as both a contest of ideas and respect for one's opponents also formed a key component of Nietzschean philosophy, where the spiritualization of enmity that emerges from agonistic struggle is essential to master morality, allowing it to affirmatively overcome the *ressentiment* and bad conscience that poisons slave morality.[2] Following Nietzsche, contemporary theorists such as William Connolly have underlined the continued significance of agonistic respect, arguing that the contest between differing viewpoints can forge "affirmative connections" in politics today.[3]

Honor is agonistic along two dimensions. First, there is a continuous contest within the competing aspects of the concept of honor itself. Honor folds within it an inspiring appeal to political action through inherited codes, concepts of patriotic duty, and democratic myths and enchantments, and yet honor also conceals in its depths the capacity to unleash destructive rage and cause immense suffering. Second, the concept of honor is central to agonism and the idea of the contest itself. To actively struggle with differing points of view in ways that can invigorate democratic politics requires the honoring of a plurality of perspectives as formidable opponents who demand respect. This inherent push and pull within honor therefore makes it both an agonistic concept and impossible to ignore in conversations about democratic agonism today. Honor resists all attempts to sweep it into the dustbin of history, tenaciously holding on to and helping to shape political imagination in the present.

Throughout this book, the constitutive role that honor plays in the contemporary political imagination has been explored through a variety of texts in visual and literary culture. Invocations of honor continue to appear in political discourse, particularly in political speeches and the Washington media, either lamenting honor's disappearance from public life or urging the public to honor its heroes. Recently, President Biden did the latter at a memorial on the 22nd anniversary of the September 11, 2001, terrorist attacks, urging his audience to revive the "power of national unity" because that's "how we truly honor those we lost on 9/11" and explicitly linking such a remaking of the political imagination as an antidote to the "poisonous politics of difference and division" that permeate the political present.[4] President Biden followed a familiar approach put forward by contemporary theorists of honor discussed in this book who see honor as a clear solution to the problems of contemporary politics. Philosopher Kwame Anthony Appiah argues that honor plays a critical role in moral revolution and that it remains essential to political progress. Political theorist Sharon Krause sees honor as a necessary bulwark that protects liberalism and its values from tyranny by inspiring individuals to act in heroic ways to safeguard freedom. This book has differed from such approaches, which tend to smooth over honor's more problematic qualities. While there are certainly affirmative ways in which honor can inspire heroic agency in the political imagination, honor remains a costly concept to embrace as the protector and savior of contemporary politics as it can also inspire reckless acts of violence, cause immense suffering and grief, and gloss over the complexity of intersubjective power relations in profoundly destructive ways. Honor endures in the political imagination not as an antidote to the poisonous politics of polarization but as an agonistic concept that allows for the construction of powerful narratives that renew the political imagination, while simultaneously concealing and eliding injustice.

Throughout the chapters of this book, the multivalence, or conceptual slipperiness, of honor has been underscored along various dimensions.

This book began by exploring how honor can be rooted in an inherited code of tradition, which is intimately tied to subject construction and the perception of oneself as a political actor. Such a strong attachment to an internal code of honor is inherently vulnerable to the recognition of others and can blind one to the dynamics of realpolitik with catastrophic consequences. The book then explored how honor can also be tied to patriotic duty to the nation and how it serves as an anesthetic that can obscure the costs and demands of service to country. While useful in constructing a narrative of patriotism, honor is brittle and constraining and fractures easily when it encounters political complexity. The aesthetic power of honor is ornamental, linked to affect and sensation, and its function is to be skillfully deployed in the art of power. Such a realist approach to honor regards it as flexible and fungible, a form of currency to be accumulated when necessary and discarded when it becomes a hindrance. Above all, this book has fundamentally linked honor to tragedy. It has argued that honor is inspiring in its appeal to heroic action but destabilizing in its recklessness and the brutal acts of violence it can generate. Finally, it has analyzed how honor can operate as a form of nostalgia that exists in an agonistic relationship with democracy itself, where superheroic tropes of honor are invoked to redeem a fractured present but also used to remake and reinscribe those ideals in partial and insufficient ways.

Honor therefore endures in the political imagination and will continue to do so despite the many characterizations that celebrate or mourn its demise. There is a fascinating temporality to honor, in that it remains fundamentally linked to the past, from which it generates mythic narratives that continue to impact the present. However, the costs of extolling honor as a political virtue in the present remain high. Honor obscures and blinds one to the workings of power relations, functions as an anesthetic that dulls the senses, and consistently obscures and conceals the complexity of politics. It is dangerous in its propensity to justify violence in the name of heroic action, and it remains fundamentally nostalgic in its longing for the past. Yet honor persists in the present because it retains its capacity to inspire action and make and remake narratives of the political imagination that are still necessary today. Honor endures precisely because of its contested nature. It is and always has been an agonistic concept—in tension with itself, in tension with time, and in tension with democracy.

Notes

Introduction

1. Ruth Marcus, "No, John Kelly, Women Should Not Be Seen as 'Sacred,'" *Washington Post*, October 20, 2017, https://www.washingtonpost.com/opinions/no-john-kelly-women-should-not-be-seen-as-sacred/2017/10/20/3c05571c-b5d9-11e7-be94-fabb0f1e9ffb_story.html?utm_term=.6ee98ed2175d.
2. See, for instance, Robert Oprisko's detailed overview of the existing literature on honor for such an attempt to clarify and specify the concept in *Honor: A Phenomenology* (New York: Routledge, 2012).
3. Wendy Brown, *Undoing the Demos: Neoliberalism's Stealth Revolution* (Princeton, NJ: Princeton University Press, 2015), 19.
4. Peter Berger, "On the Obsolescence of the Concept of Honor," *European Journal of Sociology* 11, no. 2 (1970): 339–47.
5. John Stuart Mill, *On Liberty*, 8th ed. (Indianapolis, IN: Hackett, 1978), 52.
6. Berger, "On the Obsolescence of the Concept of Honor," 339.
7. Berger, "On the Obsolescence of the Concept of Honor," 340.
8. James Bowman, *Honor: A History* (New York: Encounter Books, 2007), 7.
9. Bowman, *Honor*, 35.
10. Bowman, *Honor*, 323.
11. Oprisko, *Honor*, 3.
12. Haig Patapan, "The Politics of Modern Honor," *Contemporary Political Theory* 17, no. 4 (2018): 459–77, doi:10.1057/s41296-017-0187-y.
13. Wendy Brown, *Politics out of History* (Princeton, NJ: Princeton University Press, 2001), 3.
14. Brown, *Politics out of History*, 3.
15. Brown, *Politics out of History*, 145.
16. Brown, *Politics out of History*, 150.
17. Kwame Anthony Appiah, *The Honor Code: How Moral Revolutions Happen* (New York: Norton, 2011), xii.
18. Appiah, *The Honor Code*, xiii.
19. Appiah, *The Honor Code*, xiii–xiv.
20. Appiah, *The Honor Code*, xvii.
21. Appiah, *The Honor Code*, 19.
22. Appiah, *The Honor Code*, 22.
23. Appiah, *The Honor Code*, 13.
24. Appiah, *The Honor Code*, 18.
25. Appiah, *The Honor Code*, 18.
26. Appiah, *The Honor Code*, 9.
27. Appiah, *The Honor Code*, 42.
28. Appiah, *The Honor Code*, 44.
29. Appiah, *The Honor Code*, 60.
30. Appiah, *The Honor Code*, 99.
31. Ibn Khaldun, *The Muqaddimah: An Introduction to History*, trans. Franz Rosenthal, abridged and ed. N. J. Dawood (Princeton, NJ: Princeton University Press, 2005), 107.
32. Sharon R. Krause, *Liberalism with Honor* (Cambridge, MA: Harvard University Press), 2002, 1.
33. Krause, *Liberalism with Honor*, ix.
34. Krause, *Liberalism with Honor*, ix.
35. Krause, *Liberalism with Honor*, x.
36. Krause, *Liberalism with Honor*, x.
37. Krause, *Liberalism with Honor*, xi.
38. Krause, *Liberalism with Honor*, xi.

39. Krause, *Liberalism with Honor*, xii.
40. Patapan, "The Politics of Modern Honor."
41. Krause, *Liberalism with Honor*, 7.
42. Smita A. Rahman, *Time, Memory, and the Politics of Contingency* (New York: Routledge, 2016).
43. Krause, *Liberalism with Honor*, 13.
44. Krause, *Liberalism with Honor*, 13.
45. Robert E. Watkins, *Freedom and Vengeance on Film: Precarious Lives and the Politics of Subjectivity* (London: I. B. Tauris, 2016), 3.
46. Watkins, *Freedom and Vengeance on Film*, 4.
47. Watkins, *Freedom and Vengeance on Film*, 8.
48. Patapan, "The Politics of Modern Honor."
49. Krause, *Liberalism with Honor*, 7.
50. Krause, *Liberalism with Honor*, 20.
51. Thomas Hobbes, *Leviathan*, ed. Richard Tuck (Cambridge: Cambridge University Press, 1996), 62.
52. Hobbes, *Leviathan*, 63.
53. Hobbes, *Leviathan*, 64.
54. Hobbes, *Leviathan*, 66.
55. Hobbes, *Leviathan*, 42.
56. Hobbes, *Leviathan*, 72.
57. Charles Louis de Secondat Montesquieu, *The Spirit of the Laws*, ed. Anne M. Cohler, Basia C. Miller, and Harold S. Stone (Cambridge: Cambridge University Press, 2009), 26.
58. Montesquieu, *The Spirit of the Laws*, 27.
59. Montesquieu, *The Spirit of the Laws*, 27.
60. Montesquieu, *The Spirit of the Laws*, 27.
61. Montesquieu, *The Spirit of the Laws*, 27.
62. Montesquieu, *The Spirit of the Laws*, 27.

Chapter 1

1. Joanna Robinson, "President Obama Talks Jon Snow and Names His Favorite *Game of Thrones* Character," *Vanity Fair*, November 17, 2015, https://www.vanityfair.com/hollywood/2015/11/obama-game-of-thrones-jon-snow-tyrion.
2. James Hibberd, "George R. R. Martin Explains Why There's Violence against Women in *Game of Thrones*," *Entertainment Weekly*, June 3, 2015, http://www.ew.com/article/2015/06/03/george-rr-martin-thrones-violence-women.
3. David Benioff and D. B. Weiss, *Game of Thrones*, season 1, episode 7, "You Win or You Die," HBO.
4. Aristotle, *Politics*, trans. Ernest Baker, Oxford World Classics (New York: Oxford University Press, 1995), bk. 1, ch. 2, p. 10.
5. Aristotle, *Nichomachean Ethics*, trans. David Ross, Oxford World Classics (New York: Oxford University Press, 2009), 5.
6. Aristotle, *Nichomachean Ethics*, 12.
7. Aristotle, *Nichomachean Ethics*, 18.
8. Aristotle, *Nichomachean Ethics*, 9–10.
9. Aristotle, *Nichomachean Ethics*, 6–7.
10. Benioff and Weiss, *Game of Thrones*, season 1, episode 1, "Winter Is Coming."
11. Benioff and Weiss, *Game of Thrones*, season 1, episode 1.
12. Aristotle, *Nichomachean Ethics*, p. 24
13. Aristotle, *Poetics*, trans. Malcolm Heath (London: Penguin Books, 1996), editor's note, p. xxxii.
14. Benioff and Weiss, *Game of Thrones*, season 1, episode 2, "The Kingsroad."
15. Georg Wilhelm Friedrich Hegel, *Aesthetics: Lectures on Fine Art*, vol. 1, trans. T. M. Knox (New York: Oxford University Press, 1975), 554.
16. Hegel, *Aesthetics*, 553.
17. Hegel, *Aesthetics*, x.
18. Benioff and Weiss, *Game of Thrones*, season 1, episode 2.
19. Hegel, *Aesthetics*, 558.
20. Judith Butler, *The Psychic Life of Power: Theories in Subjection* (Stanford: Stanford University Press, 1997), 1.

21. Benioff and Weiss, *Game of Thrones*, season 1, episode 4, "Cripples, Bastards and Broken Things."
22. Benioff and Weiss, *Game of Thrones*, season 1, episode 4.
23. Hegel, *Aesthetics*, 558.
24. Hegel, *Aesthetics*, 559.
25. Hegel, *Aesthetics*, 560.
26. Butler, *The Psychic Life of Power*, 9.
27. Patchen Markell, *Bound by Recognition* (Princeton, NJ: Princeton University Press, 2003), 14.
28. Hegel, *Aesthetics*, 561.
29. Benioff and Weiss, *Game of Thrones*, season 1, episode 5, "The Wolf and the Lion."
30. Hegel, *Aesthetics*, 559.
31. Butler, *The Psychic Life of Power*, 6.
32. Butler, *The Psychic Life of Power*, 9.
33. Markell, *Bound by Recognition*, 15.
34. Benioff and Weiss, *Game of Thrones*, season 1, episode 6, "A Golden Crown."
35. Friedrich Nietzsche, *Human, All Too Human: A Book for Free Spirits*, revised ed., trans. Marion Faber, with Stephen Lehmann (Lincoln: University of Nebraska Press, 1996), aphorism 94, p. 65.
36. Benioff and Weiss, *Game of Thrones*, season 1, episode 7.
37. Butler, *The Psychic Life of Power*, 24.
38. Benioff and Weiss, *Game of Thrones*, season 1, episode 7.
39. Benioff and Weiss, *Game of Thrones*, season 1, episode 9, "Baelor."
40. Benioff and Weiss, *Game of Thrones*, season 7, episode 7, "The Dragon and the Wolf."
41. Benioff and Weiss, *Game of Thrones*, season 3, episode 9, "The Rains of Castamere."
42. Benioff and Weiss, *Game of Thrones*, season 3, episode 5, "Kissed by Fire."
43. Benioff and Weiss, *Game of Thrones*, season 1, episode 2.
44. Benioff and Weiss, *Game of Thrones*, season 1, episode 4.
45. Butler, *The Psychic Life of Power*, 28.
46. Benioff and Weiss, *Game of Thrones*, season 5, episode 2, "The House of Black and White."
47. Benioff and Weiss, *Game of Thrones*, season 7, episode 3, "The Queen's Justice."
48. Benioff and Weiss, *Game of Thrones*, season 7, episode 6, "Beyond the Wall."
49. Markell, *Bound by Recognition*, 4.
50. Hegel, *Aesthetics*, 559.

Chapter 2

1. The image of President Trump at the CIA's Wall of Honor can be viewed at Andrea Mitchell, and Ken Dilanian, "Ex-CIA Boss Brennan, Others Rip Trump Speech in Front of Memorial Wall," *NBC News*, January 22, 2017, http://www.nbcnews.com/news/us-news/ex-cia-boss-brennan-others-rip-trump-speech-front-memorial-n710366.
2. Philip Rucker, John Wagner, and Greg Miller, "Trump, in CIA Visit, Attacks Media for Coverage of His Inaugural Crowds," *Washington Post*, January 21, 2017, https://www.washingtonpost.com/politics/trump-in-cia-visit-attacks-media-for-coverage-of-his-inaugural-crowds/2017/01/21/f4574dca-e019-11e6-ad42-f3375f271c9c_story.html?utm_term=.0c12c57c7a08.
3. Mitchell and Dilanian, "Ex-CIA Boss Brennan, Others Rip Trump Speech in Front of Memorial."
4. Robin Wright, "Trump's Vainglorious Affront to the C.I.A.," *New Yorker*, June 19, 2017, https://www.newyorker.com/news/news-desk/trumps-vainglorious-affront-to-the-c-i-a.
5. Ted Gup, *The Book of Honor: The Secret Lives and Deaths of CIA Operatives* (New York: Anchor Books, 2001), 2.
6. Gup, *The Book of Honor*, 2.
7. Brian Duffy, "The Pluperfect Spy," *U.S. News & World Report*, October 18, 1999.
8. Duffy, "The Pluperfect Spy."
9. Gup, *The Book of Honor*, 3.
10. During the Trump presidency, the possibility of collusion with Russia and obstruction of justice was investigated by Special Counsel Robert Mueller, who uncovered evidence of extensive criminal activity, detailed evidence of Russian attacks against the U.S. election system in 2016, and declined to exonerate President Trump and detailed multiple incidents where he engaged in obstruction of justice. The entire report can be viewed at Washington Post Staff, *The Mueller Report, Annotated*, 2019, https://www.washingtonpost.com/graphics/2019/politics/read-the-mueller-report/?tid=usw_passupdatepg.

11. Michael O'Connell, "FX Pushes Cryptic 'Americans' Emmy Pitch with 'The Russians Are Here' Ads," *Hollywood Reporter*, June 11, 2017, https://www.hollywoodreporter.com/live-feed/fx-pushes-cryptic-americans-emmy-pitch-russians-are-ads-1012275.
12. James Poniewozik, "Review: *The Americans* History Suddenly Feels Less Retro," *New York Times*, March 6, 2017, https://www.nytimes.com/2017/03/06/arts/television/tv-review-americans-season-5-russia-trump.html.
13. Alexander Welsh, *What Is Honor? A Question of Moral Imperatives* (New Haven, CT: Yale University Press, 2008), x.
14. See, for instance, Sharon R. Krause, *Liberalism with Honor* (Cambridge, MA: Harvard University Press, 2002). Krause's arguments are analyzed in some detail in the introduction to this book.
15. Richard Hofstadter, "The Paranoid Style in American Politics," *Harper's*, November 1964, http://harpers.org/archive/1964/11/the-paranoid-style-in-american-politics/.
16. Hofstadter, "The Paranoid Style in American Politics."
17. Hofstadter, "The Paranoid Style in American Politics."
18. Suzanne Clark, "Cold Warriors: The Nation and Literary Realism," *American Literary Realism* 33, no. 1 (2000): 34, http://www.jstor.org/stable/27747000.
19. Clark, "Cold Warriors," 47.
20. Clark, "Cold Warriors," 47.
21. Suzanne Clark, *Cold Warriors: Manliness on Trial in the Rhetoric of the West* (Carbondale: Southern Illinois University Press, 2000), 203.
22. Clark, *Cold Warriors*, 204.
23. Clark, *Cold Warriors*, 205.
24. Clark, *Cold Warriors*, 205.
25. Jacob Weisberg, *The Americans*, season 1, episode 1, "Pilot", FX.
26. Weisberg, *The Americans*, season 1, episode 1.
27. Weisberg, *The Americans*, season 1, episode 7, "Duty and Honor", FX.
28. Michael Rogin, "Kiss Me Deadly: Communism, Motherhood, and Cold War Movies," *Representations* 6, no. 1 (1984): 5, doi:10.1525/rep.1984.6.1.99p0043r.
29. Rogin, "Kiss Me Deadly," 5.
30. Weisberg, *The Americans*, season 1, episode 1.
31. Weisberg, *The Americans*, season 2, episode 13, "Echo", FX.
32. Weisberg, *The Americans*, season 2, episode 13.
33. Rogin, "Kiss Me Deadly," 5.
34. Rogin, "Kiss Me Deadly," 6.
35. Rogin, "Kiss Me Deadly," 21.
36. Weisberg, *The Americans*, season 4, episode 12, "A Roy Rogers in Franconia", FX.
37. Rogin, "Kiss Me Deadly," 3.
38. Weisberg, *The Americans*, season 4, episode 12.
39. Steven Johnston, *American Dionysia: Violence, Tragedy, and Democratic Politics* (New York: Cambridge University Press, 2015), 6.
40. Bianna Golodryga, "*The Americans*: Why a TV Show about the Cold War Is More Relevant Than Ever," *Yahoo! News*, March 16, 2017, https://www.yahoo.com/katiecouric/the-americans-why-a-tv-show-about-the-cold-war-is-more-relevant-than-ever-191819306.html.
41. Johnston, *American Dionysia*, 7.

Chapter 3

1. Michel Foucault, "What Is Critique," in *The Politics of Truth* (Los Angeles: Semiotext(e) Foreign Agents Series, 2007), 44.
2. Jacques Rancière, *Dis-agreement: Politics and Philosophy* (Minneapolis: University of Minnesota Press, 1999), 29.
3. Hilary Mantel, *Wolf Hall* (London: Fourth Estate, 2009), 31.
4. Davide Panagia, *The Political Life of Sensation* (Durham, NC: Duke University Press, 2009).
5. Mantel, *Wolf Hall*, 105.
6. Indeed, the impediment never fully goes away but has to be managed. In the final book, one of the most serious threats to Henry VIII's reign is the uprising known as the Pilgrimage of Grace that specifically targets Cromwell and his low birth and allegedly heretical beliefs for corrupting the king.
7. Mantel, *Wolf Hall*, 86.

8. Mantel, *Wolf Hall*, 183.
9. Niccolo Machiavelli, *The Prince*, in *Selected Political Writings*, trans. and ed. David Wootton (Indianapolis, IN: Hackett, 1994), 55.
10. Machiavelli, *The Prince*, 16.
11. Machiavelli, *The Prince*, 20.
12. Machiavelli, *The Prince*, 29.
13. Machiavelli, *The Prince*, 59.
14. Machiavelli, *The Prince*, 70.
15. Machiavelli, *The Prince*, 71.
16. Machiavelli, *The Prince*, 71.
17. Machiavelli, *The Prince*, 32.
18. Machiavelli, *The Prince*, 32.
19. Machiavelli, *The Prince*, 54.
20. Machiavelli, *The Prince*, 55.
21. Mantel, *Wolf Hall*, 163.
22. Mantel, *Wolf Hall*, 341.
23. Mantel, *Wolf Hall*, 631.
24. Diego A. von Vacano, *The Art of Power: Machiavelli, Nietzsche, and the Making of Aesthetic Political Theory* (Lantham, MD: Lexington Books, Rowman & Littlefield, 2007), 2.
25. von Vacano, *The Art of Power*, 4.
26. Machiavelli, *The Prince*, 6.
27. Mantel sees this lack of mobility in King Henry VIII as well. Cromwell can move anywhere and shift his perspective, but Henry can't. There is artistry in the king, but his high station prevents him from acquiring the perspective necessary for the art of power: "You could watch Henry every day for a decade and not see the same thing. Choose your prince: he admires Henry more and more.... Sometimes he seems an artist, in the way his eye ranges over his work; sometimes his hand moves and he doesn't seem to see it move. If he had been called to a lower station in life, he could have been a traveling player, and leader of his troupe" (*Wolf Hall*, 436–37).
28. Panagia, *The Political Life of Sensation*, 87.
29. von Vacano, *The Art of Power*, 5.
30. Mantel, *Wolf Hall*, 205.
31. Hanna Pitkin, *Fortune Is a Woman: Gender and Politics in the Thought of Niccolò Machiavelli* (Chicago: University of Chicago Press, 1999), 35.
32. Mantel, *Wolf Hall*, 113–14.
33. Panagia, *The Political Life of Sensation*, 123.
34. Panagia and Rancière, "Dissenting Words: A Conversation with Jacques Rancière", *Diacritics* 30, no. 2 (2000): 113–126, in Panagia, *The Political Life of Sensation*, 6.
35. Mantel, *Wolf Hall*, 114.
36. Mantel, *Wolf Hall*, 115.
37. Mantel, *Wolf Hall*, 85.
38. Panagia, *The Political Life of Sensation*, 2.
39. Mantel, *Wolf Hall*, 230.
40. Plato, *Republic*, trans. Benjamin Jowett (New York: Dover, 2000), 218–19.
41. Mantel, *Wolf Hall*, 61–62.
42. Mantel, *Wolf Hall*, 61.
43. Pitkin, *Fortune Is a Woman*, 5.
44. Mantel, *Wolf Hall*, 39.
45. Panagia, *The Political Life of Sensation*, 5.
46. Panagia, *The Political Life of Sensation*, 10.
47. Mantel, *Wolf Hall*, 577.
48. Mantel, *Wolf Hall*, 577.
49. Mantel, *Wolf Hall*, 640.
50. Mantel, *Wolf Hall*, 605.
51. Mantel, *Wolf Hall*, 584–85.
52. Stephen Alford, "A Man It Would Be Unwise to Cross: Thomas Cromwell," *London Review of Books*, November 6, 2019, https://www.lrb.co.uk/the-paper/v40/n21/stephen-alford/a-man-it-would-be-unwise-to-cross.
53. Mantel, *Wolf Hall*, 517.
54. Mantel, *Wolf Hall*, 517.

55. Panagia, *The Political Life of Sensation*, 2.
56. Hilary Mantel, *Bring Up the Bodies* (New York: Henry Holt, 2012), 243.
57. Rancière, *Dis-agreement*, 29.
58. Jason Frank, "Logical Revolts: Jacques Rancière and Political Subjectivization," *Political Theory* 43, no. 2 (2015): 250, https://doi.org/10.1177/0090591715573417.
59. Mantel, *Wolf Hall*, 377.
60. Mantel, *Wolf Hall*, 394.
61. Mantel, *Wolf Hall*, 378.
62. Frank, "Logical Revolts," 251.
63. Miguel Vatter, *Between Form and Event: Machiavelli's Theory of Political Freedom* (New York: Fordham University Press, 2014), 133.
64. Vatter, *Between Form and Event*, 7.
65. Machiavelli, *The Prince*, 11.
66. Machiavelli, *The Prince*, 21.
67. Machiavelli, *The Prince*, 48.
68. Machiavelli, *The Prince*, 48.
69. von Vacano, *The Art of Power*, 27.
70. Machiavelli, *The Prince*, 76.
71. Vatter, *Between Form and Event*, 134.
72. Mantel, *Wolf Hall*, 610.
73. Hilary Mantel, *The Mirror and the Light* (New York: Henry Holt, 2020), 692.
74. Mantel, *The Mirror and the Light*, 692.
75. As Clair Wills notes in her review, in this final book "his personality has been raised to the level of a theme, that of the commoner made good, a heroic cipher for the age." Clair Wills, "Ghost Story: On 'The Mirror and the Light,' the Third Volume in Hilary Mantel's Life of Thomas Cromwell," *New York Review of Books*, July 6, 2020, https://www.nybooks.com/articles/2020/05/14/hilary-mantel-mirror-light-ghost-story.
76. Mantel, *Wolf Hall*, 359.
77. Jacques Rancière, "Politics, Identification, and Subjectivization," in *The Identity in Question*, ed. John Rajchmann (New York: Routledge, 1995), 68.
78. Jacques Rancière, *Staging the People*, trans. David Fernbach (London: Verso, 2021), 26.
79. Mantel, *Wolf Hall*, 525.
80. Mantel, *Wolf Hall*, 526.
81. Mantel, *Wolf Hall*, 527.
82. Machiavelli, *The Prince*, 55.
83. Mantel, *Wolf Hall*, 320–21.

Chapter 4

1. For a discussion of the "pastness" of tragedy and its temporality, see Simon Critchley, *Tragedy, the Greeks, and Us* (New York: Pantheon Books, 2019), 14.
2. For a much deeper engagement with the politics of temporality, see Smita A. Rahman, *Time, Memory, and the Politics of Contingency* (London: Routledge, 2014).
3. Sharon R. Krause, *Liberalism with Honor* (Cambridge, MA: Harvard University Press, 2002), 6.
4. Krause, *Liberalism with Honor*, 27.
5. For a detailed critique of liberal agency and a creative and thought-provoking reading of misinterpellated agency as an alternative to ideas of redemption, see James R. Martel, *The Misinterpellated Subject* (Durham, NC: Duke University Press, 2017).
6. Martel, *The Misinterpellated Subject*, 150.
7. Hannah Arendt, *The Human Condition*, 2nd ed. (Chicago: University of Chicago Press, 1998), 205.
8. Dana R. Villa, "Beyond Good and Evil: Arendt, Nietzsche, and the Aestheticization of Political Action," *Political Theory* 20, no. 2 (1992): 275, http://www.jstor.org/stable/192004.
9. Villa, "Beyond Good and Evil," 276.
10. Villa, "Beyond Good and Evil," 281.
11. Bonnie Honig, "The Politics of Agonism: A Critical Response to 'Beyond Good and Evil: Arendt, Nietzsche, and the Aestheticization of Political Action' by Dana R. Villa," *Political Theory* 21, no. 3 (1993): 529, http://www.jstor.org/stable/191802.
12. Joseph Campbell, *The Hero with a Thousand Faces*, commemorative ed. (Princeton, NJ: Princeton University Press, 2004), 3.

13. Campbell, *The Hero with a Thousand Faces*, 3.
14. Critchley, *Tragedy, the Greeks, and Us*, 14.
15. Critchley, *Tragedy, the Greeks, and Us*, 14.
16. Friedrich Nietzsche, *Thus Spoke Zarathustra*, trans. Walter Kaufmann (New York: Penguin Books, 1978), 159.
17. For a more detailed analysis of Nietzsche's Zarathustra, see my previous work, *Time, Memory and the Politics of Contingency* (New York: Routledge, 2015), ch. 3.
18. Jean-François Drolet, "Ennobling Humanity: Nietzsche and the Politics of Tragedy," *Journal of International Political Theory* 10, no. 3 (2014): 232, https://doi.org/10.1177/1755088214541034.
19. Drolet, "Ennobling Humanity," 232.
20. See Nietzsche's *Attempt at a Self-Criticism* in Friedrich Nietzsche, *The Birth of Tragedy and The Case against Wagner*, trans. with commentary by Walter Kaufmann (New York: Vintage Books, 1967). See also Paul J. M. van Tongeren, "A Splendid Failure: Nietzsche's Understanding of the Tragic," *Journal of Nietzsche Studies*, no. 11 (Spring 1996): 23–34.
21. Nietzsche, *The Birth of Tragedy*, 35.
22. Nietzsche, *The Birth of Tragedy*, 35.
23. Drolet in his reading of *The Birth of Tragedy* notes that Nietzsche uses the German word *schein* to denote appearance and the representation that is central to the Apollonian ("Ennobling Humanity," 236), but it is interesting to note how often the word appears in the literature around honor. As I mentioned in the introduction to this book, Hegel also invokes *schein* in his lectures on aesthetics, to underline this glowing capacity of honor and why it is so closely tied to the idea of the subject itself, who is profoundly attached to the shining within itself. There is also a clear connection here to the aesthetic idea of honor as ornament or adornment in Machiavelli, as discussed in chapter 3.
24. Nietzsche, *The Birth of Tragedy*, 42.
25. Nietzsche, *The Birth of Tragedy*, 45.
26. Nietzsche, *The Birth of Tragedy*, 43.
27. Nietzsche, *The Birth of Tragedy*, 43.
28. Nietzsche, *The Birth of Tragedy*, 46.
29. Nietzsche, *The Birth of Tragedy*, 67.
30. Nietzsche, *The Birth of Tragedy*, 46.
31. Drolet, "Ennobling Humanity," 235.
32. Drolet, "Ennobling Humanity," 235.
33. Nietzsche, *The Birth of Tragedy*, 60.
34. Drolet, "Ennobling Humanity," 236.
35. Friedrich Nietzsche, *Homer's Contest*, in *The Portable Nietzsche*, ed. and trans. Walter Kaufmann (1954; London: Penguin, 1977), 32.
36. Nietzsche, *Homer's Contest*, 32.
37. Robert Oprisko, *Honor: A Phenomenology* (New York: Routledge, 2012), 65.
38. Oprisko, *Honor*, 65.
39. Ari Kohen, *Untangling Heroism: Classical Philosophy and the Concept of the Hero* (New York: Routledge, 2014), 5.
40. Nietzsche, *Homer's Contest*, 33.
41. Nietzsche, *Homer's Contest*, 35.
42. Nietzsche, *Homer's Contest*, 36.
43. Bernard M.W. Knox, *The Heroic Temper: Studies in Sophoclean Tragedy*, paperback ed. (Los Angeles: University of California Press, 1983), 1.
44. Knox, *The Heroic Temper*, 27.
45. Knox, *The Heroic Temper*, 27.
46. Knox, *The Heroic Temper*, 28.
47. Knox, *The Heroic Temper*, 50–51.
48. Knox, *The Heroic Temper*, 52.
49. Weil, quoted in Bernard Knox's introduction to Homer, *The Iliad*, trans. Robert Fagles, introduction and notes by Bernard Knox (New York: Penguin Books, 1990), 29.
50. Weil, quoted in Knox's introduction to Homer, *The Iliad*, 29.
51. Knox, introduction to Homer, *The Iliad*, 63.
52. Homer, *The Iliad*, 77.

53. Gregory Nagy, *The Best of the Achaeans: Concepts of the Heroic in Archaic Greek Poetry*, revised ed. (Baltimore: Johns Hopkins University Press, 1998), 72.
54. Homer, *The Iliad*, 80.
55. Homer, *The Iliad*, 81.
56. Homer, *The Iliad*, 82.
57. Homer, *The Iliad*, 82.
58. Homer, *The Iliad*, 83.
59. Homer, *The Iliad*, 83.
60. Homer, *The Iliad*, 83.
61. Homer, *The Iliad*, 84.
62. Homer, *The Iliad*, 89.
63. Nietzsche, *Homer's Contest*, 38.
64. Homer, *The Iliad*, 255.
65. Homer, *The Iliad*, 261.
66. Homer, *The Iliad*, 263.
67. Homer, *The Iliad*, 263.
68. Homer, *The Iliad*, 268.
69. Homer, *The Iliad*, 272.
70. Homer, *The Iliad*, 272–73.
71. Nagy, *The Best of the Achaeans*, 69.
72. Nagy, *The Best of the Achaeans*, 33.
73. Nagy, *The Best of the Achaeans*, 33.
74. Homer, *The Iliad*, 467.
75. Homer, *The Iliad*, 470.
76. Homer, *The Iliad*, 499.
77. Jonathan Shay, *Achilles in Vietnam: Combat Trauma and the Undoing of Character* (New York: Scribner, Simon & Schuster, 1994), 77.
78. Shay, *Achilles in Vietnam*, 31.
79. Shay, *Achilles in Vietnam*, 21.
80. Shay, *Achilles in Vietnam*, 31.
81. Shay, *Achilles in Vietnam*, 39.
82. Shay, *Achilles in Vietnam*, 53.
83. Shay, *Achilles in Vietnam*, 77.
84. Homer, *The Iliad*, 519.
85. Shay, *Achilles in Vietnam*, 90.
86. Bernard Knox, foreword to Homer, *The Iliad*, 33.
87. Knox, introduction to Homer, *The Iliad*, 63.
88. Shay, *Achilles in Vietnam*, 97.
89. Kohen, *Untangling Heroism*, 35.
90. Kohen, *Untangling Heroism*, 36.
91. Nietzsche, *Homer's Contest*, 38.
92. Knox, *The Heroic Temper*, 57.

Chapter 5

1. Elisabeth Anker, *Ugly Freedoms* (Durham, NC: Duke University Press, 2022).
2. EIU, *Democracy Index 2021: The China Challenge*, https://www.eiu.com/n/campaigns/democracy-index-2021/?utm_source=economist&utm_medium=daily_chart&utm_campaign=democracy-index-2021, accessed September 1, 2022.
3. Ari Kohen, "Tony Stark and the Classical Heroism of the Marvel Cinematic Universe," in *Politics of Marvel*, ed. Lilly Goren and Nicholas Carnes (Lawrence: University of Kansas Press, 2022), 36.
4. A. O. Scott, "Are the Movies Liberal?," *New York Times*, June 2, 2022, https://www.nytimes.com/2022/06/02/movies/liberal-hollywood-dog.html?referringSource=articleShare.
5. Neal Curtis, "Superheroes and the Mythic Imagination: Order, Agency and Politics," *Journal of Graphic Novels and Comics* 12, no. 5 (2021): 360–374, doi:10.1080/21504857.2019.1690015, 360.
6. Lilly Goren and Nicholas Carnes, "An Introduction to the Politics of the Marvel Cinematic Universe," in *Politics of Marvel*, ed. Lilly Goren and Nicholas Carnes (Lawrence: University of Kansas Press, 2022), 5.
7. Goren and Carnes, "An Introduction to the Politics of the Marvel Cinematic Universe," 8.

8. Curtis, "Superheroes and the Mythic Imagination," 361.
9. Curtis, "Superheroes and the Mythic Imagination," 361.
10. See, for example, the review-bombing of *Ms. Marvel* online before it was even released, a pattern that seems to be repeating itself even more strongly with the latest Disney Plus Series, *She Hulk*. Paul Tassi, "'She Hulk' Is Getting Review-Bombed Even Harder Than 'Ms. Marvel,'" *Forbes*, August 18, 2022, https://www.forbes.com/sites/paultassi/2022/08/18/she-hulk-is-getting-review-bombed-even-harder-than-ms-marvel/?sh=2b0621e351a4.
11. Curtis, "Superheroes and the Mythic Imagination," 361.
12. Curtis, "Superheroes and the Mythic Imagination," 361.
13. Curtis, "Superheroes and the Mythic Imagination," 371.
14. Robert Jewett, and John Shelton Lawrence, *The American Monomyth* (New York: Anchor Press/Doubleday, 1977), xx.
15. Jewett and Lawrence, *The American Monomyth*, 195.
16. J. Richard Stevens, *Captain America, Masculinity, and Violence: The Evolution of a National Icon*, Television and Popular Culture (Syracuse, NY: Syracuse University Press, 2015), 7, https://www-jstor-org.duproxy.palni.edu/stable/j.ctt1j1nwb0.
17. Laurie M. Johnson, and Dan Demetriou, *Honor in the Modern World: Interdisciplinary Perspectives* (Lanham, MD: Lexington Books, 2016), ProQuest Ebook Central, 1.
18. Johnson and Demetriou, *Honor in the Modern World*, 1.
19. James Bowman, *Honor: A History* (New York: Encounter Books, 2006), 7.
20. Bowman, *Honor*, 172.
21. Bowman, *Honor*, 189.
22. Bowman, *Honor*, 224.
23. Bowman, *Honor*, 305.
24. Bowman, *Honor*, 246.
25. Jason Dittmer, *Captain America and the Nationalist Superhero: Metaphors, Narratives, and Geopolitics* (Philadelphia: Temple University Press, 2013), 10, http://www.jstor.org/stable/j.ctt14bstb0.4..
26. Dittmer, "Introducing Nationalist Superheroes," 22.
27. Richard Reynolds, *Superheroes: A Modern Mythology* (Jackson: University Press of Mississippi, 1992), 18.
28. Mika LaVaque-Manty, "Dueling for Equality: Masculine Honor and the Modern Politics of Dignity," *Political Theory* 34, no. 6 (2006): 715–16, http://www.jstor.org/stable/20452507.
29. Carl Boggs and Tom Pollard, *The Hollywood War Machine: US Militarism and Popular Culture* (Boulder, CO: Paradigm, 2007), ix.
30. Joe Thomas and Shannon French, "Honor in Military Culture—A Standard of Integrity and Framework for Moral Restraint," in *Honor in the Modern World: Interdisciplinary Perspectives*, ed. Laurie Johnson and Dan Demetriou (Lanham, MD: Lexington, 2016), 271.
31. Thomas and French, *Honor in Military Culture*, 271.
32. Thomas and French, *Honor in Military Culture*, 273.
33. https://goarmywestpoint.com/sports/2015/3/6/GEN_2014010170.aspx, Accessed on March 26, 2021.
34. Boggs and Pollard, *The Hollywood War Machine*, ix.
35. Boggs and Pollard, *The Hollywood War Machine*, ix
36. Boggs and Pollard, *The Hollywood War Machine*, 19.
37. Roger Stahl, *Militainment, Inc.: War, Media, and Popular Culture* (New York: Routledge, 2009), 6.
38. Brett Pardy, "Selling Marvel's Cinematic Superheroes through Militarization," *Stream: Culture/Politics/Technology* 8, no. 2 (2016): 29, http://journals.sfu.ca/stream.
39. Reuben Baron, "The MCU's Relationship with the Military, from Iron Man to Captain Marvel," CBR, March 16, 2019, https://www.cbr.com/captain-marvel-mcu-military-relationship/2/.
40. Yann Roblou, "Review of *Captain America, Masculinity, and Violence: The Evolution of a National Icon*, by J. Richard Stevens," *Journal of Cold War Studies* 22, no. 2 (2020): 173–75, muse.jhu.edu/article/756832.
41. Benjamin Svetkey, "Barack Obama: Celebrity in Chief," *Entertainment Weekly*, November 21, 2008, http://www.ew.com/ew/article/0,,20241874,00.html, quoted in Stevens, *Captain America, Masculinity, and Violence*, 257.
42. Stevens, *Captain America, Masculinity, and Violence*, 261.
43. Marvel Studios, *Captain America: The First Avenger*, Paramount, 2011.

44. Anthony Russo, quoted in Alex Pappademas, "The Political Avenger: Chris Evans Takes on Trump, Tom Brady, Anxiety and Those Retirement Rumors," *Hollywood Reporter*, March 27, 2019, https://www.hollywoodreporter.com/features/chris-evans-talks-trump-tom-brady-anxiety-retirement-rumors-1196705.
45. Matthew Vernon, "Subversive Nostalgia or Captain America at the Museum," *Journal of Popular Culture* 49, no. 1 (2016): 120.
46. Norman Austin, "Homeric Nostalgia," *Yale Review* 98, no. 2 (April 2010): 37–64, 37 https://doi.org/10.1353/tyr.2010.0033.
47. Austin, "Homeric Nostalgia," 36.
48. Marvel Studios, *Captain America, the Winter Soldier*, Walt Disney Studios Motion Pictures, 2014.
49. Austin, "Homeric Nostalgia," 38.
50. Lilly Goren, "Nostalgia, Nationalism, and Marvel Superheroics," in *Politics of Marvel*, ed. Lilly Goren and Nicholas Carnes (Lawrence: University of Kansas Press, 2022), 95.
51. Laurie M. Johnson, *Honor in America? Tocqueville on American Enlightenment*, Honor and Obligation in Liberal Society: Problems and Prospects (Lanham, MD: Lexington Books, 2017), xiii.
52. Christopher Galdieri, "Captain America vs James Madison," in *Politics of Marvel*, ed. Lilly Goren and Nicholas Carnes (Lawrence: University of Kansas Press, 2022), 72.
53. Galdieri, "Captain America vs James Madison," 73.
54. Galdieri, "Captain America vs James Madison," 74.
55. Marvel Studios, *Captain America: Civil War*, Walt Disney Studios Motion Pictures, 2016.
56. Wilson Carey McWilliams, "Honor in Contemporary American Politics," in *The Democratic Soul: A Wilson Carey McWilliams Reader*, ed. Patrick J. Deneen and Susan J. McWilliams (Lexington: University Press of Kentucky, 2011), 319 http://www.jstor.org/stable/j.ctt2jcjt0.22.
57. McWilliams, "Honor in Contemporary American Politics," 320.
58. McWilliams, "Honor in Contemporary American Politics," 321.
59. McWilliams, "Honor in Contemporary American Politics," 324.
60. Jason Frank, *The Democratic Sublime: On Aesthetics and Popular Assembly* (New York: Oxford University Press, 2021), 2.
61. Frank, *The Democratic Sublime*, 3.
62. Frank, *The Democratic Sublime*, 5.
63. Frank, *The Democratic Sublime*, 154.
64. Frank, *The Democratic Sublime*, 155.
65. Frank, *The Democratic Sublime*, 155.
66. Marvel Studios, *The Falcon and the Winter Soldier*, Walt Disney Studios Motion Pictures, TV Miniseries, Disney Plus, episode 1, "New World Order," 2021.
67. Terry Gross, "Novelist Zadie Smith on Historical Nostalgia and the Nature of Talent," *Fresh Air*, January 20, 2017, https://www.npr.org/2017/01/20/510600755/novelist-zadie-smith-on-historical-nostalgia-and-the-nature-of-talent.
68. Goren, "Nostalgia, Nationalism, and Marvel Superheroics," 99–100.
69. Goren, "Nostalgia, Nationalism, and Marvel Superheroics," 98.
70. W. E. B. Du Bois, "Of Our Spiritual Strivings," in *The Souls of Black Folk*, Oxford World Classics (New York: Oxford University Press, 2007), 8.
71. Marvel Studios, *The Falcon and the Winter Soldier*, episode 2, "The Star-Spangled Man."
72. James Baldwin, *The Fire Next Time* (New York: Vintage Books, 1993), 5.
73. Baldwin, *The Fire Next Time*, 5–6.
74. Marvel Studios, *The Falcon and the Winter Soldier*, episode 4, "The Whole World Is Watching."
75. Baldwin, *The Fire Next Time*, 7.
76. Marvel Studios, *The Falcon and the Winter Soldier*, episode 5, "Truth."
77. Svetlana Boym, *The Future of Nostalgia* (New York: Basic Books, 2001), xiii.
78. See, for example, Alyssa Rosenberg's opinion piece in the *Washington Post*, "Black Panthers, Captain America, Police Chiefs and Lawmakers: Who Can Really Change the World?," May 12, 2005, https://www.washingtonpost.com/opinions/2021/05/12/black-panthers-captain-america-police-chiefs-lawmakers-who-can-really-change-world/.
79. Marvel Studios, *The Falcon and the Winter Soldier*, episode 5, "Truth."
80. Marvel Studios, *The Falcon and the Winter Soldier*, episode 6, "One World, One People."

81. Marvel Studios, *The Falcon and the Winter Soldier*, episode 6, "One World, One People."
82. Boym, *The Future of Nostalgia*, 8.
83. Boym, *The Future of Nostalgia*, 49.
84. See Smita A. Rahman, *Time, Memory, and the Politics of Contingency* (New York: Routledge, 2014).

Conclusion

1. Heather L. Reid, John Serrati, and Tim Sorg, "Conflict and Competition: Agon in Western Greece: Selected Essays from the 2019 Symposium on the Heritage of Western Greece," *Parnassos Press—Fonte Aretusa* 5 (2020): xiii, https://doi.org/10.2307/j.ctv15tt78p.
2. The master and slave morality, the nature of *ressentiment*, the bad conscience, and the spiritualization of enmity are all discussed extensively in Nietzsche's *On the Genealogy of Morals* (New York: Vintage, 1989).
3. William E. Connolly, *Capitalism and Christianity, American Style* (Durham, NC: Duke University Press, 2008), 58.
4. Nandita Bose, "Biden Asks Americans to Honor Sept. 11 Dead by Rejecting Extremism," Reuters, September 11, 2023, https://www.reuters.com/world/us/us-marks-sept-11-attacks-with-pentagon-world-trade-center-site-events-2023-09-11/.

Bibliography

Alford, Stephen. "A Man It Would Be Unwise to Cross: Thomas Cromwell." *London Review of Books*, November 6, 2019. https://www.lrb.co.uk/the-paper/v40/n21/stephen-alford/a-man-it-would-be-unwise-to-cross.
Anker, Elisabeth. *Ugly Freedoms*. Durham, NC: Duke University Press. 2022.
Appiah, Kwame Anthony. *The Honor Code: How Moral Revolutions Happen*. New York: Norton, 2011.
Arendt, Hannah. *The Human Condition*. Introduction by Margaret Canovan. 2nd edition. Chicago: University of Chicago Press, 1998.
Aristotle. *Nichomachean Ethics*. Translated by David Ross. Oxford World Classics. New York: Oxford University Press, 2009.
Aristotle. *Poetics*. Translated by Malcolm Heath. London: Penguin Books, 1996.
Aristotle. *Politics*. Translated by Ernest Baker. Oxford World Classics. New York: Oxford University Press, 1995.
Austin, Norman. "Homeric Nostalgia." *Yale Review* 98, no. 2 (April 2010): 37–64. https://doi.org/10.1353/tyr.2010.0033.
Baldwin, James. *The Fire Next Time*. New York: Vintage Books, 1993.
Baron, Reuben. "The MCU's Relationship with the Military, from Iron Man to Captain Marvel." CBR, March 16, 2019. https://www.cbr.com/captain-marvel-mcu-military-relationship/2/.
Benioff, David, and D. B. Weiss. *Game of Thrones*. Seasons 1–8. Aired 2011–19 on HBO.
Berger, Peter. "On the Obsolescence of the Concept of Honor." *European Journal of Sociology* 11, no. 2 (1970): 339–347.
Boggs, Carl, and Tom Pollard. *The Hollywood War Machine: US Militarism and Popular Culture*. Boulder, CO: Paradigm, 2007.
Bose, Nandita. "Biden Asks Americans to Honor Sept. 11 Dead by Rejecting Extremism." Reuters, September 11, 2023. https://www.reuters.com/world/us/us-marks-sept-11-attacks-with-pentagon-world-trade-center-site-events-2023-09-11/.
Bowman, James. *Honor: A History*. New York: Encounter Books, 2007.
Boym, Svetlana. *The Future of Nostalgia*. New York: Basic Books, 2001.
Brown, Wendy. *Politics out of History*. Princeton, NJ: Princeton University Press, 2001.
Brown, Wendy. *Undoing the Demos: Neoliberalism's Stealth Revolution*. Princeton, NJ: Princeton University Press, 2015.
Butler, Judith. *The Psychic Life of Power: Theories in Subjection*. Stanford: Stanford University Press, 1997.
Campbell, Joseph. *The Hero with a Thousand Faces*. Commemorative edition. Princeton, NJ: Princeton University Press, 2004.
Clark, Suzanne. *Cold Warriors: Manliness on Trial in the Rhetoric of the West*. Carbondale, IL: Southern Illinois University Press, 2000.
Clark, Suzanne. "Cold Warriors: The Nation and Literary Realism." *American Literary Realism* 33, no. 1 (2000): 33–56. http://www.jstor.org/stable/27747000.
Connolly, William E. *Capitalism and Christianity, American Style*. Durham, NC: Duke University Press, 2008.
Critchley, Simon. *Tragedy, the Greeks, and Us*. New York: Pantheon Books, 2019.

Curtis, Neal. "Superheroes and the Mythic Imagination: Order, Agency and Politics." *Journal of Graphic Novels and Comics* 12, no. 5 (2021): 360–74. doi:10.1080/21504857.2019.1690015.

Deleuze, Gilles. *Bergsonism*. Translated by Hugh Tomlinson and Barbara Habberjam. New York: Zone Books, 1990.

Dittmer, Jason. *Captain America and the Nationalist Superhero: Metaphors, Narratives, and Geopolitics*. Philadelphia: Temple University Press, 2013. http://www.jstor.org/stable/j.ctt14bstb0.4.

Drolet, Jean-François. "Ennobling Humanity: Nietzsche and the Politics of Tragedy." *Journal of International Political Theory* 10, no. 3 (2014): 231–60. https://doi.org/10.1177/1755088214541034.

Du Bois, W. E. B. *The Souls of Black Folk*. Oxford World Classics. New York: Oxford University Press, 2007.

Duffy, Brian. "The Pluperfect Spy." *U.S. News & World Report*, October 18, 1999.

EIU. *Democracy Index 2021: The China Challenge*. https://www.eiu.com/n/campaigns/democracy-index-2021/?utm_source=economist&utm_medium=daily_chart&utm_campaign=democracy-index-2021. Accessed September 1, 2022.

Frank, Jason A. *The Democratic Sublime: On Aesthetics and Popular Assembly*. New York: Oxford University Press, 2021.

Frank, Jason A. "Logical Revolts: Jacques Rancière and Political Subjectivization." *Political Theory* 43, no. 2 (2015): 249–61. https://doi.org/10.1177/0090591715573417.

Foucault, Michel. *The Politics of Truth*. Los Angeles: Semiotext(e) Foreign Agents Series, 2007.

Golodryga, Bianna. "*The Americans*: Why a TV Show about the Cold War Is More Relevant Than Ever." *Yahoo! News*, March 16, 2017. https://www.yahoo.com/katiecouric/the-americans-why-a-tv-show-about-the-cold-war-is-more-relevant-than-ever-191819306.html.

Goren, Lilly, and Nicholas Carnes. *Politics of Marvel*. Lawrence: University of Kansas Press, 2022.

Gross, Terry. "Novelist Zadie Smith on Historical Nostalgia and the Nature of Talent." *Fresh Air*, January 20, 2017. https://www.npr.org/2017/01/20/510600755/novelist-zadie-smith-on-historical-nostalgia-and-the-nature-of-talent.

Gup, Ted. *The Book of Honor: The Secret Lives and Deaths of CIA Operatives*. New York: Anchor Books, 2001.

Hegel, Georg Wilhelm Friedrich. *Aesthetics: Lectures on Fine Art*. Vol. 1. Translated by T. M. Knox. New York: Oxford University Press, 1975.

Hibberd, James. "George R. R. Martin Explains Why There's Violence against Women in *Game of Thrones*." *Entertainment Weekly*, June 3, 2015. http://www.ew.com/article/2015/06/03/george-rr-martin-thrones-violence-women.

Hobbes, Thomas. *Leviathan*. Edited by Richard Tuck. Cambridge: Cambridge University Press, 1996.

Hofstadter, Richard. "The Paranoid Style in American Politics." *Harper's*, November 1964. http://harpers.org/archive/1964/11/the-paranoid-style-in-america.

Homer. *The Iliad*. Translated by Robert Fagles. Introduction and notes by Bernard Knox. New York: Penguin Books, 1990.

Honig, Bonnie. "The Politics of Agonism: A Critical Response to 'Beyond Good and Evil: Arendt, Nietzsche, and the Aestheticization of Political Action' by Dana R. Villa." *Political Theory* 21, no. 3 (1993): 528–33. http://www.jstor.org/stable/191802.

Ibn Khaldun. *The Muqaddimah: An Introduction to History*. Translated by Franz Rosenthal. Abridged and edited by N. J. Dawood. Princeton, NJ: Princeton University Press, 2005.

Jewett, Robert, and John Shelton Lawrence. *The American Monomyth*. New York: Anchor Press/Doubleday, 1977.

Johnson, Laurie M. *Honor in America? Tocqueville on American Enlightenment*. Honor and Obligation in Liberal Society: Problems and Prospects. Lanham, MD: Lexington Books, 2017.

Johnson, Laurie M., and Dan Demetriou. *Honor in the Modern World: Interdisciplinary Perspectives*. Lanham, MD: Lexington Books, 2016.
Johnston, Steven. *American Dionysia: Violence, Tragedy, and Democratic Politics*. New York: Cambridge University Press, 2015.
Knox, Bernard M. W. *The Heroic Temper: Studies in Sophoclean Tragedy*. Paperback edition. Los Angeles: University of California Press, 1983.
Kohen, Ari. *Untangling Heroism: Classical Philosophy and the Concept of the Hero*. New York: Routledge, 2014.
Krause, Sharon R. *Liberalism with Honor*. Cambridge, MA: Harvard University Press, 2002.
LaVaque-Manty, Mika. "Dueling for Equality: Masculine Honor and the Modern Politics of Dignity." *Political Theory* 34, no. 6 (2006): 715–40. http://www.jstor.org/stable/20452507.
Machiavelli, Niccolo. *Selected Political Writings*. Translated and edited by David Wootton. Indianapolis, IN: Hackett, 1994.
Mantel, Hilary. *Bring Up the Bodies*. New York: Henry Holt, 2012.
Mantel, Hilary. *The Mirror and the Light*. New York: Henry Holt, 2020.
Mantel, Hilary. *Wolf Hall*. London: Fourth Estate, 2009.
Marcus, Ruth. "No, John Kelly, Women Should Not Be Seen as 'Sacred.'" *Washington Post*, October 20, 2017. https://www.washingtonpost.com/opinions/no-john-kelly-women-should-not-be-seen-as-sacred/2017/10/20/3c05571c-b5d9-11e7-be94-fabb0f1e9ffb_story.html?utm_term=.6ee98ed2175d.
Markell, Patchen. *Bound by Recognition*. Princeton, NJ: Princeton University Press, 2003.
Martel, James R. *The Misinterpellated Subject*. Durham, NC: Duke University Press, 2017.
Marvel Studios. *Captain America: Civil War*. Walt Disney Studios Motion Pictures, 2016.
Marvel Studios. *Captain America: The First Avenger*. Paramount, 2011.
Marvel Studios. *Captain America, the Winter Soldier*. Walt Disney Studios Motion Pictures, 2014.
Marvel Studios. *The Falcon and the WinterSoldier*. Walt Disney Studios Motion Pictures. TV miniseries. Disney Plus, 2021.
McWilliams, Wilson Carey. *The Democratic Soul: A Wilson Carey McWilliams Reader*. Edited by Patrick J. Deneen and Susan J. McWilliams. Lexington: University Press of Kentucky, 2011.
McWilliams, Wilson Carey. "Honor in Contemporary American Politics." In *The Democratic Soul: A Wilson Carey McWilliams Reader*, edited by Patrick J. Deneen and Susan J. McWilliams, 319–26. Lexington: University Press of Kentucky, 2011. http://www.jstor.org/stable/j.ctt2jcjt0.22.
Mill, John Stuart. *On Liberty*. 8th edition. Indianapolis, IN: Hackett, 1978.
Mitchell, Andrea, and Ken Dilanian. "Ex-CIA Boss Brennan, Others Rip Trump Speech in Front of Memorial." *NBC News*, January 22, 2017. http://www.nbcnews.com/news/us-news/ex-cia-boss-brennan-others-rip-trump-speech-front-memorial-n710366.
Montesquieu, Charles Louis de Secondat. *The Spirit of the Laws*. Edited by Anne M. Cohler, Basia C. Miller, and Harold S. Stone. Cambridge: Cambridge University Press, 2009.
Nagy, Gregory. *The Best of the Achaeans: Concepts of the Heroic in Archaic Greek Poetry*. Revised edition. Baltimore: Johns Hopkins University Press, 1998.
Nietzsche, Friedrich. *The Birth of Tragedy and The Case against Wagner*. Translated with commentary by Walter Kaufmann. New York: Vintage Books, 1967.
Nietzsche, Friedrich. *Homer's Contest*. In *The Portable Nietzsche*, edited and translated by Walter Kaufmann, 32–38. London: Penguin, 1977. Originally published 1954.
Nietzsche, Friedrich. *Human, All Too Human: A Book for Free Spirits*. Revised edition. Translated by Marion Faber, with Stephen Lehmann. Lincoln: University of Nebraska Press, 1996.
Nietzsche, Friedrich. *On the Genealogy of Morals and Ecce Homo*. Translated by Walter Kaufmann. New York: Vintage, 1989.

Nietzsche, Friedrich. *Thus Spoke Zarathustra*. Translated by Walter Kaufmann. New York: Penguin Books, 1978.

O'Connell, Michael, "FX Pushes Cryptic 'Americans' Emmy Pitch with 'The Russians Are Here' Ads." *Hollywood Reporter*, June 11, 2017. https://www.hollywoodreporter.com/live-feed/fx-pushes-cryptic-americans-emmy-pitch-russians-are-ads-1012275.

Oprisko, Robert. *Honor: A Phenomenology*. New York: Routledge, 2012

Panagia, Davide. *The Political Life of Sensation*. Durham, NC: Duke University Press, 2009.

Panagia, Davide, and Rancière, Jacques. "Dissenting Words: A Conversation with Jacques Rancière", *Diacritics* 30, no. 2 (2000): 113–26.

Pappademas, Alex. "The Political Avenger: Chris Evans Takes on Trump, Tom Brady, Anxiety and Those Retirement Rumors." *Hollywood Reporter*, March 27, 2019. https://www.hollywoodreporter.com/features/chris-evans-talks-trump-tom-brady-anxiety-retirement-rumors-1196705.

Pardy, Brett. "Selling Marvel's Cinematic Superheroes through Militarization." *Stream: Culture/Politics/Technology* 8, no. 2 (2016): 23–35.

Patapan, Haig. "The Politics of Modern Honor." *Contemporary Political Theory* 17, no. 4 (2018): 459–77. doi:10.1057/s41296-017-0187-y.

Pitkin, Hanna. *Fortune Is a Woman: Gender and Politics in the Thought of Niccolò Machiavelli*. Chicago: University of Chicago Press, 1999.

Plato. *Republic*. Translated by Benjamin Jowett. New York: Dover, 2000.

Poniewozik, James. "Review: *The Americans* History Suddenly Feels Less Retro." *New York Times*, March 6, 2017. https://www.nytimes.com/2017/03/06/arts/television/tv-review-amer-icans-season-5-russia-trump.html.

Rahman, Smita A. *Time, Memory, and the Politics of Contingency*. New York: Routledge, 2014.

Rancière, Jacques. *Dis-agreement: Politics and Philosophy*. Minneapolis: University of Minnesota Press, 1999.

Rancière, Jacques. "Politics, Identification, and Subjectivization." In *The Identity in Question*, edited by John Rajchmann, 63–72. New York: Routledge, 1995.

Rancière, Jacques. *Staging the People*. Translated by David Fernbach. London: Verso, 2021.

Reid, Heather L., John Serrati, and Tim Sorg. "Conflict and Competition: Agon in Western Greece: Selected Essays from the 2019 Symposium on the Heritage of Western Greece." *Parnassos Press—Fonte Aretusa* 5 (2020): ix–xiv. https://doi.org/10.2307/j.ctv15tt78p.

Reynolds, Richard. *Superheroes: A Modern Mythology*. Jackson: University Press of Mississippi, 1992.

Robinson, Joanna. "President Obama Talks Jon Snow and Names His Favorite *Game of Thrones* Character." *Vanity Fair*, November 17, 2015. https://www.vanityfair.com/hollywood/2015/11/obama-game-of-thrones-jon-snow-tyrion.

Roblou, Yann. "Review of *Captain America, Masculinity, and Violence: The Evolution of a National Icon*, by J. Richard Stevens." *Journal of Cold War Studies* 22, no. 2 (2020): 173–75. muse.jhu.edu/article/756832.

Rogin, Michael. "Kiss Me Deadly: Communism, Motherhood, and Cold War Movies." *Representations* 6, no. 1 (1984): 1–36. doi:10.1525/ rep.1984.6.1.99p0043r.

Rosenberg, Alyssa. "Black Panthers, Captain America, Police Chiefs and Lawmakers: Who Can Really Change the World?" *Washington Post*, May 12, 2005. https://www.washingtonpost.com/opinions/2021/05/12/black-panthers-captain-america-police-chiefs-lawmakers-who-can-really-change-world/.

Rucker, Philip, John Wagner, and Greg Miller. "Trump, in CIA Visit, Attacks Media for Coverage of His Inaugural Crowds." *Washington Post*, January 21, 2017.

Scott, A. O. "Are the Movies Liberal?" *New York Times*, June 2, 2022. https://www.nytimes.com/2022/06/02/movies/liberal-hollywood-dog.html?referringSource=articleShare.

Shay, Jonathan. *Achilles in Vietnam: Combat Trauma and the Undoing of Character*. New York: Scribner, Simon & Schuster, 1994.

Stahl, Roger. *Militainment, Inc.: War, Media, and Popular Culture*. New York: Routledge, 2009.

Stevens, J. Richard. *Captain America, Masculinity, and Violence: The Evolution of a National Icon*. Television and Popular Culture. Syracuse, NY: Syracuse University Press, 2015. https://www-jstor-org.duproxy.palni.edu/stable/j.ctt1j1nwb0.
Svetkey, Benjamin. "Barack Obama: Celebrity in Chief." *Entertainment Weekly*, November 21, 2008. http://www.ew.com/ew/article/0,,20241874,00.html.
Tassi, Paul. "'She Hulk' Is Getting Review-Bombed Even Harder Than 'Ms. Marvel.'" *Forbes*, August 18, 2022. https://www.forbes.com/sites/paultassi/2022/08/18/she-hulk-is-getting-review-bombed-even-harder-than-ms-marvel/?sh=2b0621e351a4
van Tongeren, Paul J. M. "A Splendid Failure: Nietzsche's Understanding of the Tragic," *Journal of Nietzsche Studies*, no. 11 (Spring 1996): 23–34.
Vatter, Miguel. *Between Form and Event: Machiavelli's Theory of Political Freedom*. New York: Fordham University Press, 2014.
Vernon, Matthew. "Subversive Nostalgia or Captain America at the Museum." *Journal of Popular Culture* 49, no. 1 (2016): 116–35.
Villa, Dana R. "Beyond Good and Evil: Arendt, Nietzsche, and the Aestheticization of Political Action." *Political Theory* 20, no. 2 (1992): 274–308. http://www.jstor.org/stable/192004.
von Vacano, Diego A. *The Art of Power: Machiavelli, Nietzsche, and the Making of Aesthetic Political Theory*. Lantham, MD: Lexington Books, Rowman & Littlefield, 2007.
Washington Post Staff. *The Mueller Report, Annotated*. 2019. https://www.washingtonpost.com/graphics/2019/politics/read-the-mueller-report/?tid=usw_passupdatepg.
Watkins, Robert E. *Freedom and Vengeance on Film: Precarious Lives and The Politics of Subjectivity*. London: I. B. Tauris, 2016.
Weisberg, Jacob. *The Americans*. Seasons 1–6. Aired 2013–2018 on FX.
Welsh, Alexander. *What Is Honor? A Question of Moral Imperatives*. New Haven, CT: Yale University Press, 2008.
Wills, Clair. "Ghost Story: On 'The Mirror and the Light,' the Third Volume in Hilary Mantel's Life of Thomas Cromwell." *New York Review of Books*, July 6, 2020. https://www.nybooks.com/articles/2020/05/14/hilary-mantel-mirror-light-ghost-story/.
Wright, Robin. "Trump's Vainglorious Affront to the C.I.A." The New Yorker, June 19, 2017. https://www.newyorker.com/news/news-desk/trumps-vainglorious-affront-to-the-c-i-a.

Index

For the benefit of digital users, indexed terms that span two pages (e.g., 52–53) may, on occasion, appear on only one of those pages.

Achilles, 95–96, 102–3, 108–21
aesthetic approach to politics, 75–76, 78–82, 88
agency
    Americans and, 55–56, 59–61, 64–65
    Captain America and, 135, 147, 155
    definition of, 13–14
    democratic agency, 3, 13–19, 157
    Game of Thrones and, 33–34, 39–46, 48–49, 50
    honor's relation to, 1–4, 13–17, 39–46, 157
    identity and, 12
    Iliad and, 96–108, 121–24
    Krause and, 3, 13–19, 157
    liberalism and, 6, 13–17, 96–99
    limits of, 39–46
    Nietzsche and, 101–5
    power and difference as wiping away, 13–14
    tragedy and, 18–19, 20–21
    vainglory and, 18–19
agon, 98, 106–7, 156–58
All the President's Men (film), 141–42
American Dionysia (Johnston), 65
American exceptionalism, 132–35
Americans, The (television show)
    agency and, 55–56, 59–61, 64–65
    anxieties and, 62–64
    CIA and, 51–53, 54, 55–56, 65
    code of honor and, 57–58, 59–60, 63–65
    Cold War rhetoric and, 55–58
    contemporary relevance of, 54
    creation of, 54
    Elizabeth Jennings's sense of honor in, 57–58, 59–60, 63–65
    erasure of gender and domestic life and, 53–54, 56, 58, 62–65
    espionage and honor connection and, 53–55, 59, 64–65
    family and, 54–55, 57, 59–62, 64–65
    gender in, 58–62
    good and evil binary collapsed in, 57
    heroic action and, 61
    identity and, 53–54, 55–56, 57–61, 62–63
    intellectual history of honor and, 55–56
    liberalism and, 56
    masculinity and, 57, 58
    motherhood depictions during the Cold War and, 60–62
    overview of, 51–55, 64–66
    paranoia and, 55–58
    patriotism and, 62–64
    Philip Jennings's tragic worldview in, 57–58, 63–66
    politicization of the domestic realm and, 58–62
    subjectivity and, 61
    tragedy and, 62–66
    Trump speech in front of CIA memorial wall and, 51–54
Apollonian and Dionysian, 100–5, 107–8, 109–10
Appiah, Kwame Anthony
    code of honor and, 7–11
    contributions of, 7–9
    critiques of, 7–9
    on definition of honor, 9–10
    dueling and, 9–11
    elites and, 10–12
    eudaimonia and, 8–9
    foot-binding and, 11–12
    identity and, 7–10, 12
    liberalism and, 7–8
    moral revolution, honor as source of, 3, 7–8, 157
    progress and, 7–8
    reclaiming of honor and, 7–8
    recognition and, 8–10
    respect, honor as being entitled to, 9–11
    as too optimistic, 8–9
Aristotle
    aim of political science and, 30
    code of honor and, 32–33
    eudaimonia and, 8–9
    Game of Thrones and, 28–30
    hamartia and, 21–22, 27–28, 33–34

Aristotle (*cont.*)
  happiness as active form of living and, 28–29, 30
  honor as end of political life for, 30–31
  linking individual to larger group and, honor as, 30
  nobility and, 30–31
  political nature of human beings and, 28–29
  self-sufficiency and, 30
  tragic error and, 33–34
art of power. *See* power
Art of Power, The (von Vacano), 75–76
Atomistic individual, 13, 15–16, 23–24, 51–52
Austin, Norman, 139–40
Avengers: Endgame (film), 148–49

Berger, Peter, 4–5
Biden, Joe, 157
Birth of Tragedy, The (Nietzsche), 100, 101–2
Boggs, Carl, 133–35
Boleyn, Anne, 70–71, 85–86
Boseman, Chadwick, 129–30
Bowman, James, 132–33
Boym, Svetlana, 153–54
Bring Up the Bodies (Mantel), 67, 70–71, 85–86
Brown, Wendy, 3, 6–7, 14–15
Brunelleschi, Filippo, 77
Butler, Judith, 21–22, 27–28, 38, 40–44, 48–49, 117–18

Captain America (films)
  agency and, 135, 147, 155
  American exceptionalism and, 132–35
  Bucky Barnes in, 131, 136–38, 142–43, 145, 152–54
  Civil War and, 143–48
  code of honor and, 131–32, 133–34, 136–38, 140–41, 142–45, 148
  democratic anxiety and, 125–30, 138–48, 152, 155
  duty's relation to honor and, 125–26, 131–38
  Endgame and, 148–49
  erosion of honor culture and, 131–33
  Falcon and the Winter Soldier and, 148–54
  family and, 136, 145, 151–52, 153–54
  First Avenger and, 131–38
  heroic action and, 126–27, 135, 155
  Hollywood War Machine and, 134–35
  honor'ing the past in the present and, 148–54
  identity and, 129–30, 132–33, 135–36, 137–38, 140–43
  ideology in, 133–36
  liberalism and, 127–28, 145–46
  MCU and, 127–30, 134–35
  militarism and, 130, 131–38
  modernization of Steve Rogers in, 138–42
  myth and, 127–43, 145, 147–49, 151–54
  narrative overview of, 131
  nationalist and patriotic disjunction in, 144–46
  nostalgia and, 138–48, 150–51
  ornamental honor rejected in, 138
  overview of, 125–26, 154–55
  patriotism and, 131–38
  Peggy Carter in, 137–38, 140–41, 145, 148–49
  racial dimensions of, 150–54
  redemption and reforging in, 153–54
  representation and, 129–30, 150–54
  role of honor in modern life and, 131–33
  Sam Wilson in, 134–35, 142–43, 149–55
  speculative fiction and, 128–29
  superhero genre and, 127–31
  tragedy and, 127
  Winder Soldier and, 142–48
Carnes, Nicholas, 128–29
chivalric honor, 21–22, 27–28, 36–37
Clark, Suzanne, 57, 58
code of honor
  Americans and, 57–58, 59–60, 63–65
  Appiah and, 7–11
  Aristotle and, 32–33
  Captain America and, 131–32, 133–34, 136–38, 140–41, 142–46, 148
  dueling and, 10–11
  erosion of, 10–11
  Game of Thrones and, 26–27, 28–29, 32–33, 35, 36, 40, 41–42, 45–46
  Iliad and, 10, 94–95, 122–23
  incommensurability between political intrigues and, 27, 37
  Krause and, 17
  overview of, 7–12, 157–58
  progress and, 10–12
  recognition and, 17
  Wolf Hall and, 67–68, 78
Cold War Moms, 55, 58–62
Cold War rhetoric, 55–58
Connolly, William, 156
Critchley, Simon, 99
Curtis, Neal, 127–28, 129–30

Day After, The (film), 56
democratic agency, 3, 13–19, 157
democratic anxiety, 3, 13–14, 125–30, 138–48, 152, 155

INDEX   179

Dionysian and Apollonian, 100–5, 107–8, 109–10
dishonor, 34–35, 41, 45–49, 70–71, 82–83, 108, 111, 112
distribution of the sensible, 69, 86–89, 91
domestic realm, politicization of the, 58–62
Du Bois, W. E. B., 151–52
dueling, 4–5, 9–11
Duke of Wellington, 10–11
duty's relation to honor, 62–64, 125–26, 131–38

Earl of Winchelsea, 10–11
eudaimonia, 8–9

Falcon and the Winter Soldier (television show), 148–54
family
  Americans and, 54–55, 57, 59–62, 64–65
  Captain America and, 136, 145, 151–52, 153–54
  erasure of gender and domestic life and, 53–54, 56, 58, 62–65
  Game of Thrones and, 28–38, 42, 45–48
  gendered dimensions of, 58–62
  honor as taking toil on, 2–3
  Iliad and, 108–9, 119–20
  motherhood depictions during the Cold War and, 60–62
  political imaginary and, 2–3
Federalist Papers, The, 144–45
Feige, Kevin, 135–36
foot-binding, 7–9, 11–12
fortuna, 73–74, 86–90, 92–93
Foucault, Michel, 38, 68–69, 79–80, 108–9
French, Shannon, 133–34, 148

Galdieri, Christopher, 144–45
Game of Thrones (television show)
  agency and, 33–34, 39–46, 48–49, 50
  Aristotle and, 28–30
  Bran the Builder in, 31–33, 34–35
  Cersei Lannister in, 37, 39, 44–47
  chivalric honor and, 27–28, 36–37
  code of honor and, 26–27, 28–29, 32–33, 35, 36, 40, 41–42, 45–46
  complex legacy of honor and, 46–49
  concluding scenes of Stark in, 45
  critique of honor as binding and blinding and, 27–28, 40
  as cultural phenomenon, 25–26
  death of Stark in, 46–48
  demonstration of honor and, 40
  dishonor of Stark and, 34–35, 41, 42–43, 45–50
  displacement and, 35–38
  executions in, 37–38, 43–44, 46–48
  family and, 28–38, 42, 45–48
  hamartia and, 27–28, 33–34
  hand of the King and, 39–46
  happiness as active form of living and, 28–30
  House Stark in, 29
  identity and, 27–28, 29–30, 31, 34, 42, 44
  inherited past and, 27–35
  inspiration for, 25–26
  Jon Snow as symbol of dishonor in, 34–35, 48–49
  journey south in, 35–38
  justice in the community and, 31–32
  limits of honorable agency and, 39–46
  ontological condition of vulnerability and, 41
  opening episode of, 32–34, 37, 46–47
  overview of, 25–28, 50
  playing the game of thrones and, 27, 45–46
  political intrigue as incompatible with honor in, 37
  political life and, honor as end of, 28–29, 30–31
  politics of recognition and, 39–46
  popularity of, 25–26
  power and, 26–27, 38, 40–41, 43–45, 46–47
  as rebuttal to Disneyland Middle Ages, 26–27
  recognition and, 27–28, 36, 39–46
  relationality and, 40–41
  reworking of fantasy genre in, 25–27
  Robb Stark in, 47–48
  Robert Baratheon in, 27–28, 34–35, 41–43
  Sansa Stark in, 35–37, 46–47
  self-sufficiency and, 28–32
  singularity as implicit in principle of honor and, 41
  spinoff of, 25–26
  subjectivity and, 27–28, 35–38, 40, 42–43
  tradition and, 28–37
  tragedy and, 26–28, 33–34
  vulnerability and, 41–44
  "Winter is coming" saying in, 29–32
gender, 1, 3–4, 22, 55, 57, 58, 60–62, 108, 132–33
Goren, Lilly, 128–29, 142, 150–51

hamartia (tragic error), 21–22, 27–28, 33–34
Hegel, GWF
  chivalric honor and, 21–22, 27–28, 36
  demonstration of honor and, 40
  end of history and, 96
  identity and, 8–9

Hegel, GWF (*cont.*)
  limits of politics of honor and, 40
  power and, 40–41
  recognition and, 8–9, 36
  relationality and, 40–41
  singularity as implicit in principle of honor and, 41
  subjectivity and, 38, 40
Henry VIII, 22–23, 67–68, 70–72, 89
heroic action
  Americans and, 61
  Captain America and, 126–27, 135, 155
  definition of, 98–99
  heroic temper and, 95, 106–7, 109–10, 113–14, 121
  Homeric contest and, 105–8
  Iliad and, 96–99, 101–2, 103–4, 106–8, 113–14, 117–18, 121–24
  Krause and, 96–97
  liberalism and, 6–7, 56
  myth and, 6–7, 99, 105–6
  Nietzsche and, 100–8
  norms of, 106
  overview of, 6
  political imagination and, 157
  self-forgetting and, 99
  stripping away of, 6
  tragic and, 98–99
Hero with a Thousand Faces (Campbell), 99
Hobbes, Thomas, 14–19, 94
Hofer, J., 139–40
Hofstadter, Richard, 56
Hollywood War Machine, 134–35
Homer. *See Iliad, The* (Homer)
Homeric contest, 105–8
Homer's Contest (Nietzsche), 113
honor
  affirmative and tragic conception of, 3–4
  agency and, 1–4, 13–17, 39–46, 157
  agonism's relation to, 156–58
  as being entitled to respect, 9–11
  as binding and blinding, 3–4, 27–28, 50, 73–74, 95–96, 147, 155
  as central to contemporary political discourse, 1–3
  chivalric honor, 1–2, 21–22, 27–28, 36–37
  complex legacy of, 46–49
  conservative and traditionalist pull of, 5–6
  contributions of current volume on, 3, 6–7
  cultural honor, 5, 132–33
  definition of, 3, 5–6, 143–44
  dishonor and, 34–35, 41, 45–49, 70–71, 82–83, 108, 111, 112
  dueling and, 9–11
  enduring appeal of, 1–24, 156–58
  foot-binding and, 7–9, 11–12
  glory and, 16–20
  heroic action and, 3, 6–7, 13, 19–20
  identity and, 12
  inheritance and, 16–20
  intellectual history of, 55–56
  liberalism and, 3, 6, 12, 13–16
  masculinity and, 1, 5, 58, 108, 132–33
  moral revolutions and, 7–9
  motivation for current volume on, 2–3
  as multivalent, 6–7, 94–95, 157–58
  myth and, 6–7, 19–20, 24
  nostalgia and, 1, 6–7
  as obsolete, 4–7, 156
  ornamental honor, 3–4, 70–75, 82–86, 89, 90, 105–6, 111–12, 138
  overview of, 1–4, 156–58
  pastness and, 4–7
  polarization and, 1–2
  political imagination and, 1–4, 20–21, 156–58
  popular culture and, 2–3
  power and, 3–4, 7–13, 17–18, 157–58
  prior scholarship contrasted with current volume on, 3, 4–6
  rationalism and, 6, 12–13
  reflexive honor, 5
  research questions of current volume on, 1–3
  sacredness and, 1
  as safeguard of democratic freedom, 13, 55–56, 121, 157
  self-respect and, 17
  as slippery concept, 3, 5–6, 20–21, 94, 156, 157–58
  as source of moral revolution, 3, 7–8
  structure of current volume on, 3–4, 21–24
  temporality of, 4–5
  theoretical approach of current volume on, 3
  tradition and, 7–12
  tragic theory of, 3–4, 20–24, 100–4, 156–58
  typology and phenomenology of, 5–6
  See also Americans, The (television show); *Captain America* (films); code of honor; *Game of Thrones* (television show); *Iliad, The* (Homer); *Wolf Hall* (Mantel)
Honor (Bowman), 5
Honor Code, The (Appiah), 7–8
honor culture, 131–33
Honor in the Modern World (Johnson and Demetriou), 131–32
House of the Dragon (television show), 25–26

Human Condition, The (Arendt), 98

Ibn Khaldun, 12
identity
　agency and, 12
　Americans and, 53–54, 55–56, 57–61, 62–63
　Appiah and, 7–10, 12
　asabiyah and, 12–14, 19–20
　Captain America and, 129–30, 132–33, 135–36, 137–38, 140–43
　codes of honor and, 12
　Game of Thrones and, 27–28, 29–30, 31, 34, 42, 44
　group identity, 12, 56
　honor and, 12
　Iliad and, 94
　politics of, 57
　recognition and, 8–9
　social identity and, 9–10
　Wolf Hall and, 74–75, 79–80, 82–83, 91–92
ideology, 58, 61–64, 133–36
Iliad, The (Homer)
　Achilles in, 95–96, 102–3, 108–21
　Agamemnon contrasted with Achilles in, 110
　agency and, 96–108, 121–24
　agon and, 98, 106–7
　Apollonian and Dionysian and, 100–5, 109–10
　battlefield honor and, 120–21, 122–23
　berserk state and trauma in, 117–19, 120–21
　body politic, honor's role in, 105
　centrality of honor in, 95
　code of honor and, 10, 94–95, 122–23
　conflict and political action and, 98
　dueling concepts of honor in, 111
　etymology of Achilles's name in, 116
　excellence as meriting honor and, 105–6
　family and, 108–9, 119–20
　force as true hero of, 108
　gendered dimensions of, 108
　grief of Achilles in, 108–21
　gritty realism of, 108
　Hector in, 106, 108–9, 113, 115, 116, 119–21, 122–23
　heroic action and, 96–99, 101–2, 103–4, 106–8, 113–14, 117–18, 121–24
　heroic temper and, 95, 106–7, 109–10, 113–14, 121
　Homeric contest and, 105–8
　identity and, 94
　legacy of, 95, 108
　liberalism and, 96–99, 103–4
　linear account of time and, 96–99
　masculinity and, 108
　myth and, 99, 105–6
　Nietzsche and, 98, 100–4
　norms of heroic action and, 106
　Odysseus in, 108–9, 114, 117–18
　ornamental honor in, 3–4, 70–71, 85–86, 89, 90, 105–6, 111–12
　overview of, 94–96, 121–24
　power and, 102, 108–9
　rage and, 108–21
　recognition and, 101–3, 111–12
　redemptive and teleological aspect of honor and, 96–99
　savior role and, 94–95
　scholarship on honor and, 96, 105–6
　shame and, 108, 111–12, 114
　tragedy and, 95, 98–99, 100–4, 108–10, 113–14, 121–24
　virtue of honor and, 100–4, 109–10
　women in, 108

Jewett, Robert, 130–31
Johnson, Laurie, 143–44
Jordan, Michael B., 127

Kelly, John, 1
Kiernan, V. G., 10–11
Knox, Bernard, 106–7
Kohen, Ari, 105–6, 121, 127
Krause, Sharon
　atomistic individual and, 15–16
　codes of honor and, 17
　critiques of, 14–19
　definition of agency and, 13–14
　democratic agency and, 3, 13–19, 157
　heroic action and, 96–97
　inheritance of modernity and, 16–19
　liberalism revitalized and, 3, 13–19, 157
　power and, 17–18
　pursuit of honor and, 18–19
　safeguard conception of honor and, 13
　vainglory and, 18–19

Lawrence, John Shelton, 130–31
Leviathan (Hobbes), 17–18
liberalism
　agency and, 6, 13–17, 96–99
　Americans and, 56
　Appiah and, 7–8
　atomistic individualism and, 13, 15–16, 23–24, 51–52
　Captain America and, 127–28, 145–46
　development of, 14–15

liberalism (cont.)
  heroic action and, 6–7, 56
  Hobbesian critique of honor and, 14–15
  honor and, 3, 6, 12, 13–16
  Iliad and, 96–99, 103–4
  Krause and, 3, 13–19, 157
  linear account of time and, 97–98
  myth and, 6
  necessity of heroic action and, 13
  power and, 17–18, 56
  rationalism and, 6, 13
  rehabilitation of, 3, 13–19, 20–21, 157
Liberalism with Honor (Krause), 13
Locke, John, 14–15

Machiavelli, Niccolo
  aesthetic approach to politics and, 16–17, 76–77
  becoming and, 87–88
  fortuna and, 73–74, 86–90
  honor as way of managing enemies and, 72–74
  nobility as clinging most to tradition and, 72–73
  ornamental politics and, 70–75
  power and, 70–72
  Prince, 22–23, 70, 72–73, 87–88
  recognition and, 73
  theoria and, 77–78
  Wolf Hall and, 70–75, 85
Manchurian Candidate, The (film), 60–61
Mansfield, Harvey, 1
Mantel, Hilary, 3–4, 22–23, 67–70. See also *Wolf Hall*
Marcus Aurelius, 73
Markell, Patchen, 27–28
Martel, James, 97–98
masculinity, 1, 57, 58, 108, 132–33
McWilliams, Carey, 146–47
Medici, Lorenzo de', 76
militarism, 130, 131–38
Mill, John Stuart, 4–5
Mirror and the Light, The (Mantel), 67, 70–71, 89
Montesquieu (Charles Louis de Secondat), 16–17, 19–20
More, Thomas, 70–71, 78–85
motherhood depictions during the Cold War, 3–4, 22, 55, 60–62
Muqaddimah (Ibn Khaldun), 12
myth
  Captain America and, 127–43, 145, 147–49, 151–54

  heroic action and, 6–7, 99, 105–6
  honor and, 3–4, 6–7, 19–20, 24
  Iliad and, 99, 105–6
  liberalism and, 6
  myth-making, 3–4, 6–7, 19–20, 24, 125–26

Nagy, Gregory, 109–10, 116
Nicomachean Ethics (Aristotle), 27–28, 30
Nietzsche, Friedrich
  Achilles and, 102–3
  agency and, 101–5
  agon and, 106–7, 156
  Apollonian and Dionysian and, 100–5, 107–8, 109–10
  Birth of Tragedy and, 100, 101–2
  heroic action and, 100–8
  Homeric contest and, 106–8
  honor as second in three phases of morality and, 43–44
  Iliad and, 98, 100–4
  norms of heroic action and, 106
  redemption and, 103–4
  ressentiment and, 100–1, 156
  scope of work of, 100–1
  tragic core of honor and, 100–4
  virtue of honor and, 100–4
  Zarathustra character of, 100–1
nostalgia, 1, 6–7, 138–48, 150–51

Oprisko, Robert, 5–6, 105–6
ornamental honor, 3–4, 70–75, 82–86, 89, 90, 105–6, 111–12, 138

paranoia, 55–58
Patapan, Haig, 6, 16–17
patriotism, 3, 19–22, 53–55, 62–65, 131–38, 144–46, 153–54, 157–58
Peterson, Jordan, 1
Plato, 69, 80–81
political imagination and honor, 1–4, 20–21, 156–58. See also *Americans, The* (television show); *Captain America* (films); *Game of Thrones* (television show); *Iliad, The* (Homer); *Wolf Hall* (Mantel)
Political Life of Sensation (Panagia), 77
politicization of the domestic realm, 58–62
Politics (Aristotle), 28–29
Pollard, Tom, 133–35
Poniewozik, James, 54
power
  agency as wiped away by, 13–14
  art of, 22–23, 67–71, 74–78, 83–86, 87–89, 90–91, 92–93, 157–58

Game of Thrones and, 26–27, 38, 40–41, 43–45, 46–47
honor and, 3–4, 7–13, 17–18, 157–58
Iliad and, 102, 108–9
Krause and, 17–18
liberalism and, 17–18, 56
Machiavelli and, 70–72
Wolf Hall and, 70–78, 82–86
Prince, The (Machiavelli), 22–23, 70, 72–73, 87–88

Rancière, Jacques, 69, 86–87
rationalism, 6, 12–13, 80–81, 100–1, 155
recognition
    Appiah and, 8–10
    code of honor and, 17
    Game of Thrones and, 27–28, 36, 39–46
    Hegel and, 8–9, 36
    identity and, 8–9
    Iliad and, 101–3, 111–12
    limits of, 39–46
    politics of, 39–46
    Wolf Hall and, 73, 77
Redford, Robert, 141–42
Roblou, Yann, 135
Rogin, Michael, 60–61
Russo, Anthony, 138–39
Russo, Joe, 138–39

Scott, A. O., 127–28
self-sufficiency, 28–32, 99
shame, 11–12, 108, 111–12, 114
Shay, Jonathan, 117–18, 119, 120–21
Smith, Zadie, 150
Song of Ice and Fire, A (Martin), 25–26
Spirit of the Laws, The (Montesquieu), 19
subjectivity, 2–3, 7–9, 13–16, 27–28, 35–38, 40, 42–43, 61, 97–98, 120–21
superhero genre, 127–31
Superheroes (Reynolds), 133

theoria, 77–78
Thomas, Joe, 133–34
Tocqueville, Alexis de, 146–47, 148
tragedy
    agency and, 18–19, 20–21
    Americans and, 57–58, 62–66
    Captain America and, 127
    Game of Thrones and, 26–28, 33–34
    hamartia and, 21–22, 27–28, 33–34
    heroic action and, 98–99
    honor, tragic theory of, 3–4, 20–24, 100–4, 156–58

    Iliad and, 95, 98–99, 100–4, 108–10, 113–14, 121–24
    tragic error, 21–22, 27–28, 33–34
Trump, Donald, 51–54

Undoing the Demos (Brown), 3

Villa, Dana, 98
virtue of honor, 46–47, 100–4, 109–10
von Vacano, Diego, 75–76, 77, 88

Watkins, Robert, 15–17
Weil, Simone, 108
Weisberg, Jacob, 54
Welsh, Alexander, 55–56
Wolf Hall (Mantel)
    aesthetic approach to politics and, 75–76, 78–82, 88
    Anne Boleyn and, 70–71, 85–86
    art of power and, 75–78
    becoming and, 87–88
    birthright honor and, 68–69, 71–73
    Cardinal Wolsey in, 70–72, 79–80
    central drama of, 78
    class dimensions of, 67–69
    code of honor and, 67–68, 78
    contingency and, 86–90
    decorative and dispensable nature of honor in, 75–76
    disidentification and, 87–89
    distribution of the sensible and, 69, 86–89, 91
    food preparation and digestion and, 79–81
    fortuna and, 73–74, 86–90
    Henry VIII in, 67–68, 71–72, 89
    historical context of, 67
    honor as currency in, 67–69
    identity and, 74–75, 79–80, 82–83, 91–92
    low station of Cromwell in, 67–68
    Machiavellian conception of Cromwell and, 70–75, 85
    managing enemies and, honor as way of, 72–73
    margins of aesthetic approach to power and, honor as, 70–72
    More's views of the sensory and, 70–71, 78–85
    nobility as clinging most to tradition and, 72–73
    ornamental honor and, 70–75, 82–86
    othering and, 67–68
    overview, 67–70, 90–93
    perspective and, 77–78, 81–82

Wolf Hall (Mantel) (*cont.*)
   political and social skills of Cromwell in, 69–70
   political life of sensation and, 78–82, 85–86
   power and, 70–78, 82–86
   rationalism and, 80–81
   reception of, 69–70
   recognition and, 73, 77
   reputation of Cromwell and, 72
   reshaping of honor in, 68–69
   revisionism of Tudor era and, 67
   spheres of sensation and thought combined and, 83
   theoria and, 77–78
Wright, Source, 51–52
Wylie, Philip, 61–62